Refugees
in the
United States

Refugees
in the
United States

A Reference
Handbook

EDITED BY David W. Haines

Greenwood Press

WESTPORT, CONNECTICUT • LONDON, ENGLAND

Library of Congress Cataloging in Publication Data

Main entry under title:

Refugees in the United States.

    Bibliography: p.
    Includes index.
      1. Minorities—United States—Handbooks, manuals, etc.
2. Refugees—United States—Handbooks, manuals, etc.
3. United States—Foreign population—Handbooks, manuals,
etc. I. Haines, David W.
E184.A1R43 1985   305.8′00973   84-12794
ISBN 0-313-24068-X (lib. bdg.)

Library of Congress Catalog Card Number: 84-12794
ISBN: 0-313-24068-X

First published in 1985

Greenwood Press
A division of Congressional Information Service, Inc.
88 Post Road West
Westport, Connecticut 06881

Printed in the United States of America

10 9 8 7 6 5 4 3 2 1

Contents

Preface

More than one and a half million refugees have resettled in the United States over the past twenty-five years. The purpose of this volume is to provide to both the general reader and the specialist a basic understanding of the experience of these refugees, the cultures and societies from which they come, the nature of their exodus and transit to the United States, the problems they face, and the successes they achieve in adjusting to a new society.

There are some commonalities in the adjustment of refugees to the United States: first, they arrive and are resettled through a complex but increasingly uniform program of services and assistance; second, the obstacles they must overcome in their initial adjustment to a new country are not dissimilar; and third, all face the long-term process of moving toward integration into at least some domains of American society. These commonalities of adjustment are addressed in the three chapters of Part I.

However, although there are common patterns in the experience of refugees in the United States, the key to understanding their situation lies in an appreciation of the wide diversity of their experience—not only the diversity in the societies from which they come and the paths that have brought them to this country, but also in their potentially divergent futures. Thus Part II provides separate examinations of the major refugee groups that have arrived during the past twenty-five years, including not only those officially designated as refugees, but also those Cubans and Haitians arriving in 1980 who received the indeterminate status of entrant, and the numerous Salvadorans and Guatemalans living illegally within this country while the government generally denies their claims to be bona fide refugees.

Several features of this book derive from its primary purpose of serving as a reference volume for both the general reader and the specialist. First, the different chapters of Part II all respond to a common framework provided to each of the contributors. Each chapter entails sequential discussions of the historical and social background of the people in question, the reasons for and nature of their exodus as refugees, and key aspects of their adjustment to living in the United

States. This enables relatively easy comparison among the groups. Second, particular emphasis in the chapters of Part II is placed on the backgrounds of the refugee populations. All too frequently, refugees (and other immigrants) are viewed as blank tablets on their arrival in the United States, or their background is reduced to such simple quantified measures as age, years of education, or previous occupation. The material presented in Part II quickly dispels any notion of the adequacy of such an approach. Third, the nature of a reference volume implies a multiplicity of reader uses and needs. Although many readers may seek a lucid and reliable overview of a particular group, others may seek a more general understanding of several (or all) refugees in the United States. To meet such needs not only are the chapters of Part I provided, but also an appended annotated bibliography on the rapidly evolving literature on refugees in the United States. Rather than being exhaustive, this appendix provides a selective, pre-screened set of readily available items that should suffice for all but the expert.

Acknowledgments for a work of this kind are necessarily many. My major debts are to Joshua Haines for encouraging me to undertake this effort, and to Karen Rosenblum for cogent and illuminating assessments of the three chapters that constitute Part I. Key help was provided by Mary Sive and Cynthia Harris of Greenwood Press, the former for sound advice on the overall shape of the volume and the latter for smooth management of the editorial process. Careful readings of Chapter 1 by Phil Holman and Christie Cohagen were invaluable in improving the discussion of what remains a particularly complicated program. Mary Kahler's assistance in typing and editing the volume was essential in ensuring its completion.

The major acknowledgment must, however, go to the contributors. Providing a coherent overview of a particular refugee population is a difficult task; it requires bridging issues of sociocultural background; the depredations, exigencies, and complex politics of exodus and asylum; and the nature of adjustment to a new society. When this must be done with a balance of accessibility to the general reader and the substantive depth that provides a contribution to the scholarly literature, the task is rendered more difficult. Yet they have done well in conveying the complexities of the experience of refugees as they must be related—in the specific circumstances of particular refugee populations.

PART I

CONTEXT AND OVERVIEW

Refugees and the Refugee Program

The resettlement of refugees in the United States is part of a broader global situation. Although the United States accepts more refugees for permanent re-settlement than any other country and is the major contributor to international refugee relief efforts, its efforts are dwarfed by the number of refugees world-wide—close to eight million—and partially overshadowed by the greater per capita resettlement efforts of Canada and Australia, and the greater per capita financial contributions of seven other countries (USCR 1983:63). The presence of refugees in the United States is not only one part of this wider global situation, but is also only the last stage of an often extended and dangerous period of flight and temporary asylum elsewhere.

Despite these qualifications, the United States' acceptance and resettlement of well over two million refugees since the end of the Second World War is a significant national achievement. This chapter provides an overview of the re-settlement effort, turning first to the history of the program, second to the central roles that characterize the U.S. resettlement effort, and third to some of the issues that have informed the dialogue about the refugee program, particularly since 1980. The succeeding two chapters turn away from such programmatic considerations and toward general patterns in the adjustment of the refugees themselves.

REFUGEE RESETTLEMENT IN THE UNITED STATES

Throughout American history, people have come to the United States to escape intolerable conditions elsewhere and to seek a better life. The early American laissez-faire immigration policy necessitated no distinction between refugees and other immigrants; all were allowed entry. As a consequence, refugees suffered the same fate as other immigrants when increasing restrictions culminated with a virtual closing of America's doors in the 1920s. This became an issue of particular concern in the late 1930s as Jews attempted to flee the Nazis but were generally denied entry to the United States, a particularly bleak episode within the period of restricted immigration.

Events at the end of the Second World War brought the first elements of a separate refugee program into existence (see Reimers 1982; McHugh 1979). Responding to the presence of numerous displaced persons in Europe, the United States initially moved to expedite resettlement through existing and very limited quotas, and subsequently opened the door much wider to these refugees with the Displaced Persons Act of 1948 (under which approximately 400,000 persons entered) and then the Refugee Relief Act of 1953 (under which close to 200,000 persons, mostly fleeing from communist-dominated Eastern Europe, came to the United States). Several features of U.S. refugee policy became clear during this period: first, admissions were to be handled separately from general immigration; second, admissions focused almost entirely on political refugees from communism; and third, lacking any government program of domestic assistance for refugees after arrival, help to refugees in adjusting to American society necessarily came from the private sector. Indeed, under these laws, refugees could not be admitted unless it was guaranteed that they would not become public charges. The role of voluntary agencies, such as the U.S. Catholic Conference, became critical, for it was they who provided the necessary guarantees for refugees who lacked close relatives or friends already in the United States.

When Soviet forces suppressed a general insurrection in Hungary in late 1956 and refugees fled into Austria, the same policy prevailed, as President Eisenhower agreed to admit the first of what ultimately became nearly 40,000 refugees. Even though the federal government opened and operated a processing facility at Camp Kilmer in New Jersey, the federal effort continued to be delimited to entry, processing, and transportation costs to final destinations. Again it was the voluntary agencies that took responsibility for resettlement once the refugees left Camp Kilmer. Indeed the federal government was explicit that even the forty dollars per capita it was willing to give to voluntary agencies for the transportation of refugees to their final destination did not "constitute a precedent for giving payment to the voluntary agencies for similar costs for other refugee movements" (Taft, North, and Ford 1979:55).

Initially, the situation of those fleeing Castro's victory in Cuba two years later appeared similar to previous refugee flows; Cuban émigrés were allowed entry, but the federal government remained uninvolved with subsequent settlement. However, important differences quickly provoked changes in policy: The Cuban refugee flow was a large one, refugees came directly to U.S. shores, and they resettled predominantly in Miami. In addition, many refugees had strong prior U.S. contacts.

This combination of factors of contiguity, flow, and previous U.S. contact yielded a more direct federal government involvement. By the end of 1960 more than 100,000 Cubans had arrived in the United States, most in the Miami area. President Eisenhower, in December, opened the Cuban Refugee Center in Miami. Soon after his inauguration, in January 1961, President Kennedy directed his

Secretary of Health, Education, and Welfare, Abraham Ribicoff, to assess the Cuban refugee situation. The resulting nine-point plan became the core of the federal refugee program for many years and was reflected in the Migration and Refugee Assistance Act of 1962, which provided the continuing authorization for the Cuban program as well as for basic U.S. commitments to support international refugee relief efforts (Thomas 1965; McHugh 1979). The organizational key was a continuing Cuban Refugee Program whose central office remained in Miami, but with a small office, largely for liaison, in Washington, D.C. The programmatic key was, for the first time, the provision for federal reimbursement of state and local agency expenditures for cash assistance, medical assistance, social services, and educational assistance provided to Cuban refugees.

For the next decade the Cuban Refugee Program remained the sole program of domestic assistance to refugees in the United States. From 1959, when Castro formally took over the Cuban government, through 1971 the number of Cuban refugees entering the United States remained close to 50,000 per year, higher in 1962 but lower in the three years after the Cuban missile crisis of October 1962. In fiscal year 1972, however, the number of arrivals was half that amount, and in the following year was again reduced by half, to about 13,000.

By 1975, the number of arriving Cubans was down to 8,500. However, the fall of the American-supported governments in the countries of former French Indochina led to the entry of 130,000 (almost entirely Vietnamese) refugees into the United States, first through staging areas in the Pacific, then to processing centers in the continental United States, and then into communities under the sponsorship of the voluntary agencies. Again the U.S. decision to allow entry was population specific, and again a separate program was created with its own legislation (Indochina Migration and Refugee Assistance Act), although based on the authorities in the Migration and Refugee Assistance Act of 1962. Again, as well, the situation was seen as a one-time event, and initial events appeared to bear out this presumption. There were only 14,500 arrivals in 1976, and in 1977, the number of refugees from Indochina was only 2,500 (less than the Cuban inflow of 3,000 that year). However, 1978 saw the beginnings of a rise in inflow that would peak at 167,000 in 1980 before declining to around 50,000 by 1983. This was a combination of two factors: first, the plight of the boat refugees from Vietnam that generated worldwide attention; and second, a more complete U.S. response to the plight of Laotian and Cambodian refugees who had been left in temporary asylum camps in Thailand, many since 1975.

One other refugee flow of the 1970s merits particular attention, that of Soviet Jews. The origins of this exodus lay in the 1971 easing by the Soviet Union of the procedures for obtaining exit visas. Although Jewish émigrés officially declared their intention to go to Israel, many came to the United States. In 1973, approximately 1,500 Soviet Jews came to the United States; this figure doubled in 1974 and had doubled again by 1977, when Soviets outnumbered both Cuban and Indochinese entries. The number doubled again to 12,000 in 1978, and more than doubled again to 29,000 in 1979, before beginning a similarly rapid decline.

As with other refugee flows, the U.S. response was population specific and entailed separate legislation and a distinct program of domestic assistance.

By the late 1970s, a number of distinct changes had thus occurred in the refugee situation. First, the Cuban program had been declining and did not appear to justify its own separate existence as a program. Second, the influx from Indochina was becoming a continuing flow and one of proportions that, on an annual basis, dwarfed even the early Cuban program. Third, the significant number of Soviet refugees, then still growing, may have suggested that the multiplicity in origin of the refugee flow was to be the continuing pattern. The stage was set for a reworking and combination of the legislative authorities under which these different refugee programs operated. The result was the Refugee Act of 1980, which incorporated the U.N. definition of a refugee into U.S. law; established a single program of post-arrival assistance for all refugee groups in the United States; established an annual consultation procedure between Congress and the administration regarding admissions; set goals for the resettlement effort; and made a variety of other management, program, and admissions changes and clarifications (cf. Anker 1984; Kennedy 1981).

No sooner was the Refugee Act passed and signed by President Carter, in early 1980, than events outstripped its provisions. In late March, a busload of Cubans crashed into the Peruvian embassy in Havana, seeking asylum. By late April the Cuban government had opened the port of Mariel to all Cubans wishing to emigrate to the United States. By the end of May, 94,000 Cubans had crossed by boat to Florida; by October, the total reached 125,000. The federal government ultimately determined that these people, and the Haitians who arrived during the same period, were not refugees within the meaning of the just-passed Refugee Act. However, a distinct legal category was created for them by Congress: "Cuban/Haitian Entrant (Status Pending)." Such entrants became eligible for the same services and assistance as were refugees, and there was considerable—although far from complete—overlap in the administration of these two programs, termed the Refugee Resettlement Program (RRP) and the Cuban/Haitian Entrant Program (CHEP).

Other events also put pressure on this recently reformulated U.S. refugee program. Probably most important was the large number of refugees who arrived from Southeast Asia. During 1980 and 1981, about 300,000 refugees from Cambodia, Laos, and Vietnam arrived in the United States and were resettled on a normal flow basis (i.e., without the kinds of processing centers that were used in 1975). This was a massive effort and there were, not surprisingly, concurrent and later emerging problems. A severe recession in the early 1980s compounded the difficulty of economic adjustment, noticeably driving up the unemployment rate of refugees (more than double that of the nation as a whole).

As the program began to deal with the aftereffects of resettling the Southeast Asian refugees, the flow of refugees entering the United States began declining in numbers and shifting in ethnic composition. In fiscal year 1983, the number of arriving Southeast Asian refugees dropped to about 50,000, remaining roughly the same in the first half of 1984 and in the projections for 1985. The shifts in the relative proportion of different groups were also significant. Approvals for admission from Vietnam declined from 65,000 in 1981 to 27,000 in 1982 and to 23,000 in 1983. Admissions from Cambodia, however, vacillated more sharply; from 38,000 in 1981, the number of Cambodians dropped to 6,000 in 1982 but rose to 22,000 in 1983. The number of Laotians approved for admission dropped from 20,000 in 1981 to 3,600 in 1982, rising to 5,600 in 1983. The decline for Soviet refugees was similarly steep, from 11,000 in 1981 to 2,800 in 1982 and to 1,400 in 1983. Given these declines, smaller refugee populations became somewhat more visible than they had been previously. Most noticeable were the Poles, increasing from 2,000 in 1981 to 6,600 in 1982 and to 5,800 in 1983. Refugees from Afghanistan, Ethiopia, and Romania all maintained levels around a 3,000-to-4,000 figure annually through this period, despite the overall decrease in refugee admissions (ORR 1984).

The net result was that, by mid-1984, the flow of Southeast Asian refugees appeared to be normalized at around 50,000 per year, and there was a reasonably stable mix of other countries represented among refugee arrivals. The large Southeast Asian influx of 1980 and 1981 was receding somewhat reluctantly into the past, as were the numerous problems associated with the "entrant" Cubans and Haitians of 1980. Over the quarter century from the origins of the Cuban program about one and a half million legal refugees had been resettled in the United States, the vast majority either from Cuba or from Vietnam (Vietnamese and ethnic Chinese), with smaller but still sizable populations of Cambodians (mostly Khmer but with a few ethnic Chinese), Laotians (about evenly split between lowland ethnic Lao and various highland groups, the majority of whom are Hmong), and Soviet Jews.

ROLES IN THE RESETTLEMENT EFFORT

Despite improvements in the Refugee Act, the refugee resettlement effort continues to be characterized by complexity, considerable organizational overlap, and a flexibility that at times approaches diffuseness. It is perhaps a misnomer even to call resettlement a single program; rather it is a series of discrete activities by a wide variety of organizations and individuals bound together in a common goal of providing assistance to meet the particular needs of refugees. Refugee resettlement in the United States is thus better understood by an attention to its diversity than by attempts to see it as a single, logically consistent effort. This diversity extends even to the complex web of federal government, voluntary agency, and state and local government roles that provide the overall framework for resettlement efforts.

The Federal Government

Although the Refugee Act of 1980 incorporated the U.N. definition of refugees, the United States continues its historical pattern—as do other nations—of accepting for resettlement only those who are of special humanitarian concern; operationally, this has almost always meant refugees from communist countries, such as Hungary, the Soviet Union, Cuba, and Vietnam. The designation of special humanitarian concern is an aspect of both current and previous foreign policy. The American acceptance of refugees from Southeast Asia, for example, is the result not only of previous American involvement in the Indochina conflict, but also of pressure from those Southeast Asian countries, particularly Thailand, that bear the burden of providing initial, temporary asylum to refugees from Cambodia, Laos, and Vietnam.

Although admissions decisions (and international relief efforts) thus generally follow foreign policy considerations, refugees who come to the United States must adjust to a new environment and become part of domestic policy considerations. The central logic of the refugee resettlement program is that refugees, because of their forced flight, the frequent depredations of transit, and the lack of opportunity to prepare for life in a new country, need (and should be granted) sufficient transitional assistance to enable them to forge an adequate and self-sufficient life in the United States. Thus, once within the United States, program issues change from admissions decisions and relief efforts to issues of adjustment and assimilation. Program adequacy is no longer to be seen in terms of what refugees fled from, but rather how they are doing now in the United States.

This distinction between the overseas and domestic sides of the refugee program is partially replicated in the federal government's responsibilities for the program. In general, the Department of State (Bureau for Refugee Programs) has responsibility for the overseas side of the program, whereas the Department of Health and Human Services (Office of Refugee Resettlement) has responsibility for domestic assistance. However, the line is far from clearly drawn. The Refugee Act of 1980, for example, provides for a U.S. Coordinator for Refugee Affairs who is to have overall lead in policy development regarding both sides of the program; however, this individual remains physically located in the Department of State, with ambassadorial status, and the line between the Office of the Coordinator and the Bureau for Refugee Programs has often been quite porous. Furthermore, the Bureau for Refugee Programs has been expanding its role as it affects the adjustment of refugees in the United States by providing language training and cultural orientation while the refugees are still overseas. For example, most Southeast Asian refugees now spend time in refugee processing centers (the main one is in the Philippines) before entering the United States. Although the training occurs overseas, it is geared less toward the pursuit of foreign policy considerations than toward the effective adjustment of refugees. It is thus functionally an issue of domestic assistance.

The most important area of overlap in organizational responsibility involves the (reception-and-placement) grants provided by the Department of State to various voluntary agencies to support their resettlement efforts. The initial placement of refugees into the community, finding of housing and referral to necessary services, would seem to be part of the domestic assistance program, yet these are activities provided for by the Department of State grants. Thus, even within the boundaries of the United States, dual Department of State and Department of Health and Human Services responsibilities for refugees remain unresolved.

Voluntary Agencies

The continuing, partially overlapping federal responsibility pales before the more historically fundamental joint involvement in resettlement of both the federal government and various national voluntary agencies. The voluntary agencies have been of critical importance to the federal government at times when it was necessary to gather support for refugee programs rapidly and at relatively low cost. The federal government thus turned to the voluntary agencies in 1975, during the first influx of Southeast Asian refugees, providing to the agencies a set per capita amount for the initial settlement and placement of the refugees after they left the camps. This role has continued, with each arriving refugee being sponsored by one of the agencies.

A tremendous variety exists among the agencies in their structure, in the origins of their commitment to the resettlement of refugees, and in the resources that they bring to bear. Some function as secular social service agencies; others rely heavily on congregations to provide the necessary support for refugees. Although this variety, mixed with flexibility, may be the strength of the voluntary agencies (Zucker and Zucker 1980), it does pose problems when, as has been the case in recent years, there is increasing concern about uniformity and accountability in the overall resettlement effort.

State and Local Government

A final basic tension within the program involves state and local governmental roles. Above all, the domestic assistance program involves the reimbursement of state and local governmental expenditures on behalf of refugees. Under the Refugee Act this period of reimbursement for the major types of assistance is limited to three years after the refugee's arrival in the country. But the Refugee Act also makes it clear that the role of the states is to be central to the resettlement effort. In order to receive any reimbursement from the federal government, states must have a federally approved plan for providing assistance to refugees and designate a state coordinator to assure coordination of all resources toward effective resettlement. The emphasis on the central state role means a de-emphasis on direct relationships between the federal government and specific localities. The federal government, for example, has ceased direct funding of social services (such as language training and employment services); rather, the states are now awarded funds and in turn award contracts to service providers. However, in 1983, the federal government re-emphasized the role of local governments through a program of targeted assistance grants that, although awarded through the states, were to be administered at the county or equivalent level.

The resulting emphasis on the importance of both state and local governmental roles in refugee resettlement does not in itself resolve the problem of what those roles should be. One important problem regarding state and local roles is that the dichotomous public versus private and Department of State versus Department of Health and Human Services roles reappear in a new context. In some states voluntary agency affiliates also provide refugee services under contract from state government. In other cases the state provides all its social service funds to its own agencies (e.g., using community colleges for providing English language training for refugees). Thus in some places funds from the Bureau for Refugee Programs and funds from the Office of Refugee Resettlement remain separate, but in other places such funds are merged together by local affiliates of voluntary agencies that provide a wider set of services for a longer time.

There are several implications not only of state and local governmental roles, but also of the entire mixture of roles that constitute the refugee program. One is that there is a great opportunity for misunderstanding, as information passes through a considerable range of agencies and through various levels within each agency. Another is that there is concurrently a broad range of expertise within the refugee program not likely to be matched by programs that have a more unitary organization or that are even limited solely to either the public or private sector. Whether the positive or negative possibilities are more compelling depends on the overall way in which the program is viewed.

PROGRAM ISSUES

Although the refugee program is shaped by its history and by its unique organizational roles and tensions, it is also characterized by a number of issues that appear recurrently in its deliberations and frequently in public attitudes about the program (cf. Parkins 1983). Five of these issues merit particular consideration: first, the problems in defining who is and who is not a refugee; second, the perceived need for greater administrative coherence and coordination in the program; third, concerns about the frequency with which refugees receive public cash assistance; fourth, widespread concerns about the effects (or impact) that refugees have on the United States in general and on the states and localities in which they settle; and fifth, the extent to which refugees should have assistance not available to other U.S. residents.

Definitions

The Refugee Act of 1980 incorporates the U.N. definition of refugees, which so classifies an individual who is unable to remain in or return to his or her country of origin because of "persecution or a well-founded fear of persecution on account of race, religion, nationality, membership in a particular social group, or political opinion." This is essentially a political definition; a refugee is someone who is persecuted by a government that disclaims his or her rights. Hungarian freedom fighters and early refugees from communist takeovers in Vietnam and Cuba clearly meet this definition. Definitional issues can, however, become complex and problematic for the United States when the following conditions occur. First, it is not always clear whether people are fleeing solely for political reasons (e.g., Jaeger 1983). Persecution may come in the form of economic sanctions, as it did for many ethnic Chinese in Vietnam, or as restricted occupational opportunities, as it did for many Jews in the Soviet Union. When the persecution is not directly life-threatening, is it still persecution within the legal definition of a refugee? Second, refugees flee not only from governments to which the United States is opposed, but also from governments with which the United States is allied. This is the case for the Salvadoreans discussed in Chapter 10 and for the Haitians discussed in Chapter 6. Acceptance of numerous refugees from these countries could be inferred to constitute acknowledgment that the United States is supporting repressive regimes. For both the Salvadoreans and the Haitians, the link to a friendly government is joined by assertions that those who flee do so only to seek broader economic opportunity rather than refuge from political persecution. Third, there are a limited number of refugees who can be accepted for resettlement by any country, even one with the resources of the United States. Thus there is a need for prioritizing different refugee groups or otherwise limiting the number of refugees granted admission to the United States. Under such pressure it is easy for those interviewing possible refugees (cf. Helton 1984) to find reasons to rule that applicants are not refugees as strictly defined by law. It is this last possibility that can cause the most confusion; the application of the legal definition comes to reflect not the experiences of the applicant for refugee status, but rather the current realities of U.S. domestic or foreign policy.

Program Coordination

The refugee program is a complex one that defies the application of simple organizational models. Since the sectors, organizations, agencies, and individuals involved are legion, there is a consequent need for coordination. Many features of the Refugee Act of 1980 were geared toward ensuring coordination and better overall accountability, the lack of which has become an almost traditional complaint against the refugee program. A stronger state role was developed as a coordinative focus for resettlement efforts (clear plans and proposals were to be developed, data and program reports were to be instituted), and clarifications were made in federal agency roles, including an initial intent to move the administration of the voluntary agency grants from the Department of State to the Office of Refugee Resettlement in the Department of Health and Human Services. Although responsibility for these grants subsequently remained with the Department of State, increased requirements for applications, reporting, and coordination were placed on the voluntary agencies. Further requirements for consultations among states and voluntary agencies were part of amendments to the Refugee Act in 1982, and in 1983 the House of Representatives voted for a clearer demarcation of the line between voluntary agency responsibilities under Department of State funds and domestic assistance activities funded by the Office of Refugee Resettlement by making the voluntary agencies more fully responsible for the initial ninety days of a refugee's residence in the United States. Whatever the merits of such continuing attempts to more rigorously structure the refugee program, the very frequency of the attempts has in itself become a major problem. A report on the state administration of the refugee program in 1982, for example, suggested that the "challenge for the states is to salvage a thread of program continuity through the many program changes" (Kogan and others 1982:160).

Use of Public Assistance

The central logic of the refugee program has always revolved around the fact that refugees tend to be highly skilled and motivated individuals who are likely to do quite well in the United States but, because of the disruptions of exodus and lack of preparation for the rigors of adjustment to a new country, will need transitional assistance. This assistance, under the current program, includes the same general kinds of assistance and services that are available to other American residents; the key difference involves federal government reimbursement of what would normally be state and local government costs. The major type of assistance by cost is cash assistance. Several events combined, from the late 1970s, to raise the frequency with which refugees were receiving, or appeared to be receiving, such cash assistance. Southeast Asian refugees arriving in the United States during the great flows of 1979 to 1982 were somewhat less equipped for a rapid transition to American society; perhaps as important, they came in numbers that strained existing program resources. Although the economic recession in the early 1980s increased refugees' difficulty in finding employment, federal government actions to cut domestic spending increased the emphasis on the rapid employment of refugees. Finally, changes in the refugee program, particularly the limitation of federal reimbursement to three years, made states and localities more aware of refugee use of public assistance. Thus, although promoting refugee economic self-sufficiency was always the goal of the refugee program, increasingly in the early 1980s this goal was inverted into the negative formulation of reducing the so-called dependency rate. Much of the program's thought and effort were devoted to reducing refugee use of cash assistance, despite existing data that have demonstrated that the use of such assistance declines over time, and despite the fact that this single dependency rate masked a number of quite different situations. Frequent receipt of assistance in certain states, for example, overshadowed far more modest receipt in most other states; frequent receipt by recent arrivals overshadowed the increased economic independence of earlier arrivals. To a considerable extent, then, the goal of the refugee program came to be the reduction of what was inferred to be its previous failure—the frequent receipt by refugees of the very assistance that the refugee program had decided to make available to them because of their reasonable and expectable needs in adjusting to the United States.

The Effects of Refugees

Second only to the dependency problem has been the perceived problem of the impact that refugees have had both on the country as a whole and on particular states and localities. The resettlement of refugees does have effects at the national level and in the localities in which refugees settle. Changes occur; some are slight, some significant. Some are positive, some are—at least initially—negative. However, it is probable that the net effects over time are modest; refugees are too small a segment of the overall immigrant population to have large effects on a national level. It is also likely that these net effects are positive, whether in terms of cultural contributions, useful labor provided, or even taxes paid. Finally, although there are distinct financial costs over the short run, the federal government's commitment to reimburse states for their cash and medical assistance expenditures on behalf of refugees for three years is an acknowledgment of this.

As with the issue of refugee use of cash assistance, however, a number of factors have come together to make the effects that refugees have a more important issue than would seem to be merited. One factor is that with the recurrent gearing up and phasing down of the program, reflecting rapid changes in levels of refugee influx, there are recurring changes in the kind and level of effects that refugees have. More important, during the peak years of the Southeast Asian influx there were indeed significant effects in some localities; almost overnight, for example, schools faced new language groups, neighborhoods discovered new constituencies. At the same time, recession brought unemployment and, with lack of jobs, the usual and predictable public concern about immigration in general and the extent to which newcomers were taking jobs away from the native born. (Ironically, the reverse has often been the case, as refugees were strongly affected by last-hired, first-fired practices.) Concurrent with the recession were significant cuts in social programs, raising an analogous concern that refugees were taking away from other needy populations an important portion of an ever-shrinking array of human services resources.

The resulting sensitivity to the effects that refugees have has fostered a widespread emphasis on the word "impact," a term that appears to connote effects that are both large and negative (cf. Finnan and Cooperstein 1983). Typically, examples of impact involve competition for scarce resources, whether of housing, as in New Orleans and Denver (Afton 1980; Ragas 1980), or of fisheries, as along the Gulf and central California coasts (Starr 1981; Orbach and Beckwith 1982). The archetypal example of refugee impact is Miami, where the dense concentration of Cuban refugees arriving through the 1960s and 1970s drastically altered residential patterns, economic structure, and political voting patterns.

Whatever the merits of concerns about impact, the issue continues to have rippling effects throughout the refugee program, leading to specific federal policies regarding (limited) placement of refugees in so-called impacted areas, and provision of targeted assistance grants in addition to normal refugee social service funds to (generally) the same localities.

Equity

A final issue that has become a focal point in the refugee program is equity. Although potentially a broad concept, equity for the refugee program involves the question of whether, or the extent to which, refugees should receive assistance not available to other U.S. residents. Equity has interesting implications when dealing with refugees, because the purpose of the refugee program is to provide transitional assistance to people who, by definition, need special help. Yet concern about equity was a major rationale in the 1982 limitation of a special refugee cash assistance program to the first eighteen months of a refugee's residence in the United States (rather than the previous thirty-six months) and again a rationale in 1983 arguments by the Department of Health and Human Services that there should not be a special medical assistance program for refugees despite the presence of a strong legislative basis (in the Refugee Act) for such a program and continuing Congressional interest.

As with dependency and impact, the ideas underlying the issue are more telling than the explicit meaning. Key to any discussion of equity is the presence of a comparison group. For refugees, this has now apparently become other disadvantaged American groups. Refugees have traditionally been the relative elites of their countries of origin, prior at least to changes in government. The notion of transitional and essentially remedial assistance to a former (and at least potentially future) middle-class population appears to have been lost. Concerns about equity also tend to overshadow concerns about effectiveness. Programs on behalf of refugees can be argued against on the basis of equity even though such programs might be effective.

The issue of equity thus shares with those of dependency and impact a kind of negative quality that involves the phrasing of the refugee program in terms of the reduction of its problems rather than the achievement of its positive goals. The paths of adjustment that refugees take in the United States can easily become confused with these internal issues and dynamics of the refugee program. Although the decision to allow entry to refugees is crucial, and the domestic assistance provided is no doubt helpful, the program's effects become thinner over time as refugees exercise their own skills toward their own goals, within the opportunities and constraints presented by American society.

REFERENCES

Afton, Jean
1980   Vietnamese Immigrants in Denver: Two Seasons of Fieldwork in Sun Valley.
        In *Processes of Transition: Vietnamese in Colorado*. Edited by Peter Van
        Arsdale and James Pisarowicz. Austin, Texas: High Street Press.
Anker, Deborah
1984   The Development of U.S. Refugee Legislation. In *In Defense of the Alien*, Vol.
        VI. Edited by Lydio F. Tomasi. New York: Center for Migration Studies. Pages
        159–166.
Finnan, Christine, and Rhonda Cooperstein
1983   *Southeast Asian Refugee Resettlement at the Local Level: The Role of the Ethnic
        Community and the Nature of Refugee Impact*. Menlo Park, California: SRI
        International.
Helton, Arthur C.
1984   Political Asylum Under the 1980 Refugee Act: An Unfulfilled Promise. In *In
        Defense of the Alien*, Vol. VI. Edited by Lydio F. Tomasi. New York: Center
        for Migration Studies. Pages 201–206.
Jaeger, Gilbert
1983   The Definition of "Refugee": Restrictive Versus Expanding Trends. *World
        Refugee Survey* 1983:5–9.
Kennedy, Edward M.
1981   The Refugee Act of 1980. *International Migration Review* 15(1):141–156.
Kogan, Deborah, Patricia Jenny, Mary Vencill, and Lois Greenwood
1982   *Study of the State Administration of the Refugee Resettlement Program*. Berke-
        ley, California: Berkeley Planning Associates.
McHugh, Catherine
1979   *Review of U.S. Refugee Resettlement Programs and Policies*. Washington,
        D.C.: U.S. Government Printing Office. (Report prepared for the Senate Com-
        mittee on the Judiciary by the Congressional Research Service.)
Orbach, Michael K., and Janese Beckwith
1982   Indochinese Adaptation and Local Government Policy: An Example from Mon-
        terey. *Anthropological Quarterly* 55(3):135–145.
ORR (Office of Refugee Resettlement)
1984   *Report to the Congress: Refugee Resettlement Program*. Washington, D.C.:
        U.S. Department of Health and Human Services.
Parkins, C. Richard
1983   Issues in Refugee Resettlement. In *Immigrants and Refugees in a Changing
        Nation: Research and Training*. Edited by Lucy Cohen and Mary Ann Gross-
        nickle. Washington, D.C.: Catholic University of America. Pages 15–22.
Ragas, Wade R.
1980   Housing the Refugees: Impact and Partial Solutions to the Housing Shortages.
        Journal of Refugee Resettlement 1(1):40–48.
Reimers, David M.
1982   Recent Immigration Policy: An Analysis. In *The Gateway: U.S. Immigration
        Issues and Policies*. Edited by Barry R. Chiswick. Washington, D.C.: American
        Enterprise Institute for Public Policy Research. Pages 13–53.

Starr, Paul D.
1981   Troubled Waters: Vietnamese Fisherfolk on America's Gulf Coast. *International
          Migration Review* 15(1):226–238.
Taft, Julia, David North, and David Ford
1979   *Refugee Resettlement in the United States: Time for a New Focus.* Washington,
          D.C.: New TransCentury Foundation.
Thomas, John F.
1965   U.S.A. as a Country of First Asylum. *International Migration* 3(1):5–15.
USCR (U.S. Committee for Refugees)
1983   *World Refugee Survey.* New York: American Council for Nationalities Service.
Zucker, Norman L., and Naomi F. Zucker
1980   *The Voluntary Agencies and Refugee Resettlement in the U.S.: A Report to the
          Select Commission on Immigration and Refugee Policy.* Kingston: University
          of Rhode Island.

Initial Adjustment

Although the federal government's role in refugee resettlement has grown and changed, and although the numbers and origins of refugees to the United States have shifted, the initial difficulties of adjusting to a new society remain a constant. These difficulties are, in many ways, similar to those faced by immigrants to the United States, both those arriving in recent years and those in the hundred years from 1820 to 1920 whose descendants form such a major portion of American society. However, the very nature of refugee status, the typical rapidity and danger of exodus, and the inexorably permanent separation from home country militate for a consideration of the uniqueness of refugees in their resettlement.

The precise way in which refugees adjust to the United States varies as would be expected simply from the divergent social and cultural heritages that they bring with them. There is also variation because of the different faces that American society presents to particular refugee populations. Yet there are also some commonalities. This chapter presents an overview of the initial adjustment of refugees based on the wide range of research (quantitative and qualitative, sophisticated and rudimentary) that currently exists. Reflecting numbers, material is most extensive for Southeast Asian and Cuban refugees, far less so for Soviet refugees, and extremely limited for other, smaller groups. The net result is a research emphasis on the three major refugee populations of the past twenty-five years. The general question to be addressed is the overall shape of the initial adjustment that refugees make to American society. The answer requires separate attention to the capabilities, expectations, and values that refugees bring with them, the way in which they come to the United States, the kind of reception they receive, and the kinds of problems they are likely to encounter.

WHAT THEY BRING

General Population Characteristics

Much of the nature of refugee adjustment to the United States hinges not on cultural particulars or personal experiences, but rather on such general population characteristics as age and sex. The elderly, for example, are likely to lack familiarity with English and with American customs and may find adapting to new ways particularly difficult. Children, on the other hand, are likely to adjust faster to new customs, possibly at the expense of their relations with parents. Women, by virtue of their roles as wives and mothers, may remain confined within their homes and thus cut off from experiences that would help them acculturate to their new society. The relative proportion of the sexes and of particular age-groups thus helps determine the kinds of problems most likely to affect given refugee groups.

The Cuban, Southeast Asian, and Soviet refugees differ markedly in terms of such general demographic characteristics. They also differ both from the general U.S. population and from immigrants to the United States as a whole. Age differences are the greatest. As Taft, North, and Ford (1979:18) pointed out in their seminal report on the U.S. refugee program, the U.S. population had a median age of almost twenty-nine in 1975 and immigrants arriving that year had a median age of about twenty-four. Cuban refugees who had arrived since the late 1960s were considerably older, with a median age of over thirty-seven; Southeast Asian refugees were considerably younger, with a median age under twenty. Soviet refugees were in between, with a median age two years greater than that of the U.S. population as a whole. In terms of the proportion of the population under age fifteen, the differences are similarly striking. Both the U.S. population and arriving immigrants in 1975 had about one-fourth of their members under the age of fifteen, but for both Cuban and Soviet refugees less than a fifth of the population was under the age of fifteen. For Southeast Asian refugees arriving in 1975, well over a third (38.7 percent) were under the age of fifteen, as has continued to be the pattern (e.g., ORR 1983, 1984). Southeast Asian refugees are thus a far younger population, with a far larger number of children, than the general U.S. population or the even older Cuban and Soviet refugee populations. This has direct implications for the ability to find employment adequate to meeting household financial need.

Occupational and Educational Background

The second set of factors that can influence adjustment to the United States involves the skills and competencies that refugees bring with them. Probably the most important of these involves occupational background. For all three refugee populations during their initial years of exodus to the United States, more than two-thirds of those who had been in the labor force in their country of origin had been in white-collar occupations. For the U.S. population as a whole, only half of those in the labor force are in white-collar occupations. Perhaps more important are the percentages who were in professional and technical occupations. For the U.S. labor force, the relevant figure is about 15 percent, but for all the refugee populations, the figure is much higher. Of Cuban refugees, one in four had been in a professional or technical occupation; for

Vietnamese refugees almost a third and for Soviet refugees more than a third had been in equivalent occupations (Fagen and Brody 1964; HIAS 1980; OSI 1977).

Educational levels are corresponding high, especially considering the relative lack of educational opportunities in most countries from which refugees come. A systematic sample of the roster of the Cuban Refugee Center (Miami) in 1963 indicated that more than 14 percent of male refugees over the age of sixteen had completed four years of college. An additional 22 percent had completed high school, with or without subsequent college education. Less than 5 percent had completed no more than the third grade (Fagen and Brody1964:392). Data from a survey of 1,574 Southeast Asian refugee heads of household in Illinois (Kim 1980:33) present a not dissimilar picture. Fewer Southeast Asian refugees had completed college (8.3 percent) but more had completed high school (32.8 percent). Only 7 percent lacked any formal education. Data from a 1980 national survey of 1,032 Southeast Asian refugee households give similar aggregate figures but also illustrate important differences among the different Southeast Asian nationalities. For Vietnamese males, almost 14 percent had completed college and over 40 percent had completed at least the first of the two high school degrees. For the Cambodians and Laotians, the figures were generally lower. Among Laotian males, for example, only half as many had completed college and about one-fourth as many had completed high school (OSI 1981).

As a generality then, refugees come to the United States with relatively high levels of occupational skills and, especially as compared with their compatriots in country of origin, quite high educational levels. This generalization tends to be less true of later arrivals from both Cuba and Southeast Asia. There are also limitations in the extent to which prior education and occupation are relevant to the demands of the U.S. situation. Nevertheless, the general picture remains of relatively well-skilled populations. Perhaps as important, however, are the variations within particular refugee populations. Those without education or particularly relevant occupational skills—such as the farmers and fishers who constitute a small but significant portion of recent flows from Southeast Asia— face greater difficulties as they adjust to life in the United States.

Life Experiences, Values, and Expectations

The third set of factors that influence the adjustment process includes the life experiences of refugees in country of origin, their basic values, and their expectations about and goals for life in the United States. Cuban, Southeast Asian, Soviet, and the other, smaller refugee populations differ both from one another and from mainstream American society. Those from the Soviet Union, for example, have spent their lives under a planned, socialist economy. The state has restricted many of their freedoms, including the practice of their religion. It has also, however, met many of their basic needs (including employment) without requiring great initiative by the individual (e.g., Osborn 1976). Soviet refugees thus have little experience that bears directly on the self-initiated job search that is important in the American labor market. Cubans, on the other hand, come from a society that, prior to 1959, shared many features with that of the United States. In particular, early Cuban refugees had experience with the workings of an open, competitive, capitalist economy. Aspects of American society, such as entrepreneurship, that may elude a Soviet refugee may come as second nature to someone from Cuba (e.g., Portes 1969). Cambodians, Laotians, and Vietnamese come to the United States having spent their entire lives under a situation of continuing, if intermittent, war, preceded by three or more generations of French colonial rule. Although refugees from all three countries come to the United States to escape communist domination, their personal histories are markedly different and likely to affect the continuing course of their lives in the United States.

The values that refugees hold also affect adaptation to the United States. Perhaps the most important set of values relates to the ways in which refugees define themselves. For most of the refugees, individualism per se is less valued than it is by Americans. Rather, the individual is an integral part of ongoing social units, particularly those of the family. The importance of the "honor" of the Cuban family, for example, has been a spur to the quest for economic success in the United States. Husbands and wives cooperate in constructing a self-sufficient and productive life in the United States (e.g., Boone 1980; Prohias and Casal 1973). Even more so for many Southeast Asian refugees, the individual appears as less important than the social group. Success in the United States can be defined more as a familial attribute than as an individual attribute.

Expectations that refugees hold about their new lives in the United States can have important effects. Rita Simon's (1981a, 1981b) research on Vietnamese and Soviet refugees in Chicago is instructive. Both Vietnamese and Soviet parents had high expectations for the academic and occupational success of their children. The parents were also concerned that their traditions remain alive in succeeding generations, as witnessed by their desire that their children marry within the ethnic group. The dual expectations of success and cultural maintenance set a standard against which future experiences will be judged and toward which resources will be allocated.

Such values and expectations can both hinder and facilitate adjustment. On the positive side, teachers note the considerable respect and effort they find among Vietnamese children. On the negative side, refugees who have lived under a pervasive state bureaucracy (as in the Soviet Union) may have little understanding of the independence of private agencies in the United States, such as the voluntary agencies that have resettled them. The effects of such previous life experiences, current values, and future expectations, whether positive or negative, are also difficult to predict. Their importance, however, is clear.

Family and Kinship

The final set of factors involves the primary web of social relationships within which the adjustment of the individual refugee takes place. The most important of these involves the family, both as a household and as an extended set of kin. Much of the importance of the family stems directly from such demographic considerations as fertility. Southeast Asian refugees, for example, have more children than do mainstream American families; Soviet refugees have fewer (e.g., Gordon 1983; R. Simon 1981b). Automatically, then, Vietnamese refugee households are larger, include more dependents, and will experience problems in the areas of housing, education, and household incomes. At least as important, however, is the way in which the family functions as the nexus of social identity.

The structuring of roles within the household also has important effects. One of the most critical roles is that of the adult woman. For example, Cuban women have entered the U.S. labor force in large numbers, and this has been attributed to the flexibility in their roles as wives and mothers. Specifically, employment is seen as a way to contribute to the family without sacrificing rights and obligations within the home (Ferree 1979; Boone 1980). Similar flexibility in the wife's role has been noted for the Vietnamese (Hoskins 1975). If refugees bring with them to the United States the belief that women's work outside the home is both acceptable and important, then the family has an additional wage earner and enhanced flexibility in achieving economic self-sufficiency.

A final aspect to kinship involves the multiplicity of function and extent of inclusion that characterize many refugee families. The structure of Vietnamese and Hmong kinship is of particular interest in indicating this. For both groups, kinship is organized along patrilineal lines. This does not mean that the family itself is patriarchal, but rather that blood relations between males are used to extend the family back to distant ancestors and laterally to include distant cousins. For both the Hmong and the Vietnamese, these sets of relatives linked through males can be extensive. The resulting kin group functions as a unit for a variety of social, political, economic, and ritual activities. In Vietnamese villages a particularly large kin group could act as the framework for the economic and political life of an entire village (Hickey 1964). For the Hmong, the extension of the kin group and the multiplicity of its functions are even greater. Leadership, for example, may be the result of belonging to a particular family and is likely to be validated through a series of (polygynous) marriages to women of other clans or family alliance groups (Geddes 1976; LeBar, Hickey, and Musgrave 1964; Dunnigan 1980).

For the Hmong and Vietnamese, then, the family extends directly into the areas that in the United States would be characterized as the arena of the community. It is a comment on the diversity of Southeast Asian cultures that the Lao and Khmer do not particularly resemble the Hmong and Vietnamese. The Khmer show some preference for relatively small nuclear households and, if anything, a tendency to extend the family through female, rather than male, blood relations. Khmer kinship terminology and residence patterns actually show considerable similarity to those of the United States. One result is that, for the Khmer, "community" may be quite similar to the American situation and relatively separate from kin relations.

As in the area of values and expectations, the different refugee populations differ both from one another and, by and large, from American society. In some cases such distinctive characteristics will facilitate adjustment; in other cases they may make it more difficult. In yet other cases, they may simply make the adjustment process different.

Exodus and Transit

Refugees are refugees because they flee from situations of danger. Flight is often chosen rapidly, and even when the dangers are not excessive it involves clandestine actions, social and financial losses, and a severe separation from homeland. All refugees share this experience, and it conditions their adjustment to a new country. However, there are great variations among refugees as to the precise nature of exodus and the nature and duration of the transit to the United States. For the Cubans, the United States has usually been the country of first asylum, although during the mid-1960s some Cubans came to the United States by way of other countries, particularly Spain. For Soviet and Southeast Asian refugees, however, arrival in the United States is the result of a long and complex transit.

Soviet Jews have perhaps the most routine transit. All those desiring to emigrate from the Soviet Union must apply for exit visas to Israel. The time period from application to acceptance varies considerably, as does the overall likelihood of success, which has declined drastically since the mid-1970s. During this period the potential émigré is, as Simon points out in Chapter 11, largely cut off from Soviet society, denied work, and subject to harassment. When exit is approved the émigré goes first to Vienna, and it is only then that any desire to go to the United States can be made known. All Soviet refugees coming to the United States are technically "break-offs" (*noshrim*) from emigration to Israel. When their desire to *not* go to Israel is made known, they are transferred to Rome for processing to the Western countries, including the United States. The entire process, from visa application to arrival in the United States, can be lengthy. The émigré is likely to be exposed to some material hardship and considerable ideological pressure (Jacobson 1978; GAO 1977).

For Southeast Asian refugees, transit has been particularly difficult. The initial exodus (largely Vietnamese) from Southeast Asia in 1975 followed the fall of the American-supported governments and occurred under panic conditions (Kelly 1977; Liu, Lamanna, and Murata 1979). People were caught up in the exodus with little, if any, prior planning. Families were splintered and fortunes were lost. Those going to the United States were transported to camps in the Pacific and then to others in the continental United States before being resettled by the voluntary agencies into local communities. Material needs, however, were met with considerable success, and at least some provision was made for orientation and language training. Later Indochinese refugees have faced different sets of problems. Many refugees from Laos and Cambodia in 1975 faced long stays in camps of temporary asylum in Thailand rather than rapid movement to resettlement countries. Camp conditions were frequently poor, with little security, limited supplies, and limited opportunity for planning a future in a country of final asylum. The increasing exodus by boat in 1978 added further dangers and deprivation. Many boats sank on the way; others experienced the thefts, rapes, and murders of Thai pirates. Boats approaching land were sometimes pushed back to sea. Refugees reaching shore found themselves placed in overcrowded camps with an uncertain future (Grant and others 1979; Burton 1983; USCR 1984).

WHAT THEY FACE

The Situation in the United States

Refugees come to the United States with varying background characteristics, bring different skills and abilities, and arrive through a wide range of migration experiences. They also come to the United States at different times and settle in different parts of the country in varying numbers. In essence, they come to different Americas; they adjust to different environments. Their very reception by the American varies. The early Cuban refugees came as exiles from a communist nation strongly opposed by the U.S. government. Their stay was initially viewed as temporary (contingent on the fall of Castro), and they enjoyed strong political support. Southeast Asian refugees also fled from new communist governments, but they brought memories of an unpopular war. They also came at a time when Asian immigration had risen significantly after the 1965 revisions to the Immigration and Nationality Act. Refugees became, to most, a visible part of a far larger Asian presence. Soviet refugees, having lived their lives in a secular society, must face a Jewish community that supports them extensively but also tends to expect from them a religiosity with which they have no experience. Thus refugees not only bring their own set of expectations with them but are also affected by the expectations about them held by both American society as a whole and the particular Americans with whom they interact, whether as sponsors, as colleagues, as neighbors, or as friends.

Refugees also face, as have immigrants throughout American history, economies that are at different stages of growth or constriction. Cuban refugees generally fared better in terms of employment prospects in the early 1960s than did Southeast Asian refugees in the late 1970s. The situation was particularly bleak for Southeast Asian refugees in the early 1980s. Although the public might consider that refugees were taking jobs from Americans, the extent to which refugees were first laid off suggests that this was not generally the case. Case-study material notes the extent to which refugees lacked the necessary seniority to make it through the recession (e.g., the situation of refugees in the light aircraft industry in Wichita, Kansas, as described in Finnan and Cooperstein 1983). National surveys of Southeast Asian refugees by the Office of Refugee Resettlement showed correspondingly high unemployment rates for refugees of

24 percent in fall 1982 and somewhat down to 18 percent in fall 1983 (ORR 1983, 1984).

The overall shape and specific elements of public policy also have important effects on refugee adjustment. Different refugee populations and the same refugee population at different times have been subject to varying domestic resettlement provisions and regulations—much less varying admissions criteria and overseas training and maintenance. Cubans, for example, were allowed to congregate heavily in the Miami area. With Southeast Asian refugees, on the other hand, considerable efforts were initially made to disperse the refugees throughout the United States, and this has remained a concern ever since. The specifics of the kinds of assistance available to refugees also make a difference. Support to early Cuban refugees was direct and localized in Miami through the Cuban Refugee Center. Soviet and, to a lesser extent, some other non-Cuban, non-Southeast Asian refugees have received support through a matching grant program. Southeast Asian refugees have been particularly subject to the constant vacillations in federal assistance programs that were discussed in Chapter 1.

Finally, the adjustment of refugees is subject to the particular features of the communities in which they settle. This is true both in terms of the resources available (jobs, housing) and in terms of more general features of the local environment. Starr and Roberts (1982) have demonstrated that such general community characteristics as ethnic heterogeneity and low median educational levels significantly affect the nature of Vietnamese refugee adjustment. It is also likely that the resources of an established ethnic community make a difference. The lack of an ethnic base may cause smaller refugee groups to have adjustment problems, but it is also an area in which the different Southeast Asian refugee groups have had difficulties. Even for the Vietnamese, there was little in the way of an established ethnic base in the United States before the initial exodus of 1975.

Problems

The variety of possible situations and responses in the United States, coupled with the range of skills and characteristics that refugees bring with them, ensures that the resettlement and adjustment of the refugees is a complex, multifaceted process. It can be smooth; it is more likely to be characterized by a variety of problems, some serious. Health itself can be a problem. A survey of ninety Soviet émigrés in Baltimore led Gilison (1979:24) to note their arrival ''with a backlog of medical problems.'' Health status has been of particular concern for Southeast Asian refugees. Anemia and skin, respiratory, and gastrointestinal problems were often joined by more serious conditions, such as malaria, hepatitis, and tuberculosis (Erickson and Hoang 1980; Catanzaro and Moser 1982; CDC 1980; GAO 1983). Concerns about refugee health have since led to improved medical screening overseas, before refugee entry into the United States.

Other problems have more to do with the availability of resources in the United States. Housing itself can be a problem. There may be problems of affordability, of availability, or of availability of appropriate housing—a problem for large refugee families, as it tends to be for all large families in the United States. Even if housing is available, its location may be less than ideal in terms of employment or even in terms of safety. Many Southeast Asian refugee families, for example, have moved into high-crime areas because of their need for modest-cost, multibedroom, rental housing. Although this causes the refugees themselves problems, it may rebound to the benefit of the neighborhood as a whole, as when refugees moving into San Francisco's Tenderloin area had the net effect of stabilizing a previously transient area, making it safer for all (Finnan and Cooperstein 1983).

Much of the difficulty that Southeast Asian refugees have in regard to housing results from their relatively large families and the consequent mismatch between their housing needs and an American rental housing market affected by the dual trends toward condominium conversion and market responses to shrinking U.S. household size (Haines 1980; Ragas 1980; Masnick and Bane 1980; HUD 1980). Nearly two-thirds of (1,237) Southeast Asian refugee respondents in an Illinois survey, for example, rated housing as a serious (31 percent) or very serious (31 percent) problem, whereas only 11 percent of a sample of Soviet refugees in Detroit expressed any dissatisfaction with housing (Kim 1980:99; Gitelman 1978).

Although health represents, in essence, an aftereffect of exodus and transit, and housing, a potential mismatch between particular household needs and available community resources, a problem area perhaps more fundamental to refugee resettlement is the area of orientation or, more precisely, reorientation. In adjusting to the United States, refugees must learn how to deal with American society in general and with the variety of institutions and people who hold the key to the success of the adaptation, whether they be potential employers, medical personnel, neighbors, government officials, or friends. The basic rule of thumb generally holds true: The greater the cultural differences between the United States and a refugee's country of origin, the more difficult the adjustment. Orientation is the bridge across these cultural differences.

Refugees themselves express the need for orientation. For example, a survey of 697 Southeast Asian refugee clients in California included questions about which areas refugees felt they needed help in coping with (Human Resources Corporation 1979). More than a third (37 percent) of the refugees who left Southeast Asia before 1978 indicated a need to learn about life in the United States. The proportion was even higher (41 percent) among those who left in 1978 and 1979. Furthermore, almost half (47 percent) of the more recent arrivals indicated that they needed help in dealing with agencies and services. Finally, half of the recent arrivals (but only 40 percent of the earlier arrivals) expressed the need for help in dealing with education. Education, especially for immigrants and refugees, can be a basic mechanism for orientation. English itself—the most frequently mentioned area of need—is also an aspect of orientation. Notably, the respondents stressed orientation problems far more frequently than they did family problems or personal emotional problems.

One of the particularly difficult areas involves the refugees' interaction with those who seek to aid them. Many refugees, because of their prior experiences, have little understanding of social services as they are organized in the United States. American social services often emphasize an interventionist but benign counseling approach that may be alien to refugees. Soviet refugees, for example, have spent their lives under a government that supplies a variety of basic material needs but is also relatively unresponsive to their demands. Such refugees are likely to perceive that social service agencies in the United States owe them a considerable amount of material aid but will be slow and unresponsive in furnishing that aid. Greenberg echoes the comments of many service providers when he notes:

Agency staff members are accustomed (to some degree) to an "adversary" element when working with families who are dependent on an agency for financial assistance. But, many of the Soviet immigrants tend to play their cards "closer to the vest," and seem less ready to reveal their plans, aspirations and feelings—or even furnish verification of obligations for which they seek financial assistance. Some are unwilling to accept a worker's decision and insist on going to the "highest authority." (Greenberg 1976:141)

Because of such a lack of fit between the refugee's perceptions of the agency and the agency's perceptions of the refugee client, the refugee is thus kept at a distance from the very people who are attempting to facilitate his or her adjustment.

Similar problems in dealing with social service agencies exist for Southeast Asian refugees. Many, particularly those of non-elite background, have limited exposure to American-style social services and the ideas on which they are based. Such lack of exposure is reflected in refugee perceptions of agency helpfulness. Of 530 Vietnamese refugees interviewed in California in 1977 (Aames and others 1977:73), the majority felt that the agency with which they were dealing had helped them at least a little. However, the ranking of agency helpfulness varied in terms of the class background of the refugees in Vietnam. Those who placed themselves close to the top of the social system in Vietnam had significantly more favorable views of the agency. Only 27 percent indicated that the agency had been of "no real help." For those who had been at the middle levels of Vietnamese society, this figure rose to 34 percent, and for those at the lower levels, it was 44 percent. Although the differences are not great, they suggest the obvious: Relatively upper-class refugees are better attuned to the nature, appropriate behavior, and likely outcomes of social service agency support in the United States.

Employment

Ultimately, refugees must find the financial resources necessary to support themselves and their households. For most—excluding the few who were able to bring their wealth with them—this entails work. Although the employment of individuals is not necessarily sufficient to enable the self-sufficiency of the household, the latter is dependent on the former. And although there have been great concerns about refugees' ability to find work, particularly during the recession of the early 1980s, Bach and Bach's (1980:31) succinct statement regarding the earlier Southeast Asian refugees remains appropriate: There is "sufficient cause for optimism." Case-study and small-survey data for Soviet refugees throughout the 1970s have indicated high rates of participation in the labor force and reasonable success in actually finding employment (e.g., Gilison 1979; Gitelman 1980; Feldman 1977). The major survey effort on these refugees (Simon and Simon 1982) also had positive findings. The success of the initial Cuban refugees was reflected in 1970 census data, showing a labor force participation rate of 84 percent for Cuban-born males, the highest rate for any reported group and well above the figure of 77 percent for U.S. males combined. Cuban-born women had a labor force participation rate of 51 percent, a full 10 percentage points higher than the U.S. average for women (Urban Associates, Inc. 1974:102). Later data for Cubans arriving in 1973-74 also indicated rapid employment (Portes, Clark, and Bach 1977).

The employment experiences of the initial influx of Southeast Asian refugees in 1975 were similarly positive. By 1977, the refugees, mostly Vietnamese, had achieved labor force participation and unemployment rates similar to the general U.S. population (OSI 1977; Stein 1979; Marsh 1980; Montero 1979). By 1980, the data, reflecting the situation of 1975-79 arrivals, was somewhat less favorable. Interviews conducted with 605 Vietnamese, 216 Cambodian, and 211 Laotian refugee heads of household in 1980 (OSI 1981) indicated labor force participation rates for males of about 60 percent with some variation by country of origin and for females a range from a low of 26.7 percent (Laotian) to a high of 42.4 percent (Vietnamese). Unemployment rates were also somewhat high compared with the general U.S. population.

On the surface, the data appear to indicate relatively low rates of labor force participation and significant differences among the three national groups. However, the implications of the data are modified when the effects of length of residence are considered. Recent arrivals are likely to have low rates of labor force participation, thus obscuring the gains made by earlier arrivals. If the same Opportunity Systems, Inc., data are reorganized by length of residence, the labor force participation rates are clarified. Specifically, the combined labor force participation rate (both males and females) for 1975 arrivals was 64 percent, about the national average, whereas for 1979 arrivals it was only 32 percent. Length of residence also has significant effects on unemployment rates. For 1975 arrivals, the rate was less than 4 percent, compared with 17 percent for 1979 arrivals (OSI 1981).

A variety of succeeding survey efforts have indicated the same general patterns in the increase in labor force participation and employment by Southeast Asian refugees over time. Particularly useful are annual survey data by the Office of

Refugee Resettlement, which indicate both the extent to which more recent arrivals have difficulty in finding employment and the way in which particular entry cohorts do make progress from year to year. The percentage of working-age adults who arrived in 1980 who held jobs in 1981 was 42 percent, in 1982 was 46 percent, and in fall 1983 was 51 percent. For those arriving in 1979, the equivalent percentages were 45 percent in 1981, 51 percent in 1982, and 58 percent in 1983. All three surveys indicated that refugees arriving before 1979 worked at about the same frequency as the general U.S. population, although they did experience a higher unemployment rate (ORR 1982, 1983, 1984; cf. Dunning 1982; Kim 1980).

For Southeast Asian refugees, as for others, a variety of factors condition the ability to seek and find work. Age is an important factor. Preliminary analysis on Southeast Asian refugees, for example, suggests that they are disproportion-ately in the labor force in the middle years of adulthood and out of the labor force as youths and as those over age forty-five compared with the general U.S. population (Bach 1980). Household roles and responsibilities are an important factor with women typically in the labor force less frequently than men. With refugees this gap is sometimes narrowed because of noticeably strong labor market involvement by women, particularly true of Cubans and perhaps of Vietnamese as well. Health problems can keep people from employment, as can disadvantageous locations or simple lack of knowledge about the American world of work.

Two factors, however, merit particular attention. The first is English language competence. For most refugee groups, English language competence appears to be an essential element in successful employment. Comprehensive data on Soviet refugees are lacking, but case-study material supports the importance of English for obtaining employment (e.g., Feldman 1977; Gilison 1979; Gitelman 1978; Gilison 1976). For Cubans, the importance of competence in English is less clear. The Cuban National Planning Council's needs assessment stressed the continuing need for more English language training, particularly for the adult population. English was cited as the first of four major needs for the Cuban population of Dade County, Florida (Hernandez 1974). This is suggestive, es-pecially since Dade County is an area of dense Cuban settlement. The area approximates a fully bilingual environment, and the need for English competence should thereby be significantly reduced. Other research on Cubans in the Miami area, however, is less clear on the importance of English language competence as a determinant of rates of employment (e.g., Portes and Bach 1980). For Cubans elsewhere, the issue is also clouded by the wide use of Spanish in many areas of the United States.

The importance of English language competence for employment is clearer for Southeast Asian refugees. Data from interviews with 1,032 Southeast Asian refugees in 1980 show the significant effects of English language competence on both labor force participation and unemployment (OSI 1981). Only a fifth of the Cambodian, Laotian, and Vietnamese refugees who could not speak English were in the labor force. About half of those who spoke some English were in the labor force. Of those who spoke English well, about three-fifths were in the labor force, although the proportion was somewhat lower for Laotians (56.6 percent) and somewhat higher for Cambodians (71.8 percent). Unemployment rates (those in the labor force who could not find jobs) also reflected levels of English language competence. The unemployment rate for Laotians with no English ability was 37 percent. The rate dropped to 11 percent for those with some English and to 7 percent for those who spoke English well. For Vietnamese, the corresponding figures were 16 percent (no English), 11 percent (some English), and 4 percent (spoke English well). For Cambodians, the respective figures were 11 percent, 9 percent, and 5 percent.

The second general factor affecting employment involves the skills that refugees bring into the labor market. Case-study data from California (Finnan 1980) indicate how vocational training can be an effective bridge into productive, culturally acceptable employment. Various studies of Cubans with professional backgrounds have shown how skills-transfer programs have facilitated the employment of some refugees and how others have been successful in reapplying their skills to the U.S. situation (e.g., Moncarz 1973a, 1973b; Wey and Newport 1964; Wey and Hardin 1965). The importance of occupational skills is widely noted by refugees themselves. The national needs assessment of the Cuban National Planning Council had as two of its four major designated needs, problems involving vocational/professional training (Hernandez 1974). The responses of Southeast Asian refugees to questions about barriers to employment also emphasize job skills. Almost half of 1,200 refugee respondents in Illinois (in 1979) rated lack of job-skills training programs as a "very serious" problem; an additional one-fourth rated it as a "somewhat serious" problem (Kim 1980:90). Responses from a 1979 survey of service providers in California placed a similarly strong emphasis on the need for job skills. Service providers were asked: "What do you think are the major barriers for the refugees to become economically self-supporting?" Virtually all the 153 service providers (97 percent) mentioned lack of English language competence. The second most common comment (89 percent) was that refugees lack job skills relevant to the U.S. labor market (Human Resources Corporation 1979:23). Further, the third most frequently cited barrier (52 percent) was a tight job market. Lack of job skills was mentioned three times as often as welfare dependency. The importance of relevant job skills is seen perhaps more clearly in the relative success in finding work of those who are more highly skilled. Survey data from 1982 on Southeast Asian refugees, for example, show the relative success of those who had been professionals and managers (59 percent had jobs) versus those who had been students (38 percent had jobs), farmers and fishers (27 percent had jobs), laborers (28 percent held jobs), or even semiskilled blue-collar workers (41 percent held jobs) (Bach and others 1983).

For some refugees, obtaining employment is a relatively rapid process. They have the English language facility and the relevant job skills that allow easy entry into the U.S. labor force. For other refugees, obtaining employment involves overcoming serious obstacles of lack of English or difficult personal circumstances, such as health problems. For yet other refugees, employment is an unreachable and possibly irrelevant goal. The elderly and those with severe and continuing health problems are unlikely to ever seek or obtain employment (e.g., Kennedy 1976; Kahn 1980). Many refugees need and utilize different forms of public assistance during their initial adjustment to the United States. Such assistance is necessary to maintain refugee households through the period when employment is not obtainable, or when its rewards in wages and salaries are insufficient to meet household needs. According to 1970 census data, Cuban refugees utilized a higher level of general assistance than did the U.S. population. The rate was 17 percent versus 5 percent for the general U.S. population (Urban Associates, Inc. 1974). Although Cubans had rates of labor force participation well above those for the total population, their median income remained lower. That is, as a group they showed a greater inclination to work but received lower financial rewards for doing so. However, only half as many Cuban families were receiving social security. The disproportionate use of some forms of federal assistance by refugees, as by immigrants in general, is often compensated for by disproportionate underuse of others (J. Simon 1981; Kennedy and Schmulowitz 1980).

Southeast Asian refugees also utilize public assistance. Again, the utilization reflects both difficulties in obtaining employment and the limited rewards of the employment that is obtained. Southeast Asian refugee households are also relatively large. At the very least, a third of the households comprise six or more members (OSI 1981; Aames and others 1977; Kim 1980; Ragas and Maruggi 1978). Recent arrivals also appear to lack, compared with other refugees, the English language and vocational skills that facilitate finding employment. They also face an increasingly tight job market. Such refugees are likely to find that employment is difficult to obtain, financial rewards are limited, and the rewards seem even further limited because of the size of their households and the number of children they contain.

This is to say no more than that the adjustment of refugees to the United States is neither quick nor without difficulties for the refugees and the programs that attempt to serve them. The very forces that bring refugees to the United States militate against easy solutions.

REFERENCES

Aames, Jacqueline S., Ronald L. Aames, John Jung, and Edward Karabenick
1977   *Indochinese Refugee Self-sufficiency in California: A Survey and Analysis of the Vietnamese, Cambodians and Lao and the Agencies That Serve Them.* Report submitted to the State Department of Health, State of California.

Bach, Robert L.
1980   Employment Characteristics of Indochinese Refugees: January 1979. Washing-
        ton, D.C.: The Brookings Institution.
Bach, Robert L., and Jennifer B. Bach
1980   Employment Patterns of Southeast Asian Refugees. *Monthly Labor Review*
        103(10):31–38.
Bach, Robert, Linda Gordon, David Haines, and David Howell
1983   The Economic Adjustment of Southeast Asian Refugees in the U.S. *World
        Refugee Survey 1983*. Pages 51–55.
Boone, Margaret S.
1980   The Uses of Traditional Concepts in the Development of New Urban Roles:
        Cuban Women in the United States. In *A World of Women*. Edited by Erika
        Bourguignon. New York: Praeger.
Burton, Eve
1983   Surviving the Flight of Horror: The Story of Refugee Women. *Indochina Issues*
        No. 34.
Catanzaro, Antonino, and Robert John Moser
1982   Health Status of Refugees from Vietnam, Laos, and Cambodia. *Journal of the
        American Medical Association* 247(9):1303–1308.
CDC (Center for Disease Control)
1980   Health Screening of Resettled Indochinese Refugees—Washington, D.C., Utah.
        Morbidity and Mortality Weekly Report 29(1):4, 9–11.
Dunnigan, Timothy
1980   The Importance of Kinship in Hmong Community Development. Paper pre-
        sented at the annual meetings of the American Anthropological Association,
        Washington, D.C.
Dunning, Bruce B.
1982   *A Systematic Survey of the Social, Psychological and Economic Adaptation of
        Vietnamese Refugees Representing Five Entry Cohorts, 1975-1979*. Washing-
        ton, D.C.: Bureau of Social Science Research.
Erickson, Roy V., and Giao Hoang
1980   Health Problems Among Indochinese Refugees: Results of 194 Comprehensive
        Evaluations. Paper presented at the First National Conference on Indochinese
        Education and Social Services, Arlington, Virginia.
Fagan, Richard R., and Richard A. Brody
1964   Cubans in Exile: A Demographic Analysis. *Social Problems* 11(4):389–401.
Feldman, William
1977   Social Absorption of Soviet Immigrants: Integration or Isolation. *Journal of
        Jewish Communal Service* 54(1):62–68.
Ferree, Myra Marx
1979   Employment Without Liberation: Cuban Women in the United States. *Social
        Science Quarterly* 60:35–50.
Finnan, Christine Robinson
1980   A Community Affair: Occupational Assimilation of Vietnamese Refugees. *Jour-
        nal of Refugee Resettlement* 1(1):8–14.

Finnan, Christine, and Rhonda Ann Cooperstein
1983   *Southeast Asian Refugee Resettlement at the Local Level: The Role of the Ethnic Community and the Nature of Refugee Impact.* Menlo Park, California: SRI International.

GAO (U.S. General Accounting Office)
1977   *Report to the Congress: U.S. Assistance Provided for Resettling Soviet Refugees.* Washington, D.C.
1983   *Improved Overseas Medical Examinations and Treatment Can Reduce Serious Diseases in Indochinese Refugees Entering the United States.* Washington, D.C.

Geddes, William R.
1976   *Migrants of the Mountains.* Oxford: Clarendon Press.

Gilison, Jerome M.
1979   Summary Report of the Survey of Soviet Jewish Émigrés in Baltimore. Baltimore, Maryland: Baltimore Hebrew College.

Gilison, Jerome M., Ed.
1976   *The Soviet Jewish Émigré: Proceedings of the National Symposium on the Integration of Soviet Jews into the American Jewish Community.* Baltimore, Maryland: Baltimore Hebrew College.

Gitelman, Zvi
1978   Soviet Immigrants and American Absorption Efforts: A Case Study in Detroit. *Journal of Jewish Communal Service* 55(1):72–82.
1980   Soviet Jewish Immigrants to the United States: Profile, Problems, Prospects. Paper presented at the annual conference of YIVO, New York City.

Gordon, Linda W.
1983   New Data on the Fertility of Southeast Asian Refugees in the United States. *P/AAMHRC Research Review* 2(1):3–6.

Grant, Bruce, and others
1979   *The Boat People: An "Age" Investigation.* New York: Penguin Books.

Greenberg, Martin
1976   Agency Concerns: The Special Problems Confronting Agencies in Providing Services to Immigrants from the USSR. In *The Soviet Jewish Émigré.* Edited by Jerome Gilison. Baltimore, Maryland: Baltimore Hebrew College.

Haines, David
1980   Mismatch in the Resettlement Process: The Vietnamese Family Versus the American Housing Market. *Journal of Refugee Resettlement* 1(1):15–19.

Hernandez, Andres R., Ed.
1974   *The Cuban Minority in the U.S.* Washington, D.C.: Cuban National Planning Council.

HIAS (Hebrew Immigrant Aid Society)
1980   Statistical Abstract, Vol. 21. New York, New York.

Hickey, Gerald C.
1964   *Village in Vietnam.* New Haven, Connecticut: Yale University Press.

Hoskins, Marilyn W.
1975   Vietnamese Women: Their Roles and Their Options. In *Being Female.* Edited by Dana Raphael. The Hague: Mouton.

HUD (U.S. Department of Housing and Urban Development)
1980   *How Well Are We Housed?: Large Households.* Washington, D.C.

Human Resources Corporation
1979   *Evaluation of the Indochinese Refugee Assistance Program in Private Agencies in California.* San Francisco, California.

Jacobson, Gaynor I.
1978   Soviet Jewry: Perspectives on the "Dropout" Issue. *Journal of Jewish Communal Service* 55(1):83–89.
Kahn, Arthur L.
1980   Indochina Refugees Receiving Supplemental Security Income. U.S. Department of Health, Education, and Welfare, Social Security Administration, Research and Statistics Note No. 6.
Kelly, Gail Paradise
1977   *From Vietnam to America: A Chronicle of the Vietnamese Immigration to the United States.* Boulder, Colorado: Westview Press.
Kennedy, Lenna D.
1976   Supplemental Security Income Payments to Indochina Refugees. U.S. Department of Health, Education, and Welfare, Social Security Administration, Research and Statistics Note No. 23.
Kennedy, Lenna, and Jack Schmulowitz
1980   SSI Payments to Lawfully Resident Aliens, 1978-79. *Social Security Bulletin* 43(3):3–10.
Kim, Young Yun
1980   *Population Characteristics and Service Needs of Indochinese Refugees.* Vol. 3 of the Research Project on Indochinese Refugees in the State of Illinois. Chicago: Travelers Aid Society of Metropolitan Chicago.
LeBar, Frank, Gerald Hickey, and John Musgrave, Eds.
1964   *Ethnic Groups of Mainland Southeast Asia.* New Haven, Connecticut: Human Relations Area Files Press.
Liu, William T., Maryanne Lamanna, and Alice Murata
1979   *Transition to Nowhere: Vietnamese Refugees in America.* Nashville, Tennessee: Charter House.
Marsh, Robert E.
1980   Socioeconomic Status of Indochinese Refugees in the United States: Progress and Problems. *Social Security Bulletin* 43(10):11–20.
Masnick, George, and Mary Jo Bane
1980   *The Nation's Families: 1960-1990.* Cambridge, Massachusetts: Joint Center for Urban Studies of MIT and Harvard University.
Moncarz, Raul
1973a   A Model of Professional Adaptation of Refugees: The Cuban Case in the U.S., 1959-1970. *International Migration* 11(4):171–182.
1973b   Cuban Architects and Engineers in the United States. *International Migration* 11(4):184–190.
Montero, Darrel
1979   *Vietnamese Americans: Patterns of Resettlement and Socioeconomic Adaptation in the United States.* Boulder, Colorado: Westview Press.
ORR (Office of Refugee Resettlement)
1982   *Report to the Congress: Refugee Resettlement Program.* Washington, D.C.: U.S. Department of Health and Human Services.
1983   *Report to the Congress: Refugee Resettlement Program.* Washington, D.C.: U.S. Department of Health and Human Services.
1984   *Report to the Congress: Refugee Resettlement Program.* Washington, D.C.: U.S. Department of Health and Human Services.

OSI (Opportunity Systems, Inc.)
1977   *Fifth Wave Report: Vietnam Resettlement Operational Feedback.* Washington, D.C.
1981   *Ninth Wave Report: Indochinese Resettlement Operational Feedback.* Washington, D.C.
Osborn, Robert J.
1976   The Soviet Social Environment and American Contrasts. In *The Soviet Jewish Émigré.* Edited by Jerome Gilison. Baltimore, Maryland: Baltimore Hebrew College.
Portes, Alejandro
1969   Dilemmas of a Golden Exile: Integration of Cuban Refugee Families in Milwaukee. *American Sociological Review* 34:505–518.
Portes, Alejandro, and Robert L. Bach
1980   Immigrant Earnings: Cuban and Mexican Immigrants in the United States. *International Migration Review* 14(3):315–341.
Portes, Alejandro, Juan M. Clark, and Robert L. Bach
1977   The New Wave: A Statistical Profile of Recent Cuban Exiles to the United States. *Cuban Studies* 1:1–32.
Prohias, Rafael, and Lourdes Casal
1973   *The Cuban Minority in the U.S.: Preliminary Report on Need Identification and Program Evaluation.* Boca Raton: Florida Atlantic University.
Ragas, Wade R.
1980   Housing the Refugees: Impact and Partial Solutions to the Housing Shortages. *Journal of Refugee Resettlement* 1(1):40–48.
Ragas, Wade R., and Vincent Maruggi
1978   Vietnamese Refugee Living Conditions in the New Orleans Metro Area. University of New Orleans, Division of Business and Economic Research, Working Paper No. 111.
Simon, Julian
1981   New Evidence Shows Immigrants Benefit U.S. Citizens: Supplemental Report to the Select Commission on Immigration and Refugee Policy. Urbana: University of Illinois.
Simon, Rita J.
1981a   Refugee Families' Adjustment and Aspirations: A Comparison of Soviet Jewish and Vietnamese Immigrants. Urbana: University of Illinois.
1981b   Mothers and Adolescent Daughters: Interactions and Aspirations Among Recent Immigrants and American Families. Urbana: University of Illinois.
Simon, Rita J., and Julian L. Simon
1982   *The Soviet Jews' Adjustment to the United States.* New York: Council of Jewish Federations.
Starr, Paul, and Alden Roberts
1982   Community Structure and Vietnamese Refugee Adaptation: The Significance of Context. *International Migration Review* 16(3):595–618.
Stein, Barry N.
1979   Occupational Adjustment of Refugees: The Vietnamese in the United States. *International Migration Review* 13(1):25–45.
Taft, Julia Vadala, David S. North, and David A. Ford
1979   *Refugee Resettlement in the U.S.: Time for a New Focus.* Washington, D.C.: New TransCentury Foundation.

Urban Associates, Inc.
1974   *A Study of Selected Socio-economic Characteristics of Ethnic Minorities Based on the 1970 Census, Vol. 1: Americans of Spanish Origin*. Washington, D.C.: U.S. Department of Health, Education, and Welfare, Office of the Assistant Secretary for Planning and Evaluation.
USCR (U.S. Committee for Refugees)
1984   *Vietnamese Boat People: Pirates' Vulnerable Prey*. New York: American Council for Nationalities Service.
Wey, Herbert W., and Henry N. Hardin
1965   The Professional Preparation and Placement of Cuban Refugee Teachers. Coral Gables, Florida: University of Miami.
Wey, Herbert W., and John F. Newport
1964   The Professional Preparation and Placement of Cuban Refugee Teachers. Coral Gables, Florida: University of Miami.

Toward Integration into American Society

Because of the urgency with which refugee resettlement often occurs, and the narrow temporal focus of the federal government's involvement with refugees, the adjustment of these people to the United States is often viewed as a short-term process—if not in actuality, then at least as an ideal. Any attention to previous immigration to the United States, however, makes evident the long-term nature of the accommodation that newcomers make to American society. Indeed, the process is multigenerational and its outcomes are far from predictable. Adjustment is subject not only to the internal social dynamics of the immigrants, but also to a wide range of factors in the receiving society that can either encourage assimilation (even if in the negative way experienced by German-Americans during the Second World War) or retard it (as in the various forms of ghettoization historically experienced by Asian-Americans).

Between these long-term, multigenerational aspects of integration into American society and the far shorter-range concerns discussed in Chapter 2 lies a middle stage of adjustment. Once refugees have succeeded in crafting an accommodation to a new environment—or perhaps simply have passively survived the inevitable problems and traumas of dislocation—they must move forward in new lives. They are no longer fully strangers, but rather another element in the complex class and ethnic fabric of American life. They are no longer operating in an unknown environment, but rather trying to modify traditional goals and values and to work this new environment to meet these goals. Although one can argue about the nature or dimensions of assimilation or about the extent to which at least some members of given immigrant groups retain allegiance—either cultural or political—to their country of origin, it is inarguable that most do become American; the gaining of citizenship in itself is a far from arbitrary proxy for this.

Plausibly, there is some point in time at which it could be hypothesized that refugees move into this middle stage of adjustment to the United States. Attention to economic concerns might suggest a period of between two and three years as the starting point on the basis of the fact that the average refugee household

apparently moves above the poverty line at about that time. Another point might
be that at which refugees participate in the labor force at about the same rate as
the overall U.S. population—about four years currently. Attention to so-called
mental health issues might suggest a similar period of four years when at least
one study suggests that general alienation significantly declines. Other compu-
tations of the transition point could be based on cultural adjustment, for which
a good proxy would be English language competence.

Any such date is at least partially arbitrary and certainly a crude generalization,
considering the wide variety of refugee groups and the great variations in the
U.S. economy and society that they enter. But it remains useful to suggest that
the initial set of issues given in Chapter 2 does shift toward longer-range considerations. This chapter thus addresses those elements of this middle stage of
adjustment that are critical and about which at least some information is available.
The chapter turns first to economic issues, focusing on occupation and income;
second to issues of the family and the ethnic community; and third to aspects
of individual personal adjustment, usually treated in the United States under the
rubric of mental health. As in Chapter 2, the focus is limited to the three major
refugee groups to the United States, those from Cuba, Southeast Asia, and the
Soviet Union.

OCCUPATION AND INCOME

Initial economic adjustment to the United States and the achievement of minimal economic self-sufficiency hinge on participation in the labor force and the
obtaining of employment. Quite typically, for refugees, as for the general U.S.
population, this entails more than one wage earner per family. These jobs are
frequently at the minimum-wage level. Longer-term economic success, on the
other hand, depends more on the level of employment. Even two minimum-
wage jobs, for example, are less than sufficient for the relatively large households
that characterize at least Southeast Asian refugees. And although unemployment
is a significant problem for refugees, underemployment is probably a more
pervasive one.

Downward Occupational Mobility

Cuban, Southeast Asian, and Soviet refugees have come to the United States
with relatively high occupational and educational backgrounds. However, during
their first few years in the United States they have significant difficulties in
obtaining employment commensurate with their skills and abilities. Barry Stein,
reviewing the existing research on refugee resettlement in the United States,
notes the extent of this downward occupational mobility and its implications for
refugee adjustment. The achievement of a level of employment consistent with
prior occupational status is, he suggests, "of crucial importance to the degree

of assimilation and satisfaction a refugee achieves in his resettlement'' (Stein 1979:25). However, such a transfer of occupational status is difficult:

The highly skilled refugees, who represent a majority of most refugee waves,...have many barriers to successful resumptions of their careers. The major obstacles to the transfer of foreign-acquired skills are non-recognition of degrees and skills, licensing restrictions by trades and professions, the extensive retraining needed to adjust to national differences, the greater language demands of professional, managerial, and sales work, and the non-transferability of certain skills. (Stein 1979:39)

The obstacles to finding employment commensurate with existing skills are many. The extent of the resulting downward occupational mobility is worth noting. The initial influx of Southeast Asian refugees occurred in 1975. About two years later, in the summer of 1977, Opportunity Systems, Inc. (OSI 1977) conducted its Fifth Wave Survey of 607 Vietnamese heads of household. Despite a full two years of residence in the United States the results indicated high levels of downward occupational mobility. Nearly half of those surveyed claimed professional or managerial occupations in Vietnam. Less than one in ten had an equivalent occupation in the United States. Specifically, 30 percent had been professional in Vietnam, but only 7 percent were in professional employment in the United States. For managers, the corresponding drop was from 15 percent to 2 percent. The compensating rises were in blue-collar work, both skilled and unskilled. Those working as craftsmen, for example, rose from 14 percent in Vietnam to 30 percent in the United States. The general finding was a decided shift away from professional and managerial occupations toward blue-collar work of all skill levels.

More recent data come from Opportunity Systems, Inc.'s Ninth Wave Survey (OSI 1981), conducted during October and November of 1980 with a random sample of 1,032 Southeast Asian refugees of all three national groups. The data also show significant levels of downward occupational mobility. For Cambodians and Vietnamese, the percentage in professional and managerial occupations in the United States was about half of what it had been in country of origin; for Laotians, it was about a fourth. All three national groups experienced significant drops in those in clerical and sales work. The result, as in the previous survey on Vietnamese refugees, was a significant shift away from white-collar work as a whole. For Cambodians, the drop in white-collar work from country of origin to the United States was from 63 percent to 24 percent; for Laotians, it was from 76 percent to 28 percent; and for Vietnamese, it was from 72 percent to 43 percent. The one positive finding was the relatively high proportion of Vietnamese refugees who had reattained professional employment in the United States. The figure (21 percent) is triple that from the 1977 survey (7 percent). Nevertheless, the overall finding is again significant downward occupational mobility, tempered somewhat by the longer length of residence of the Vietnamese refugees.

Cuban refugees experienced a similar pattern of downward occupational mobility after their resettlement. Research on the initial flow of Cuban refugees (e.g., Fagen, Brody, and O'Leary 1968) indicated high occupational levels in country of origin. Although later arrivals had somewhat lower occupational and educational backgrounds (cf. Prohias and Casal 1973), a survey conducted in Miami in 1966 still indicated that nearly half the refugees resettled by that time had been in professional or managerial occupations in Cuba (University of Miami 1967). The same survey also found that only 13 percent were in professional or managerial occupations in the United States. Data from the 1970 census corroborate this with a finding that about 14 percent of the Cuban work force in Miami was in professional or managerial occupations. As with Southeast Asian refugees, there was a net shift toward blue-collar work and away from highly skilled white-collar work. However, the data also suggest differences between the Cuban and Southeast Asian experience. Both populations had about a fourth of their work force in clerical and sales work in country of origin; only for the Cubans was this proportion maintained in the United States. The data also indicate, although tentatively, that Southeast Asian refugees may have had correspondingly more success than Cubans in obtaining skilled rather than unskilled blue-collar jobs.

Soviet refugees also have experienced the same kind of downward occupational mobility. A variety of case-study material indicates difficulties in transferring occupational status in the Soviet Union to the United States. For example, a survey of ninety émigrés in Baltimore indicated the highly skilled occupations in which the refugees had been employed in country of origin. More than a third had been in positions that required supervision of more than ten persons. Many of these were in the engineering professions. However, only half of those in such positions in the Soviet Union had obtained related employment in the United States (Gilison 1979). A survey of 123 Soviet émigrés in Detroit had different but related findings. Only about a fourth of those surveyed expressed any satisfaction with their current jobs, despite the fact that nearly half thought that their standard of living had improved since coming to the United States. Questions about self-identification by class also indicated a strong sense on the part of the refugees that their occupational status had declined drastically in the United States (Gitelman 1978).

The net implication of the existing data is that Cuban, Southeast Asian, and Soviet refugees all experience considerable downward occupational mobility during their early years in the United States. Although there is some indication, as with the Vietnamese refugees, that this process is partially reversed over time, the reachievement of employment commensurate with existing skills and abilities is neither a rapid nor inevitable process. This has direct implications for the amounts of income available to individuals and thus to households.

Income Levels

During their first years in the United States, refugees not only have difficulty in obtaining jobs, but even when successful receive relatively low wages. A survey conducted in 1977 of Vietnamese who arrived in 1975 indicated that almost 85 percent of those working were working forty hours a week or more. Nevertheless, almost a fifth had a weekly income lower than would be expected from working at the then minimum wage of $2.30 per hour (OSI 1977; cf. U.S. Bureau of the Census 1980). This was, however, a far more favorable picture than that presented in earlier surveys (e.g., OSI 1976). Similar data came from a survey of 1,034 Southeast Asian refugees conducted in California, also in 1977. The percentage of Vietnamese refugees earning less than $2.50 per hour (twenty cents above the then minimum wage) was 19; for Cambodians, the equivalent figure was 16 percent. For Chinese-Vietnamese and for Laotians, the situation was worse. Well over a third of both groups (38 percent for Chinese-Vietnamese and 40 percent for Laotians) were receiving wages lower than $2.50 per hour (Aames and others 1977).

English language competence has a particularly pronounced effect on wage and salary income, as it does on other aspects of employment. For example, a survey of 671 Vietnamese heads of household in late 1979 indicated the way in which English language competence affects wages. About 60 percent of those who spoke no English earned less than $150 per week. Less than 30 percent of those who spoke some English and less than a fourth of those who spoke English well earned less than $150 per week (OSI 1979). The proportions of those earning more than $200 per week were 11 percent (no English), 44 percent (some English), and 61 percent (good English). Data from a survey of 1,182 refugee households in 1982 also indicate how income rises sharply with improved English language competence. Those with no English fluency earned an average weekly wage of $159. This rose to $186 for those who had a little English and to $224 for those who spoke and understood the language well (ORR 1982:24). English competence thus remains as important for long-term adjustment as for initial adjustment.

Individual wages and salary income do not, however, directly determine the adequacy of household income. One household may do fairly well financially by combining the minimal wages of several working household members, whereas another household may do poorly if a single wage earner making a less modest salary must support numerous nonworking dependents. Data from the 1970 census concerning Cuban refugees are illustrative. Cubans had high rates of labor force participation for both men and women. They also had a rate of intact marriages about at the national rate (Urban Associates, Inc. 1974; Prohias and Casal 1973). The result was that household income was fairly high despite unremarkable individual wage and salary levels. Household structure itself becomes an important contributor to successful adjustment. Annual surveys by the Office of Refugee Resettlement have consistently shown that Southeast Asian refugee household structure has strong correlations with use of public assistance, both because of the presence of numerous dependents and because of the availability of more than one wage earner (ORR 1982, 1983, 1984). Research on Southeast Asian refugees in California in 1977 has similar implications. Overall family size was found to be inversely related to household self-sufficiency, and the ratio of adults to family size was found to be positively related to self-sufficiency. In both cases the relationships were statistically significant (Aames and others 1977).

It is for Southeast Asian refugees that the gap between individual wage and salary income and household needs is likely to be the greatest. Compared with Cuban and Soviet refugees, those from Southeast Asia are a relatively young population, with large numbers of children. Because household size is large, household need is great. Data from Kim and Nicassio's (1980) survey of 1,627 refugee households in Illinois are helpful. Combining all Vietnamese, Hmong, Lao, and Cambodian arrivals from 1975 until the time of the survey, in 1979, more than a fourth had monthly household incomes under $400. Another fourth had household incomes between $400 and $700. The average household size was 4.2 persons. These are low household incomes, considering the fact that the basic nonfarm poverty line for a family of four at that time was $7,412 (U.S. Bureau of the Census 1980), or about $620 per month.

Household income varied among the Cambodians, Hmong, Lao, and Vietnamese. For the Vietnamese, about 47 percent of the households had incomes below $700 per month. For the Lao, the equivalent figure was 52 percent, and for the Cambodians (with an average household size of only 3.6 persons), it was 72 percent. For the Hmong, the situation was most serious. Almost 70 percent of the households, with an average size of 5.5 persons, had a monthly income under $700. By comparison, the poverty line for a family of five was about $730 per month (U.S. Bureau of the Census 1980).

The general situation and the variation among the ethnic groups, however, appear less serious when the effects of length of residence are taken into consideration. For all four ethnic groups, the household incomes of those in the United States for less than two years remain under an estimated median monthly figure of $600. For those in the second year of residence, the estimated median household incomes for all four groups were within a $12 range, from $513 to $525. Household income continued to rise with length of residence, averaging about $900 per month for 1975 arrivals. The general indication, then, is that household incomes are low during the first two years of residence but, by rough comparison with national poverty lines, reach a crossover point during the third year of residence and continue to rise thereafter.

Occupational Satisfaction

Refugees experience significant downward occupational mobility when coming to the United States. This causes direct financial problems in terms of finding employment that provides sufficient income for household needs. The existing data indicate that income gradually rises and that there may be some reversal of the drop in occupational levels. However, it is unlikely that most refugees can achieve a level of occupational status in the United States that matches their experience in country of origin. Refugees face barriers of health, age, English language competence, licenses and credentials, and even appropriateness of former employment to the U.S. labor market. Ultimately, during the course of the middle stage of adjustment, refugees must make a compromise between the occupations that would be equivalent to those held in country of origin and occupations that are possible in the United States.

The importance of occupational satisfaction is indicated by the widely noted adjustment problems of refugees who come from high-status occupations and thus have most difficulty in reachieving previous levels. Stein (1979) suggests that for most refugees, the higher the previous occupational status, the more difficult the adjustment. Various studies of Southeast Asian refugees have pointed out the particular problems encountered by high-status refugees who are unable to find work of equivalent status in the United States (e.g., Lin, Tazuma, and Masuda 1979; Vignes and Hall 1979). One survey of 350 Vietnamese refugees suggested that both educational and social status in country of origin have negative effects on refugee mental health (Starr and others 1979). That is, those of high status in Vietnam were having particular difficulty in developing a balanced personal adjustment to their new situation in the United States.

Much of the case-study material on Soviet émigrés in the United States indicates the problems caused by employment that is below the level of work available in country of origin. Downward occupational mobility was, for example, coupled with low job satisfaction among 123 émigrés in Detroit (Gitelman 1978). Only 28 percent of the respondents were satisfied or very satisfied with their current jobs. Soviet refugees in general have been described as difficult social service clients because of their high expectations about employment in the United States. They come from a society in which occupation is the key to general status (Gilison 1976) to a society in which there is extensive, and to them alien, job mobility. They are characterized as sometimes unwilling to take employment that is inconsistent with their prior experience in the Soviet Union (e.g., Fisher 1975; Hawks 1977; Parker 1979). That is, they show some unwillingness to accept the need for compromise in terms of occupational goals or the time necessary to achieve professional-level occupations.

Many refugees do have high, and perhaps unrealistic, expectations about level of employment in the United States. However, other refugees have made compromises between desired and possible employment. Their ability to do so appears contingent on two factors: first, a situation in country of origin that is, in some respects, similar to the United States; and second, sufficient time in the United States to understand the remaining differences. These two factors—length of time in the United States and degree of similarity to the United States of the society from which they come—apply most clearly to the situation of the early Cuban refugees, and it is for them that the data on occupational satisfaction are clearest. Focusing on integration into U.S. society, Portes's (1969) now-classic research with forty-eight Cuban refugee families in Milwaukee in the late 1960s unraveled key elements in the dynamics of occupational satisfaction. The major finding of the research was that the level of integration was statistically best predicted by the current socioeconomic status of the families. This would suggest that those refugees with previously high occupational status, because of difficulty in equaling that status in the United States, were having problems. However, the data indicated that the degree of satisfaction with current employment had a relativistic aspect.

What seems to make this comparative level effective in leading to integration is that individuals take into account a series of other factors in their subjective comparisons of situations. First of all, they consider the rapidity of the ascent in the United States. . . . Second, they consider the difficulties of their point of departure. . . . Third, they take into account an alternative situation which could have been worse had they gone to a different country or even to another place in this country. (Portes 1969:513)

That is, the determination of the suitability of current occupation lay in a rational assessment of factors that included both the rough equivalence of present and prior occupation and the difficulties in achieving present occupation given the inevitable effects of relocation in a new country.

Rogg's (1974) analysis of interviews with 250 Cubans in West New York, New Jersey, provides additional information. The survey findings indicated high levels of downward occupational mobility for the refugees, as would be expected. However, the respondents also expressed relatively high levels of satisfaction with their current employment. As in Milwaukee, the refugees were making a compromise between what could be expected on the basis of their prior occupation and what was realistic in terms of the U.S. labor market. Furthermore, the research suggested that it was the presence of a strong ethnic community that facilitated this relative satisfaction with current employment. Specifically, the ethnic group functioned as a reference group through which the refugees could judge if current employment was satisfactory. Rogg suggests that this research:

supports current theories of assimilation that show that one crucial factor in the assimilation of refugees is the strength of the community. Indeed, a strong ethnic community can favorably influence the adjustment of its members by providing a comparison referent which does not demean the refugees' sense of worth as well as by providing psycho-social strength and satisfactions to its members. (Rogg 1971:481)

That is, the presence of a strong ethnic community facilitated a rational assessment by the Cuban refugees of what represented a reasonable compromise between desired employment and possible employment (cf. Portes, McLeod, and Parker 1978). The literature on Cuban refugees thus suggests that the social effects of downward occupational mobility can be mitigated over time. The process is facilitated by the extent of experience with American society and with a similar economic system in country of origin. For those without experience with the U.S. situation, who come from dissimilar countries, or who lack a strong ethnic community, occupational satisfaction is likely to remain elusive.

FAMILY AND COMMUNITY

Refugee adjustment is as much a function of social groups as it is of individuals. The effects of household structure on self-sufficiency and general income levels have been indicated, as has the influence of the ethnic community in facilitating occupational satisfaction. The existing literature stresses the importance of the family to Cuban (e.g., Rumbaut and Rumbaut 1976; Szapocznik and others 1978), Southeast Asian (e.g., Haines 1982; Haines, Rutherford, and Thomas 1981), and Soviet refugees (e.g., Brodsky 1982; Hanfmann and Beier 1976). Perhaps the best documentation for the value placed on family, however, is seen in the continuing importance placed by refugees on family reunion. This has been noted, in particular, for Southeast Asian refugees. An extensive survey of Southeast Asian refugees in Illinois found that 77 percent of those questioned believed that broken families (as a result of exodus) were a "very serious" problem (Kim 1980:110). It was, from the point of view of the refugees, their most serious problem, even more than (English) language problems. Confirming data come from another survey in California in which "worry about family or friends still in homeland" was rated as the second most serious problem by the refugees interviewed (Human Resources Corporation 1979). Interestingly, the concern about missing family members is one area in which there is significant difference between the perceptions of refugees and of service providers. In both the noted surveys, service providers were also asked to assess the seriousness of various problems facing refugees and in both cases rated such family problems as significantly less serious than did the refugees.

Not only are families important to refugees, but they are also capable of easing many of the problems of adjustment to the United States. For example, the high labor force participation rates of Cuban women have contributed substantially to the economic progress of the families with which they live. In the United States they have added an explicit wage-earning element to their traditional role within the family, thereby enhancing the family's socioeconomic status. The review of interviews with 122 Cuban-born women in Dade County, Florida, led Ferree to conclude that:

there is no necessary conflict between traditional standards of female behavior and women's paid employment. Since the Cuban woman is working for her family, her employment is not seen as an expression of her independence or the loosening of traditional controls and restraints.... Because female employment is needed to maintain standards of respectability for the family, daughters are counseled to prepare for a lifetime career, and parents are willing to invest in such preparation. (Ferree 1979:48).

Boone (1980) notes a similar contribution to the family among Cuban women in the Washington, D.C., area. Wives and mothers not only fulfill traditional roles within the family, but also directly contribute to the family's economic adjustment. Similar patterns emerge among Southeast Asian refugees, particularly those from Vietnam, in which the traditional role of women is also flexible enough to include management of the home and participation in the labor market (e.g., Hickey 1964; Hoskins 1975).

Family capabilities to facilitate adjustment to the United States also extend to relatives outside the immediate household. Adult siblings among the Vietnamese not only furnish one another emotional support, but also cooperate in economic activities (e.g., Haines, Rutherford, and Thomas 1981). Extended family alliances among the Hmong take an active part in bridging the distance between refugees and U.S. service providers (e.g., Dunnigan 1982). Family ties may be particularly effective in easing the difficult adjustment of elderly refugees. For example, a survey of the Cuban elderly in Miami (Hernandez 1974) indicated that they faced severe problems of low incomes, high housing costs, and difficult personal adjustments that constituted a "trauma that few others have experienced" (ibid:171). However, the elderly themselves expressed considerable satisfaction with their current situation. Four-fifths were satisfied with their neighborhoods and about nine-tenths were satisfied with their current housing. Part of the reason for this satisfaction despite adversity probably lay in the fact that three-fifths of the respondents had children in the area and only 15 percent reported little or no contact with relatives. Again, family relations appear to ease the difficulty of adjustment.

Refugee families, however, also face problems. The incorporation of wives and mothers into the labor force may facilitate the family's economic adjustment, but it may also strain domestic relations. On the basis of research with 100 Cuban women in Miami, Gonzales notes that "conflicts between the economic pressure to work and the social need to maintain the domestic role have strained the smooth running of the traditional Cuban family" (Gonzales 1980:2). One result is the frequent usage of calmatives and tranquilizers (Page and Gonzales 1980). That is, the wives' contribution to the economic adjustment of the family is not entirely without costs.

One particular area in which refugee families face difficulties is in their relationship to their children. Children are caught between the demands of their traditional culture (represented by their parents) and American culture (represented by schools, peers, and the media). This can lead to conflict. As the Indochina Refugee Action Center's assessment of the needs of Southeast Asian refugee youth suggests, childhood and adolescence are the:

battlefields over which and in which the most severe cultural conflicts emerge. Children are the key to any group's survival as a distinct cultural unit. As "New Americans," immigrant children find themselves charged by their elders with maintaining what often appears to be an increasingly remote and irrelevant cultural heritage. (Indochina Refugee Action Center 1980:1)

The very success of Southeast Asian refugee children in the school system may cause problems at home (e.g., Ellis 1980:9). Alternately, adherence to traditional cultural values and patterns, as represented by the home, may cause problems for children and youth in adjusting to the U.S. educational system (e.g., Cejas and Toledo, Inc. 1974; Szapocznik and others 1978).

Thus although refugee families have a significant capacity to facilitate adjustment, whether in contributing to household income levels or in furnishing a supportive home environment, they face difficulties. Many families have lost members, resulting, for example, in single-parent households that are at risk both financially and emotionally (e.g., Lin, Tazuma, and Masuda 1979). Others may be intact but burdened by the different levels of accommodation to the United States that husbands, wives, and children have achieved.

The ethnic community, like the family, can function as a mediator between the refugees and the wider American society, thus facilitating the adjustment process. The ethnic community can also furnish a wide variety of quite practical support, particularly in guiding its members toward the services they need or the opportunities (e.g., jobs) they desire.

On the social side the community provides a set of people with common traditions, goals, and problems. Tran Minh Tung (1975) has stressed the importance of the ethnic community in meeting the ardent needs of Vietnamese refugees for a "sense of belonging." For the Cubans, Rumbaut and Rumbaut suggest that successful adjustment has been the result of:

the creation of a network of relationships and activities within ethnic communities in the United States, the best example of which is the extraordinarily large colony in Miami, which in turn...permits the development and maintenance of a vigorous sense of collective identity and ethnic consciousness.

They go on to suggest that such communities "permit adaptation within a supportive network of ethnic relationships and affiliations and constitute sources of psychosocial gratification to the expatriate that are unavailable outside Cuban groups" (Rumbaut and Rumbaut 1976:398).

The ethnic community not only provides a basis for a more positive self-identification and sense of belonging, but can also furnish more direct economic aid. Its networks can provide access to jobs. It can also provide the rationale through which particular jobs become desirable. Finnan (1980), for example, has described how certain features of electronics work in California have been interpreted by the Vietnamese community as signifying clean and good work, thus significantly enhancing the social acceptability of work that could be characterized instead as repetitive and undemanding. But the ethnic community can also create jobs. Wilson and Portes, for example, describe ethnic businesses in Miami. There the combination of sustained Cuban immigration and entrepreneurial skills that originated in Cuba led to significant economic benefits for both the entrepreneurs and those they hired. They suggest that such ethnic businesses can:

make use of language and cultural barriers and of ethnic affinities to gain privileged access to markets and sources of labor. These conditions might give them an edge over similar peripheral firms in the open economy. . . . The economic expansion of an immigrant enclave, combined with the reciprocal obligations attached to a common ethnicity, creates new mobility opportunities for immigrant workers and permits utilization of their past investments in human capital. Not incidentally, such opportunities may help explain why many immigrants choose to stay in or return to the enclave, foregoing higher short-term gains in the open economy. (Wilson and Portes 1980)

The ethnic community thus can draw on its own skills and resources to develop businesses that in the long run benefit both employer and employed. This ability is clearly contingent on community size. On a far smaller scale similar developments appear to be taking place in Los Angeles, home to the largest group of Vietnamese refugees in the United States. Although on a far smaller scale than for the Cubans in Miami, the Los Angeles area has seen a wide growth in Vietnamese businesses, including banking and the all-important availability of capital (Finnan and Cooperstein 1983).

Ethnic communities thus have the same dual potential that families have. Both furnish a sense of belonging and the basis for a positive self-identity. Both communities and families also make direct contributions to economic adjustment. While families pool often-minimal individual wages and salaries, communities, through enclave businesses, develop the basis for communitywide rises in income. The demonstrated tendency of refugees, like other immigrants, to cluster in particular localities has thus a social and an economic dynamic (cf. Light 1972; Portes and Bach 1980).

MENTAL HEALTH

Mental health can be seen either as an independent issue in refugee adjustment or as a proxy for the relative success of the adjustment process as a whole. For example, much of the importance of the ethnic community relates to its ability to ease the emotional pressures of transition to a new society. Occupational satisfaction also qualifies as a mental health issue. Because such potential mental health issues have already been discussed, this concluding section deals only with three core aspects of the wider mental health issue: first, the extent to which refugee mental health problems continue over time; second, the diversity in coping styles among refugee populations and between refugees and mainstream American society; and third, an initial definition of refugee personal adjustment.

Refugee exodus is a traumatic experience. It often involves a decision made within a few hours that irrevocably changes a person's life. It may occur under complete panic conditions; even when longer-range planning occurs, exodus is still usually clandestine, dangerous, and with family members left behind or lost en route. The result is that refugees are left "midway to nowhere" (Kunz 1973). The psychological manifestations are serious and multiple. Segal and Lourie (1975), for example, reported on the situation of the Indochinese refugees who reached Guam after the fall of Saigon. They noted:

feelings of grief and depression, anxiety about the welfare of separated family members, panic over an uncertain future, feelings of remorse and guilt, confusion, and a growing sense of bitterness, disappointment, and anger. The emotional burdens carried by the refugees are often reflected not only in a general sense of malaise, fatigue, and psycho-somatic complaints, but by evidences of lethargy, withdrawal and seclusion, huddling, expressions of melancholy, and crying in private. (Segal and Lourie 1975:4)

Other more quantitative research also indicated the emotional stress that the initial Vietnamese refugees were undergoing. The use of such standardized in-struments as the Cornell Medical Index (CMI) during 1975 indicated levels of overall distress for the Vietnamese refugees that were higher than those for American, British, Asian, or other migrant populations (Rahe and others 1978; Lin, Tazuma, and Masuda 1979). Further, this emotional distress did not dis-appear rapidly after resettlement. Follow-up work in 1976 indicated that CMI levels remained as high as they had been in the previous year and differed significantly only in increased levels of anger and somewhat reduced levels of inadequacy (Lin, Tazuma, and Masuda 1979; cf. Masuda, Lin, and Tazuma 1980). A survey of agencies involved in refugee mental health in 1979 also indicated the continuation of mental health problems (Pennsylvania Department of Public Welfare 1979). Among the findings from the survey were that mental health problems of refugees who had arrived in 1975 were, in many cases, only beginning to surface at the time of the survey, in spring 1979; depression (plau-sibly an aftereffect of exodus) was a major problem, but anxiety and marital conflict were also frequent problems; middle-aged refugees were at particular risk owing to the loss of traditional roles and statuses; and all smaller ethnic groups were at risk because of the lack of a strong ethnic community. All findings had in common the implication that refugee mental health problems continue and increasingly involve the problems of transition to a new society rather than the aftereffects of exodus.

A preliminary indication of the length of time needed for alleviation comes from a survey of Southeast Asian refugees in Illinois (Kim and Nicassio 1980). The researchers constructed an alienation index on the basis of answers to ten standardized statements of the refugee's life situation in the United States. The results were broken down by ethnic group and by year of arrival. The Hmong had the highest score (indicating most alienation) and the Vietnamese had the lowest. Further, when respondents were resorted according to year of entry, there was a statistically significant and inverse relationship between length of residence and alienation. However, the individual scores showed a rise through the first three years before declining in the fourth and fifth years. Although the drops for those in the fourth and fifth years of residence imply that mental health problems are ameliorated after three years in country, this finding may well reflect the social characteristics of those who arrived in 1975 and 1976.

The understanding of and solutions to refugee mental health problems are rendered difficult by the cultural divergences between different refugee populations and between refugees and American society. For Southeast Asian refugees, even the basic concepts of mental illness show little consistency with American psychological assumptions (e.g., Tran Minh Tung 1980; Westermeyer and Wintrob 1979a, 1979b). Cubans, culturally closest of the refugees to American society, also have distinctive ideas about what constitutes acceptable behavior and therefore a normal mental health status. Analysis of value orientations in two separate samples of Cubans and native-born Americans indicated significant differences along a number of dimensions. The Cubans tended to prefer lineality (e.g., hierarchical relations within the family), a present-time orientation, and subjugation to nature. The Americans, on the other hand, showed a preference for individuality, mastery over nature, and a future-time orientation (Szapocznik, Scopetta, and King 1978; Szapocznik, Kurtines, and Hanna 1979).

Compared with one another, specific refugee populations also have considerable differences. Southeast Asian refugees, for example, are often treated as a culturally homogeneous group. However, the constituent ethnic groups have distinctive cultural patterns and thus distinctive coping strategies. Data from a study of 217 Southeast Asian refugees in the Denver area are illustrative (Ossorio, Aylesworth, and Lasater 1979). The study included Vietnamese, Hmong, and Cambodian refugees and found significant differences between them. The researchers concluded that "the findings indicate that each of the three groups, Vietnamese, H'Mong, and Cambodian, has a stress pattern which is unique to that group and is a pervasive fact of life for essentially the entire adult population" (Ossorio, Aylesworth, and Lasater 1979:36). That is, different refugee populations may share similar general problems in recovering from the trauma of exodus and in adjusting to American society. However, the specifics of these problems, their general phrasing, and effective resolutions of them are likely to vary between different refugee groups. Vietnamese, Hmong, and Cambodians will have different problems and will be responsive to different solutions. Cuban refugees may be unresponsive to standard American therapeutical styles because of their cultural differences; therapists must be willing to "take charge of the therapist-client relationship, to validate hierarchical structures in the client's life context, and to intervene on behalf of the client" (Szapocznik, Scopetta, and King 1978:968). Soviet refugees are likely to lack any experience with the mental health profession as it exists in the United States (e.g., Segal 1979) and thus react to it as another bureaucracy. For all refugees, the cultural phrasing of mental health problems will differ from American categories, thus making the resolution of mental health problems an area subject to misunderstanding.

For the individual refugee, personal adjustment will take different paths. The effects of cultural background, job skills, availability of family and co-ethnics, age, and sex will all influence the result and the pace. What all these paths are likely to share is some element of balance between clinging to old beliefs and behavior, on the one hand, and uncritically accepting American ways, on the other. Le Xuan Khoa's (1979) general comment for Southeast Asian refugees may be one of the few commonalities for all refugees. Turning backward, he points out, means the inability to absorb the changes attendant on immersion in a new environment. An overly assimilative approach, however, leads ultimately to a crisis of identity as the refugee realizes he or she can never be totally American.

A balanced adjustment must lie between the two.

REFERENCES

Aames, Jacqueline S., Ronald L. Aames, John Jung, and Edward Karabenick
1977   *Indochinese Refugee Self-sufficiency in California: A Survey and Analysis of the Vietnamese, Cambodians and Lao and the Agencies That Serve Them*. Report submitted to the State Department of Health, State of California.

Boone, Margaret S.
1980   The Uses of Traditional Concepts in the Development of New Urban Roles: Cuban Women in the United States. In *A World of Women*. Edited by Erika Bourguignon. New York: Praeger.

Brodsky, Betty
1982   Social Work and the Soviet Immigrant. *Migration Today* 10(1):15–20.

Cejas and Toledo, Inc.
1974   Needs Assessment: The Prevention of Spanish-speaking Dropouts in the Target Areas of "Little Havana" and "Wynwood" (Grades 7–12). Miami, Florida.

Dunnigan, Timothy
1982   Segmentary Kinship in an Urban Society: The Hmong of St. Paul—Minneapolis. *Anthropological Quarterly* 55(3):126–134.

Ellis, Arthur E.
1980   *The Assimilation and Acculturation of Indochinese Children into American Culture*. Sacramento: California Department of Social Services.

Fagen, Richard R., Richard A. Brody, and Thomas J. O'Leary
1968   *Cubans in Exile: Disaffection and the Revolution*. Stanford, California: Stanford University Press.

Ferree, Myra Marx
1979   Employment Without Liberation: Cuban Women in the United States. *Social Science Quarterly* 60:35–50.

Finnan, Christine Robinson
1980   A Community Affair: Occupational Assimilation of Vietnamese Refugees. *Journal of Refugee Resettlement* 1(1):8–14.

Finnan, Christine, and Rhonda Ann Cooperstein
1983   *Southeast Asian Refugee Resettlement at the Local Level: The Role of the Ethnic Community and the Nature of Refugee Impact*. Menlo Park, California: SRI International.

Fisher, Leon D.
1975   Initial Experiences in the Resettlement of Soviet Jews in the United States. *Journal of Jewish Communal Service* 51(3):267–269.

Gilison, Jerome M.
1979   Summary Report of the Survey of Soviet Jewish Émigrés in Baltimore. Baltimore, Maryland: Baltimore Hebrew College.

Gilison, Jerome M., Ed.
1976   *The Soviet Jewish Émigré: Proceedings of the National Symposium on the Integration of Soviet Jews into the American Jewish Community*. Baltimore, Maryland: Baltimore Hebrew College.

Gitelman, Zvi
1978   Soviet Immigrants and American Absorption Efforts: A Case Study in Detroit. *Journal of Jewish Communal Service* 55(1):72–82.

Gonzales, Diana H.
1980   Sociocultural Adaptations Among Cuban Émigré Women in Miami, Florida. Paper presented at the annual meetings of the Caribbean Studies Association.

Haines, David W.
1982   Southeast Asian Refugees in the United States: The Interaction of Kinship and Public Policy. *Anthropological Quarterly* 55(3):170–181.

Haines, David W., Dorothy A. Rutherford, and Patrick A. Thomas
1981   Family and Community Among Vietnamese Refugees. *International Migration Review* 15(1):310–319.

Hanfmann, Eugenia, and Helen Beier
1976   Comparison of the Interpersonal Attitudes of the Russian Displaced Person and an American Group. In *Six Russian Men: Lives in Turmoil*. North Quincy, Massachusetts: The Christopher Publishing House.

Hawks, Irene Kaminsky
1977   The New Immigrant: A Study of the Vocational Adjustment of Soviet Jews. *Journal of Jewish Communal Service* 54(2):161–165.

Hernandez, Andres R., Ed.
1974   *The Cuban Minority in the U.S.* Washington, D.C.: Cuban National Planning Council.

Hickey, Gerald C.
1964   *Village in Vietnam*. New Haven, Connecticut: Yale University Press.

Hoskins, Marilyn W.
1975   Vietnamese Women: Their Roles and Their Options. In *Being Female*. Edited by Dana Raphael. The Hague: Mouton.

Human Resources Corporation
1979   *Evaluation of the Indochinese Refugee Assistance Program in Private Agencies in California*. San Francisco, California.

Indochina Refugee Action Center
1980   An Assessment of the Needs of Indochinese Youth. Washington, D.C.

Kim, Young Yun
1980   *Population Characteristics and Service Needs of Indochinese Refugees*. Vol. 3 of the Research Project on Indochinese Refugees in the State of Illinois. Chicago: Travelers Aid Society of Metropolitan Chicago.

Kim, Young Yun, and Perry M. Nicassio
1980   *Psychological, Social, and Cultural Adjustment of Indochinese Refugees*. Vol. 4 of the Research Project on Indochinese Refugees in the State of Illinois. Chicago: Travelers Aid Society of Metropolitan Chicago.

Kunz, E. F.
1973   The Refugee in Flight: Kinetic Models and Forms of Displacement. *International Migration Review* 7(2):125–146.

Le Xuan Khoa
1979   Cultural Adjustment of Indochinese Refugees. Paper presented at a seminar on "The Plight of Indochinese Refugees." University Park, Pennsylvania: Penn State University.

Light, Ivan H.
1972   *Ethnic Enterprise in America*. Berkeley: University of California Press.

Lin, Keh-Ming, Laurie Tazuma, and Minoru Masuda
1979   Adaptational Problems of Vietnamese Refugees: Health and Mental Health Status. *Archives of General Psychiatry* 36:955–961.

Masuda, Minoru, Keh-Ming Lin, and Laurie Tazuma
1980   Adaptation Problems of Vietnamese Refugees: Life Changes and Perceptions of Life Events. *Archives of General Psychiatry* 37:447–450.

ORR (Office of Refugee Resettlement)
1982   *Report to the Congress: Refugee Resettlement Program*. Washington, D.C.: U.S. Department of Health and Human Services.

1983   *Report to the Congress: Refugee Resettlement Program*. Washington, D.C.: U.S. Department of Health and Human Services.

1984   *Report to the Congress: Refugee Resettlement Program*. Washington, D.C.: U.S. Department of Health and Human Services.

OSI (Opportunity Systems, Inc.)
1976   *Second Wave Report: Vietnam Resettlement Operational Feedback*. Washington, D.C.

1977   *Fifth Wave Report: Vietnam Resettlement Operational Feedback*. Washington, D.C.

1979   *Eighth Wave Report: Indochinese Resettlement Operational Feedback*. Washington, D.C.

1981   *Ninth Wave Report: Indochinese Resettlement Operational Feedback*. Washington, D.C.

Ossorio, Peter G., Laurence S. Aylesworth, and Lane Lasater
1979   *Mental-Health-Related Needs Among the Indochinese Refugees in the Denver Metropolitan Area*. Denver, Colorado: Linguistic Research Institute.

Page, J. Bryan, and Diana H. Gonzales
1980   Drug Use Among Miami Cubans: A Preliminary Report. *Street Pharmacologist* 3(11):1–4.

Parker, Lenore
1979   From Paternalism to Pluralism: Soviet Émigrés Bewildered by Contrasting Lifestyles. *Foundation News* 17(5):38–43.

Pennsylvania Department of Public Welfare
1979   *National Mental Health Needs Assessment of Indochinese Refugee Populations*. Philadelphia, Pennsylvania: Office of Mental Health, Bureau of Research and Training.

Portes, Alejandro
1969   Dilemmas of a Golden Exile: Integration of Cuban Refugee Families in Milwaukee. *American Sociological Review* 34:505–518.

Portes, Alejandro, and Robert L. Bach
1980   Immigrant Earnings: Cuban and Mexican Immigrants in the United States. *International Migration Review* 14(3):315–341.

Portes, Alejandro, Samual A. McLeod, and Robert N. Parker
1978   Immigrant Aspirations. *Sociology of Education* 51(4):241–260.
Prohias, Rafael, and Lourdes Casal
1973   *The Cuban Minority in the U.S.: Preliminary Report on Need Identification and Program Evaluation.* Boca Raton: Florida Atlantic University.
Rahe, Richard H., John G. Looney, Harold W. Ward, Tran Minh Tung, and William T. Liu
1978   Psychiatric Consultation in a Vietnamese Refugee Camp. *American Journal of Psychiatry* 135(2):185–190.
Rogg, Eleanor
1971   The Influence of a Strong Refugee Community on the Economic Adjustment of Its Members. *International Migration Review* 5(4):474–481.
1974   *The Assimilation of Cuban Exiles: The Role of Community and Class.* New York: Aberdeen Press.
Rumbaut, Ruben D., and Ruben G. Rumbaut
1976   The Family in Exile: Cuban Expatriates in the United States. *American Journal of Psychiatry* 133(4):395–399.
Segal, Boris M.
1979   Psychiatric Services in Soviet General Outpatient Clinics. *American Journal of Psychiatry* 136(2):183–186.
Segal, Julius, and Norman Lourie
1975   The Mental Health of the Vietnam Refugees: Memorandum to Rear Admiral S. G. Morrison. Washington, D.C.: U.S. Department of Health, Education, and Welfare, National Institute of Mental Health.
Starr, Paul D., Alden E. Roberts, Rebecca G. LeNoir, and Thai Ngoc Nguyen
1979   Adaptation and Stress Among Vietnamese Refugees: Preliminary Results from Two Regions. Paper presented at the Conference on Indochinese Refugees, Fairfax, Virginia, George Mason University.
Stein, Barry N.
1979   Occupational Adjustment of Refugees: The Vietnamese in the United States. *International Migration Review* 13(1):25–45.
Szapocznik, Jose, William Kurtines, and Norma Hanna
1979   Comparison of Cuban and Anglo-American Cultural Values in a Clinical Population. *Journal of Consulting and Clinical Psychology* 47(3):623–624.
Szapocznik, Jose, Mercedes A. Scopetta, and Olga E. King
1978   Theory and Practice in Matching Treatment to the Special Characteristics and Problems of Cuban Immigrants. *Journal of Community Psychology* 6:112–122.
Szapocznik, Jose, Mercedes Arca Scopetta, Maria de los Angeles Aranalde, and William Kurtines
1978   Cuban Value Structure: Treatment Implications. *Journal of Consulting and Clinical Psychology* 46(5):961–970.
Tran Minh Tung
1975   The Vietnamese Refugees and Their Mental Health Problems: A Vantage View. Paper presented at a meeting of the District of Columbia Chapter of the Washington Psychiatric Society, Washington, D.C.
1980   The Indochinese Refugees as Patients. *Journal of Refugee Resettlement* 1(1):53–60.

University of Miami
1967   *The Cuban Immigration 1959-1966 and Its Impact on Miami-Dade County,
        Florida.* Coral Gables, Florida.
Urban Associates, Inc.
1974   *A Study of Selected Socio-economic Characteristics of Ethnic Minorities Based
        on the 1970 Census, Vol. 1: Americans of Spanish Origin.* Washington, D.C.:
        U.S. Department of Health, Education, and Welfare, Office of the Assistant
        Secretary for Planning and Evaluation.
U.S. Bureau of the Census
1980   *Statistical Abstract of the United States* (101st Edition). Washington, D.C.
Vignes, A. Joe, and Richard C. W. Hall
1979   Adjustment of a Group of Vietnamese People to the United States. *American
        Journal of Psychiatry* 136(4):442–444.
Westermeyer, Joseph, and Ronald Wintrob
1979a   "Folk" Criteria for the Diagnosis of Mental Illness in Rural Laos: On Being
        Insane in Sane Places. *American Journal of Psychiatry* 136(6):755–761.
1979b   "Folk" Explanations of Mental Illness in Rural Laos. *American Journal of
        Psychiatry* 136(7):901–905.
Wilson, Kenneth L., and Alejandro Portes
1980   Immigrant Enclaves: An Analysis of the Labor Market Experiences of Cubans
        in Miami. *American Journal of Sociology* 86(2):295-319.

PART II

THE REFUGEES

Chinese from Southeast Asia

The years 1978 to 1980 were major in the movement of Chinese out of Vietnam and Cambodia. These people found themselves at the mercy of both political and economic change within Southeast Asia and international rivalries outside. Given the pressures, they decided that they wanted out—not just out in general, but out to the United States. They have come not as a separate and distinct group, but mixed with ethnic Vietnamese and Khmer from Vietnam and Cambodia at the same time that Lao, Hmong, and other groups were also entering the United States. Once here, there is the question of their relations with the Chinese-Americans already in residence.

Overall, it is safe to say that less is known of the Chinese refugees from Southeast Asia than of any other major group from that region. Many studies exist of the Chinese people themselves, as well as a good number on the Chinese in Southeast Asia. Yet little attention has been paid to the Chinese communities in Saigon/Cholon and Phnom Penh, not to mention the smaller ones in Haiphong and Hanoi. Tsai (1968) has examined his own community in southern Vietnam in great detail, and Willmott (1967, 1970) has studied the Chinese in Cambodia, particularly Phnom Penh. I have used these major studies as well as a number of other sources to describe these Chinese communities, particularly with attention to their historical background.

This chapter brings together the information available to us on the Chinese communities of Indochina (especially Vietnam, but also Cambodia; the Chinese community in Laos does not concern us here) and joins it with data from surveys of Chinese refugee groups in the United States. The result is a description of these refugees, their lives, and their prospects in the United States.

BACKGROUND

Although Chinese have had contact with and lived on the eastern mainland of Southeast Asia for more than two millennia, the important growth of Chinese communities in Vietnam, Cambodia, and elsewhere in Southeast Asia has only come about in the past 400 years. The rise of regional and international trade in the sixteenth and seventeenth centuries, including the increasing involvement of the Europeans, brought Chinese into the ports of Vietnam, Cambodia, Thailand, the Philippines, and Indonesia (Whitmore 1983; Willmott 1967). Difficulties of trade with the Japanese and the Europeans in China led Chinese traders to Southeast Asia for easier contacts, and the fall of the Ming dynasty in China to the Manchu power, in 1644, resulted in a flood of loyalists onto the coasts of the southern seas.

The early Chinese communities formed close to the contemporary centers of power and contributed much to the growth of the capitals, as at Phnom Penh. On occasion, the Chinese (or people of Chinese ancestry) became involved in the wielding of local political power. In Vietnam the Chinese had a choice of becoming Vietnamese (being known as *Minh-huong*) or remaining Chinese. If they chose the former, they adopted Vietnamese ways and came under Vietnamese law; if the latter, they stayed in the Chinese communities and were treated as foreigners. Interestingly, the diplomatic corps of nineteenth-century Vietnam was made up largely of *Minh-huong*, including the great Phan Thanh Gian, who dealt with the French in the 1860s (Woodside 1971; Nguyen 1971).

Another important development involving the settlement of Chinese in Vietnam took place during the seventeenth century in the south (generally known as Cochin China). Vietnamese had begun settling in this area only in the previous century, and the Saigon area became Vietnamese only in the 1690s. When 3,000 Chinese arrived off the coast of central Vietnam in flight from the Manchu conquerors, in the 1670s, the local Vietnamese lord took it on himself to suggest that they keep going to inhabit open land around what is now Bien-hoa, north of Saigon. This land had been in the Cambodian domain, but the Chinese settlements there and elsewhere helped, ultimately, to bring it into the Vietnamese realm (Nguyen 1971; Tsai 1968).

Trade and Chinese settlement did not flourish to nearly the same degree around the cities of the north, the capital Thang-long (now Hanoi) and the provincial centers, during the seventeenth and eighteenth centuries. It was mainly in the mountains, near the Chinese border and in the mining areas, or along the coast that the Chinese population could be found. In the south the final quarter of the eighteenth century brought war and destruction to the Chinese communities. Out of the dynastic conflagration of the times emerged the settlement called Sai-con by the Vietnamese and T'ai-ngon by the Chinese as the major trading center of the Mekong Delta area. By 1801 the Vietnamese were calling the Chinese community there Cho-lon, or "Large Market" (Nguyen 1971; Tsai 1968; de Poncins 1957).

With the establishment of the Nguyen dynasty in the first years of the nineteenth century, the new rulers drew a sharp line between the *Minh-huong* and the Chinese sojourners. The latter were officially recognized through their *bang*. Such organizations were natural to the overseas Chinese, being based on dialect and home province. Thus the *bang* served as fairly autonomous and self-governing administrative units for the Vietnamese government, and their chiefs acted as the links between the Vietnamese bureaucracy and the Chinese population. The various chiefs accepted the responsibility for collecting taxes and controlling the flow of Chinese immigrants for the capital in Hue (Nguyen 1971; Tsai 1968).

Substantial though the Chinese population was in Vietnam by the middle of the nineteenth century, the major growth in the Chinese community came during the ninety years of the French colonial period. The European powers of the late nineteenth century, including the French, were drawing coolie labor out of China by the thousands. Encouraged by the French, the Chinese also took the opportunity to move south into better economic conditions, and from the 1860s boatloads of Chinese immigrants arrived in Vietnam (hence the Vietnamese term *nguoi tau*, ''boat people,'' for them). The French had conquered the far south of Vietnam, called by them Cochin China, in the 1860s and removed it from the control of Hue. Saigon and the Mekong Delta would officially remain a separate colony under French law into the 1940s, whereas from the 1880s the north and center (called by the French Tonkin and Annam) were ostensibly under Vietnamese administration. The Chinese tended to gather in the French-controlled areas, the south and the urban centers, particularly the ports. Hence Cholon, adjacent to Saigon; Haiphong, the French port of the north; and Hanoi, the French administrative center for Indochina, became the major places of Chinese settlement. Phnom Penh in Cambodia and to a much lesser degree Vientiane in Laos were also French administrative centers and locations of Chinese communities. Other Chinese lived in lesser population centers scattered across Vietnam and Cambodia. The main point to be made here is that the Chinese formed almost entirely an urban population and pursued economic advancement in urban occupations (Tsai 1968; Ky 1963).

The number of Chinese in the south of Vietnam grew rapidly. By 1889, almost 60,000 (according to official French count) lived scattered about the south alone. Seventeen years later the figure had doubled. Through the colonial period and into the 1950s the Chinese population of southern Vietnam greatly outstripped that of the north and center. In the early 1930s the French counted more than 200,000 Chinese immigrants in the south (with more than 70,000 *Minh-huong*), more than 50,000 in the north, but only 10,000 in the center. The Chinese community in Cambodia expanded rapidly in the 1920s as well, to more than 200,000. Twenty years later, at the end of the colonial period, the number of Chinese in southern Vietnam may have quadrupled to more than 800,000 and that in Cambodia almost doubled to more than 400,000, whereas those in the north and center of Vietnam had only grown slightly. (Some 40,000 of Chinese descent are supposed to have come south in 1954-55.) The Saigon/Cholon metropolitan area seems to have had more than 575,000 Chinese and other urban areas in the south more than 90,000; another 130,000 plus appeared to be scattered among villages of the south. Thus about 84 percent of the Chinese in southern Vietnam were urban and 16 percent, rural. Some 35,000 were in Haiphong in the north and another 15,000 were in Hanoi. The urban/rural ratio in

Cambodia was much closer, being 59 percent to 41 percent. These figures tend not to include those of Chinese descent whose families had lived in Vietnam before the French, that is, for Vietnam, the *Minh-huong* (Tsai 1968; Ky 1963; Willmott 1967).

The Chinese tendency to organize themselves by dialect group and region of birth in the homeland was accepted and reinforced by the French administration. In this way the French refrained from direct interference into Chinese affairs, unless necessary, and placed responsibility for the activities of the Chinese community in the hands of the organizational leaders, whom they could replace. These organizations, the *bang*, took care of taxation, immigration, and police matters for the French within their own groups. In Vietnam the largest group of Chinese—perhaps half—were the Cantonese from Kwangtung province in China, with the Teochiu from the northeast coast of Kwangtung almost a third. In Cambodia (as in Thailand) the situation was strongly reversed (Teochiu more than three-quarters and Cantonese a tenth). Other major dialect groups of some size (2%–10%) in Vietnam and Cambodia were Hakka, Hokkien (from Fukien province), and Hainanese (Tsai 1968; Willmott 1967; Skinner 1951). The dominant language for the entire Chinese community in Vietnam (unlike elsewhere in Southeast Asia) was Cantonese, and a large proportion of those in Cholon knew neither Vietnamese nor French (nor, later on, English) (Tsai 1968; de Poncins 1957). From the 1880s the French colonial system recognized these five dialect groups as the official congregations (*bang*), with Chinese not belonging to any of them included with the Hakka. These five remained the basic organization of the Chinese community through the colonial period. They had their own temples, schools, hospitals, and cemeteries. As Willmott (1967:84) noted for Cambodia, "a speech group was the constituency for business relationships, marriage partners, associations, and relations with the administration." Local branches of the *bang* officially served the Chinese population scattered among the towns of the countryside. Saigon, Cholon, Tra-vinh, and Long Xuyen in Vietnam, and Phnom Penh and Kompong Cham in Cambodia had branches of all five *bang*; other towns of any size had two, three, or four *bang*. Smaller towns only had one, encompassing all the local Chinese of whatever group (Tsai 1968; Willmott 1970; Skinner 1951).

The importance of the Chinese community in twentieth-century Indochina lay in its economic function. The French facilitated the Chinese participation in the colonial economy, thus greatly advancing the French extractive powers. The Chinese had greater liberties than the Vietnamese, Khmer, and Lao. They could move among the five *pays* of French Indochina (Tonkin, Annam, Cochin China, Cambodia, and Laos), and they had access to the countryside and its peasants. They handled goods and accumulated large commercial fortunes. The Chinese profited greatly from the alcohol, salt, and opium monopolies imposed by the French on Vietnamese and Cambodian societies. Not only did the Chinese merchant community help underwrite the French administration by way of the monopolies, but it was also most important in supplying the colonial structure and

instrumental in the major export from the colony, rice. With French encourage-
ment, their contacts in the rural towns and villages, their ownership of the rice-
hauling junks and the rice mills, and their monetary loans to the peasants, the
Chinese merchants controlled the movement of rice within Vietnam and Cambodia and supplied its export abroad from Saigon/Cholon (amounting to two-
thirds of French Indochina's total export value). Pepper was another agricultural
product controlled by the Chinese. Through the international network of Chinese
firms, such exports moved from the Chinese communities of Vietnam and Cambodia to Chinese firms in the major port cities of Southeast Asia and China. It
was the Chinese who kept the flow of commercial goods going into and through
the colony, profiting greatly thereby. With such advantages, the heavy bulk of
the Chinese community within Vietnam and Cambodia was involved in business
of one sort or another (Ky 1963; Ngo 1971; Murray 1980; Tsai 1968; Willmott
1967).

To quote Tsai Maw-kuey (1968:135), a Chinese from southern Vietnam, "All
observers, whatever their nationality, are in accord that in South Vietnam the
Chinese held and still hold all the levers of commerce, of industry, and of
handicrafts and that they continue to play the most important role in the economic
life of the country." Compared with other countries of Southeast Asia, the
Chinese communities in Indochina were much more heavily involved in business
than in laboring occupations (a majority in commerce and another third in industry
and artisanry). Saigon/Cholon was the hub of the Chinese economic network,
and Phnom Penh was the center of its Cambodian hinterland during the colonial
period.

As noted earlier, the major activity of the Chinese was the rice trade. Besides
the control of the rice market, Chinese merchants strongly dominated the handling
of foodstuffs in general, both wholesale and retail. Their enterprises supplied
the major cities and extended deep into the villages of the countryside. The
Chinese businessmen were also heavily involved in buying and selling numerous
other items in Vietnam and Cambodia, and diversity was one of their economic
strengths. Hundreds of Chinese firms controlled the production and trade of
textiles and wood and metal goods. (See the appendix to this chapter for detail
on the economic activities of the different dialect groups.) Fundamental to such
Chinese economic success were two elements: (1) commercial organization and
networks (within the colony and without) and (2) the extension of credit (within
their own community and to others).

The strength of the Chinese community lay, according to Tsai (1968:116), in
its "perfect internal organization...whose power and efficacy are often underestimated or ignored." Hui (as opposed to the official bang) were groups formed
to achieve any one of a number of specific goals. They were interlinked to create
an informal network or series of networks that stretched throughout the colony
and abroad. Any Chinese could belong to one such grouping or several, depending on personal interests. Three general types of hui existed: (1) by common
family name or locality of origin; (2) by professional association; and (3) by

shared interest (temples, schools, sports, etc.). Organized similarly, these groupings drew many people (and their families) into their workings and thus tied
together the diverse Chinese community. Through such contacts were social ties
and commercial links achieved, bringing trust to the relationships and providing
access, in Lim's (1984) terms, "to labour, credit, information, market outlets,
and security." Under the overarching structure of the five *bang*, such ties and
links reached from the big cities into the countryside and to other big cities, at
home and abroad. The urban connections and greater efficiency in operation led
the Chinese to be preferred intermediaries (Tsai 1968; Willmott 1967; Ky 1963;
Barton 1984).

The economic links that followed these social ties included better terms of
credit and loans and went beyond the Chinese community to link members of
the local population to the resulting economic structure. Based on the "confidence
and spirit of cooperation" built up through the commercial and social networks,
as Tsai (1968) described it, the Chinese system of credit, a "system both in-
genious and original," further tied the Chinese networks together and stretched
into the countryside. Among themselves, the Chinese merchants would often
pool funds and take turns sharing the proceeds. In the process of handling
commerce in the countryside (particularly in rice), these merchants would advance credit to their customers, mainly in the dry season, before the monsoon.
As buyer from and seller to the peasant farmers, the Chinese village shopkeeper
kept the flow of goods going in both directions, using loans of cash and other
items to maintain this flow. The village shopkeeper in turn dealt with the town
merchant, also receiving credit to facilitate local commerce. The provincial
merchant himself operated on credit extended by the major merchants in the
large cities (Saigon/Cholon, Phnom Penh). Ultimately, credit came from the
Chinese banks in these cities (Tsai 1968; Ky 1963; Willmott 1967; Barton 1984).

A major interest for all Chinese groups was education. The five *bang* had
public schools for their own members (that still required some tuition), and there
were many expensive private schools. By the end of the colonial era there were
well over 200 schools with a total of more than 50,000 students, male and
female, mainly at the primary level and spread across southern Vietnam. Cambodia had about half as many schools and students. Chinese families were
prepared to make sacrifices for their children to attend these schools, but inevitably, attendance rose and fell with commerce. The schools were enmeshed in
the local Chinese social structures. Mandarin, the official language of China,
served as the language of instruction among almost all groups, some Cantonese
being the exception, and problems existed in the quality of both teaching and
texts. The desire for education was so great that it led to overcrowding in the
classrooms. A variety of approaches (traditional, modern, nationalist, etc.) complicated the situation further. A French-Chinese high school supplied many of
the intermediaries between the colonial regime and the Chinese commercial
sector. The educational goal was mainly to provide a basic literacy and competence with numbers as well as to make contacts within the Chinese community,

thus aiding the business sector. In general, Chinese education in Indochina lagged behind that found elsewhere in Southeast Asia (Tsai 1968; Willmott 1967, 1970; Skinner 1951).

The situation of the Chinese in Vietnam and Cambodia changed considerably with independence in the mid-1950s. The next twenty years saw major restrictions placed on the Chinese community in its economic and professional pursuits. Both the Saigon and Phnom Penh regimes put important limits on the economic activities open to nonnationals (mainly the Chinese). In Vietnam, such activities included many of those dominated by the Chinese (shopkeeping, the rice trade, fish, tea, soy, transportation, scrap iron, textiles, and general dealing, among other fields). This situation affected more than 40 percent of the Chinese enterprises in Saigon/Cholon and more than 60 percent of all firms in the forbidden activities. The purpose was to convert the Chinese into Vietnamese citizens. The result was that some Chinese became Vietnamese, others officially turned their businesses over to their Vietnamese wives or children, others (illegally) found a Vietnamese to front for them, and quite a few (almost a thousand) simply closed up shop. Even though about a half million Chinese apparently accepted Vietnamese citizenship during 1956 and 1957, the economic system slowed drastically as many middlemen ceased operations. Other restrictions included immigration, travel, the practice of Western medicine, books, and schools. Cambodia, on independence, did not restrict the Chinese quite so widely as did the Vietnamese but tried to keep them out of rice, salt, shipping, general trade, secondhand dealing, and loans. It also removed the restrictions of the *bang* system, the result being a loosened boundary between the Chinese and the Khmer communities and a greater opening for Cambodian citizenship. Tighter controls did exist for Chinese schools (Tsai 1968; Willmott 1967, 1970; Fall 1959).

The disappearance of the official *bang* in both countries left the way open for the growth in variety and importance of the voluntary organizations (*hui*). At the same time, with the great decline in rice exports and the rise of American aid, both linked to the war, the economic role of the Chinese shifted somewhat from the commercial to the industrial and service sectors. Urbanization and commerce boomed. Many of the older economic pursuits thrived and grew with the flood of foreign wealth, mainly into southern Vietnamese society, but also into Cambodia (Tsai 1968; Willmott 1970). Clifton Barton (1984:48) felt "that a figure of seventy to eighty percent was a fairly accurate representation of the portion of the total volume of commercial and industrial activity that was controlled by overseas Chinese businessmen during the decade 1965-1975," and Tsai Maw-kuey (1968:76) could say in that year, "Incontestably, Cholon is, after Singapore, the greatest Chinese city outside China."

The Chinese in northern Vietnam benefited from rapprochement between Hanoi and Peking and were allowed to remain Chinese citizens at the same time as they held the same rights as Vietnamese. A well-to-do Chinese from Hanoi noted that the Chinese had the privileges, but not the disadvantages (as military duty), of their Vietnamese compatriots. The Chinese continued their urban and intermediary occupations within the context of the developing socialist system through the two decades of war. This included the privilege of visiting China and carrying on clandestine trade between the two countries. As Charles Benoit (1981:146) has noted, "their stellar success at running what amounted to an alternative economic system" meant the continuation of the Chinese community serving the Vietnamese economic system.

THE REFUGEE MOVEMENT

The mid-1970s saw little change in the situations of the Chinese communities in southern Vietnam, northern Vietnam, and Cambodia. The war in all three zones restricted the Chinese activities, as it did everybody's, but the role of the Chinese remained the same. They continued to operate in the urban sector, keep the economy going, and act as the intermediaries. With the end of the fighting, in 1975, the situation for the Chinese in northern Vietnam changed little, whereas that in the south underwent the strains of the transition from Saigon to Ho Chi Minh City. Some Chinese were in the first wave of refugees (an unpublished Michigan survey in 1980 showed that about 15 percent of Chinese respondents came before 1978). Nevertheless, the Vietnamese government policy toward the cities and the Chinese was initially moderate, particularly in comparison with that of the new Cambodian government. The fall of Phnom Penh to the Khmer Rouge in mid-April 1975 marked an immediate effort to clear from the cities not only the accumulated mass of refugees from the countryside, but the urban population as well. The Chinese were thus removed from the towns and pushed into the countryside (with no protest from Peking). Many of the Chinese left, going either east into southern Vietnam, particularly Saigon/Cholon, or west into Thailand.

The major flood of Chinese refugees came in the midst of international power struggle and Vietnamese policy change. Increasing tensions with China led initially to security measures concerning those of Chinese descent on the northern border, in late 1977 and early 1978. Then the Vietnamese government both began to speak of forcing Vietnamese citizenship (and thus military duty) on the Chinese and decided that a change in economic policy was needed. That spring the government moved directly to control the urban economic sector, one that they had largely left alone in prior years. This move took place not only in the recently reunified south, but also in the north, in Haiphong and Hanoi. Since, even in the north, it was the Chinese who were heavily involved in urban commerce, this effort to bring central control into the cities meant that the Chinese community was greatly affected. At the same time, relations between Vietnam and Cambodia worsened, and the friction along their common border became bloody. The Chinese regime was strongly behind that of Pol Pot against the Vietnamese. In addition, the fall of 1978 saw the breakdown in the talks between the Vietnamese and the United States, with the Americans formally recognizing the People's Republic of China in December. In November the Socialist Republic of Vietnam joined the Council for Mutual Economic Assistance, the eastern European economic bloc, and moved much closer to the Soviet Union.

Thus the Chinese in Vietnam were caught two ways. Official Vietnamese economic policy acted against their interests at the same time that China was beginning to lean heavily on the Vietnamese. Peking took the occasion both to make an example of the Vietnamese regarding the handling of overseas Chinese in Southeast Asia and to lean on the Vietnamese as being pro-Soviet. The Vietnamese in turn saw China on all sides of them, to the south and west (in Cambodia) as well as to the north and east. The Chinese in Vietnam, and eventually even those of longtime Chinese descent, were caught in both an economic squeeze and a security fear. They were being forced to leave the cities and any areas, particularly in the northern mountains and coasts, in which the Vietnamese thought they were a risk, a potential fifth column. They were to go to designated areas in the countryside or up into the highlands. The Chinese did not like the choices being offered them within Vietnam, and many took the opportunity to leave. The Vietnamese initially tried to calm their fears, but ethnic tensions continued to rise through 1978, and with the heavy fighting on the border in early 1979 the Vietnamese became active in getting the Chinese to leave (Grant and others 1979; Benoit 1981).

By the middle of 1978, the atmosphere of impending war and tales of good reception in China led more Chinese refugees to leave Vietnam. Rumor, panic, and propaganda sent almost 150,000 over the border from northern Vietnam into China, where they were stuck away in the hills of Kwangsi province. Thereafter, most left by sea as China closed its border, those in the north going to Hong Kong and those in the south going to Malaysia, Indonesia, or the Philippines. These were the "boat people." Technically, this was illegal emigration, but testimony indicates that Vietnamese officials took payments to allow the flow of Chinese out of the country to continue. The organization of the departure was handled through the old commercial channels, and the boats lying offshore were arranged by the local and international networks of Chinese contacts. Thus the blame for the poor conditions of the refugees must lie with both the government that allowed it to occur and the community that organized it, under however trying conditions (Grant and others 1979; Benoit 1981).

The flow of Chinese refugees continued from 1978 through 1979. Vietnam invaded Cambodia in late December 1978, hoping to end the dirty border war with Pol Pot. Teng Hsiao-p'ing then visited the United States and, on leaving, declared that China would "punish" Vietnam. The United States did not demur. The subsequent invasion led to three weeks of fighting that were bloodier than any three weeks in the first or second Indochina wars. Tensions rose steeply, and the Vietnamese began to make it clear to the Chinese that they should leave. Other Chinese refugees came out of Cambodia to the Thai border after the Vietnamese destruction of the Pol Pot regime and the subsequent fighting and famine. By 1980, thousands had left Indochina and were seeking refuge in countries beyond Asia, particularly in the United States.

The sea voyages were horrendous for the overloaded craft, and many of the refugees were lost at sea or ravaged by pirates in the Gulf of Siam. Estimates of the losses range up to 50 percent of all those who left Vietnam. Problems still remained for the survivors on their arrival at foreign shores. The countries of first asylum, particularly Malaysia, but also Indonesia, the Philippines, and Hong Kong, were nervous about taking so many illegal Chinese into their populations. The first camps for the refugees were hastily improvised in deserted locations, the island Pulau Bidong off the east coast of the Malay Peninsula being the prime example. Here the refugees were kept alive through international efforts until they could be screened and admitted into a third country for permanent settlement. Later transitional camps were set up at Bataan in the Philippines, on an island in Indonesia, and in Hong Kong for those being admitted to the United States. There the refugees received orientation to American life, English training, and instruction in some vocational skills.

The procedures whereby the Chinese refugees entered the United States were the same as those for the Vietnamese, Lao, Hmong, and others—once screened by the Immigration and Naturalization Service, they had to have personal sponsors, generally found by one of the voluntary agencies (VOLAGS) that had signed a contract with the State Department to take responsibility for the refugees. In this way the Chinese refugees were placed as single nuclear families (parents and children) in scattered localities across the country. One problem in examining the Chinese as a separate refugee group is that official records were usually kept on country of origin rather than ethnicity (Peters and others 1983), and sorting them out of the Vietnamese and Khmer refugee populations, especially the former, is often difficult.

SOCIAL AND ECONOMIC STATUS IN THE
UNITED STATES

The Chinese refugees were, on the average, the earliest of the ethnic groups coming to the United States in the second wave of Indochina emigration (1978 on). The Lao and Hmong, although they were in the Southeast Asian camps longer than the Chinese, tended to arrive here only after the boat people. The Vietnamese of the second wave mainly came later still. A study of Vietnamese, Chinese from Vietnam, and Lao refugees who arrived in the years from 1978 to 1982 conducted by the Institute for Social Research (ISR) of the University of Michigan for the Office of Refugee Resettlement (HHS) (Caplan and others 1984) shows the Chinese to have been here an average of 28.5 months, the Lao 25 months, and the Vietnamese only 23 months.

The ISR study surveyed the three refugee groups in five sites around the country (Boston, Chicago, Houston, Seattle, and Orange County, California). The resulting data provide a profile of the Chinese refugees from Vietnam and enable preliminary comparisons between this group and the Vietnamese and Lao. Of the total adult population of 4,160 in the survey, 836 were Chinese from

Vietnam (20%, compared with 50% Vietnamese and 30% Lao). Fifty-five percent of these adults were male and 45 percent female. The Chinese refugee population tended to be older than the Lao and the Vietnamese, with an average age among adults of thirty-three. Eighteen percent were sixteen to nineteen years of age, 36 percent in their twenties, 18 percent in their thirties, 13 percent in their forties, 8 percent in their fifties, and 7 percent sixty and over, a much flatter distribution than for the other two groups, which had a higher percentage of younger adults. The highest percentage of Chinese among the local survey populations lived in Seattle (39%), with Chinese making up 29 percent of the Chicago survey, 18 percent in Orange County, and only 9 percent and 8 percent, respectively, in Houston and Boston. Seventeen percent of the Chinese in the survey had moved, a percentage slightly higher than for the Vietnamese and the Lao.*

As would be expected from a historical view of the Chinese in Vietnam, they were quite heavily urban (87%), and their occupations there reflect this—31 percent of all the adults had held such urban jobs as proprietors, clerks, assistants, construction workers, auto mechanics, machine operators, and factory workers. Another 33 percent had been students. Their educational background was, however, not high—more than half the adults had had no more than a primary education in Vietnam, another 40 percent had had some secondary education but no more, and only 4 percent had even studied at a university.

Half the Chinese households (50%) were single nuclear families, and another 29 percent were extended families. The remaining fifth of the households contained at least one single, unrelated adult (whether living alone, with other singles, or with one or another type of family unit). Compared with the Vietnamese and the Lao in this survey, the Sino-Vietnamese tended to have both a higher percentage of single-person households and a higher percentage of extended family households. Yet these Chinese households were on average the smallest (5.2 persons) and had the fewest children (1.6), the fewest children under age six (0.44), and the highest percentage of adults (75%). The average age of the youngest child was over six years old, the highest of the three groups, and thus this average child was in school. Overall, the Chinese refugees from Vietnam had households that were smaller, with more adults and older children, and had moderate levels of education and occupation in Southeast Asia compared with the Vietnamese and Lao refugees.

The question of English proficiency was a major one for the refugees. Because knowledge of English was strongly correlated with education, the Sino-Vietnamese were likely to be only moderately proficient in English, and this proved to be the case. Not quite half the Chinese households (47%) had anyone who knew any English when they arrived in the United States and in less than a tenth (8%) of the households did anyone know English even fairly well. In less than a fifth of the households (17%) did half the adults know some English. These figures are slightly higher than the Lao figures but are much lower than the

* I wish to thank Mr. Bui Long Quang for his aid in providing me with these figures.

Vietnamese. The relative pattern for current English among the three ethnic groups generally follows that of arrival English, as all three groups show consistent gains. Although fewer Chinese in the survey had taken English classes in the Asian camps (14% as compared with the overall mean of 23%), there was little difference among the three groups in taking English classes in the United States (40% were currently taking classes and more than three-quarters had had such classes at one time or another). The major reasons for Chinese respondents not taking current English classes were that the respondents were too old or too busy.

The Chinese from Vietnam were more involved in general employment services (40%) than were either the Vietnamese or the Lao (28% each), whereas vocational training, which requires more education and better English, had fewer Chinese (6%) than Vietnamese (9%) but more than Lao (4%). The unemployment rate for the Chinese from Vietnam (46%) was slightly worse than that for the Vietnamese (43%) and the Lao (40%) in the sample, despite the Chinese having been in the country longer. A partial explanation for this difference might be that the smallest numbers of Chinese in the sample came from the two areas with the best economic conditions, Houston and Boston. Moreover, such aggregate figures are misleading and need to be examined in terms of the length of time the refugees have been in the country. Thus the Chinese unemployment rate dropped steadily, from more than 90 percent for those here a year or less to about 30 percent for those here between three and four years.

Another aspect of employment for the Chinese from Vietnam also reflects that for the Vietnamese and the Lao. When they are able to get work, the jobs are most often lower in status and poorer paying and have less of a future than the ones they held in Southeast Asia. If lucky, the refugee will find a similar job; more often, it will be less than what he or she had had. For example, although operating a machine is a relatively common job for the refugees here, those (like many Chinese) who used to operate machines in Vietnam have difficulty getting jobs here, undoubtedly because of poor English. The jobs obtained by the refugees tend to be in less stable sectors of the economy, where the work is part-time, seasonal, and irregular, with low wages. The Chinese hold jobs that are less likely than those held by either the Vietnamese or the Lao to have employment benefits in general (55%) or health benefits (49%), paid vacations (45%), or retirement pensions (18%) in particular; they are, however, about equal in dental plans (27%). Even though the Chinese have a higher unemployment rate than the Lao, they have been employed for a slightly longer average time (fourteen months to thirteen months) and have a slightly higher average hourly wage ($4.89 to $4.76). In general, the Chinese from Vietnam tend to fall between the Vietnamese and the Lao in job status, being lower than the former and higher than the latter (11% with high-status jobs, 9% being professionals or managers).

The Sino-Vietnamese who were not in the labor force included current students (working and nonworking), housewives, the disabled, retirees, and those who were simply not looking for work at the time. They again fell between the

Vietnamese and the Lao in the percentage of adults fitting these categories (56%), and the same is true for the percentage of students (17%).

An important aspect of the ISR study is its focus on the household rather than the individual. In the short time that the refugees had been here at the time of the survey (fall 1982), few of them, as individuals, had been able to get jobs good enough to lift them out of poverty. What is important, then, is the combination of resources the *household* was able to bring together in order to support all its individuals. Those on public assistance, for example, tended to have a mix of available resources. The Chinese from Vietnam had 67 percent of their households receiving some sort of public cash assistance and almost all of them also received food stamps. This was higher than for the Lao and slightly lower than for the Vietnamese. As with unemployment, the percentages of those on cash assistance declined steadily from the first year of residence to the fourth. Another important instance of the mix of resources for the household is the *number* of jobs held by individuals in the household. For the Chinese, as for the refugees as a whole, there is a steady and significant progression upward in the number of households having more than one job.

On this basis of mixed resources in the household, the key question is not whether any one individual (or for that matter household) receives any kind of public assistance; rather, it is whether the household has any earned income. Fifty-nine percent of the Chinese households had some form of earned income, slightly lower than for the Lao but higher than for the Vietnamese. The next question is the source of the refugee household's total income (public assistance, earned, or a combination of the two). The Chinese households were high on combined incomes, slightly low on public assistance alone, and fairly low on earned income alone. This is understandable, considering the tendency of the Chinese to live in more complex extended families. The adults of these households are pooling their resources, both earned and assistance, to further their mutual aim. Over time the number of households on only cash assistance drops sharply from the first to the fourth year of residence, the number with combined incomes peaks in the third year and then falls off, and the number on earned income alone rises from the first through the fourth year. An important point to be made here is that the search for work continues through time, irrespective of eligibility for assistance or its cutoff.

One important reason for this, besides the desire for work itself, is that earnings are needed for households to rise significantly above the federal poverty level. In general, the households in the survey averaged 79 percent of the poverty level if they received only cash assistance, 146 percent if they combined income sources, and 218 percent if they had earned income alone. Approximately the same percentages hold true if the households had no jobs, one job, or more than one job. The Chinese from Vietnam fit this pattern. Although half the Chinese households were living below the poverty level (essentially the same as the Vietnamese and the Lao), there is a steady rise in the percentage of the poverty level met from those in the country only a few months to those who had been here longer than three years.

Overall, Caplan and others (1984) suggest that among the Vietnamese, Chinese from Vietnam, and Lao in the sample, ethnicity was a less important factor than a number of others—length of time in the United States, Southeast Asian education and occupation, arrival English proficiency, site, and household composition. Arrival English, which has a certain correlation with education in Southeast Asia, was a strong predictor of economic self-sufficiency. Household composition, in terms of the number of employable adults, was also of significance. The single nuclear family had the worst economic standing, particularly if it was large, except in cases in which some of the members had a decent level of English.

Dunning (1982) examined the Sino-Vietnamese refugees in southern California and Texas within a year or two of their arrival. He found them falling short of the ethnic Vietnamese refugees (many of whom had been here since 1975) in economic performance. Actually, when compared with other 1979 arrivals, the Chinese seemed to be doing fairly well. One area Dunning examined that the ISR survey did not was sociocultural adjustment. Dunning's data show the Chinese to be more adaptive culturally to the surrounding environment than are the Vietnamese, considering the longer time spent here by the Vietnamese that were examined. Yet Peters and others (1983) have shown in their study of Sino-Vietnamese from West Philadelphia that the Chinese from Vietnam have not integrated appreciably with any surrounding groups. The area in which they live is quite mixed (blacks, whites, Asians, and native Americans) and a Chinatown exists in downtown Philadelphia. There are Korean establishments, and to quote the study (p. 1), "in the past two years there has been an explosive expansion of Southeast Asian refugee fruit and vegetable vendors as well as small food stores, many of which are owned by Sino-Vietnamese." Nevertheless, tensions have pervaded the neighborhood and exist between the Vietnamese and Chinese; the different Chinese groups from Southeast Asia (mainly Vietnam and Cambodia) have not mixed appreciably (partly owing to language differences—Cantonese vs. Teochiu), and to quote from the report again (p. 6), "in general, very little interaction or integration has occurred between the Sino-Vietnamese refugees and the local Chinatown community." First of all, few of the refugees can afford to live there, but more basically a line exists between the "Hong Kong-and-Taiwan-connected" community and the Southeast Asian Chinese. The Chinese refugees here are, for the time being, left to develop both their Chinese-ness and their American-ness pretty much on their own.

FUTURE PROSPECTS

The strength of the Chinese communities in Vietnam and Cambodia, as described earlier, lay in the strongly interlocked nature of their social and economic networks, sources of both information and funds. Barton (1984) has shown how strongly personal integrity meshed within these networks, such individual and family success depended on maintaining contacts across the community and beyond. In this vein we can see the significance of the many groups and associations, organized for a great number of social purposes, in setting the scene for such contacts to take place. Involved here were both informality and a strong sense of propriety in carrying out one's economic dealings.

What does this mean for the Chinese refugees from Southeast Asia in the United States? To succeed as they succeeded in Vietnam and Cambodia, they will have to re-form the type of networks and the access to capital that were available to them there. This has already occurred to a limited degree in some places. The *New York Times* reported on the success of some Sino-Vietnamese refugees who arrived in 1975 and linked up with contacts in New York City's Chinatown. To quote Seth Mydans (1984), "As a Chinese, Mr. Chao benefits from a worldwide network of more than 21 million overseas Chinese whose family and clan connections link them across national boundaries as a powerful economic force." According to this report, "many" of the New York Chinese refugees moved into Chinatown, where links reached out to California, Houston, Louisiana, and Washington, not to mention Singapore, Malaysia, Thailand, and Taiwan. The specific links mentioned here were Teochiu.

Such linkages do not appear to exist yet in a location like Philadelphia. However, Peters and others (1983) show that these developments may be only in a nascent stage, and the future will see much greater achievements in this direction. Certainly the "Food Cart Network" around the University of Pennsylvania would seem to be a classic case of such economic organization. But the Philadelphia area has not shown any strong tendency so far to establish the multitude of associations that flourished so successfully in Southeast Asia. As a consequence, both information and capital have been difficult to obtain.

Thus the characteristics of the Chinese refugee community in this country— urban, small and medium business backgrounds, and moderate levels of education—mean that economic success and social integration (into Chinese-American society) will depend on the opportunity and ability to reach out and make contact. Developing networks will be a key to this success. Those Chinese refugees who remain isolated, however hard-working, will be at the mercy of their poor English, undeveloped education, and lack of capital.

APPENDIX

The Chinese wholesale commerce in foodstuffs included fish products, pepper, tea, livestock, market gardening, and raising fowl (ducks in Vietnam, chickens in Cambodia). Beyond the wholesale stage lay the retail—groceries, butcher shops, street vendors, soup stalls, cafes, restaurants, and so on. Overall, the Chinese handled 85 percent of the commerce in foodstuffs and 90 percent of the preservation and sale of meat and fish. More than 1,400 firms in Saigon/Cholon alone handled textiles and their products, almost 900 firms dealt with metal products, including jewelry, and more than 200 firms were involved with wood products, including paper. The Chinese in South Vietnam handled all the textile production, almost half (48%) the commerce in textiles, almost all (98%) the commerce in metals, and 40 percent of forestry exploitation (Tsai 1968; see also Ky 1963; Tsung 1959). Willmott (1967) demonstrates a similar pattern for Cambodia.

Tsai Maw-kuey (1968), a member of the Hokkien *bang*, has broken down these economic activities in terms of the five dialect groups. Although the Cantonese and Teochiu were dominant numerically (this being the only place in Southeast Asia where the Cantonese were the largest group), the Hokkiens were dominant in commercial circles. The other two groups (Hakka and Hainanese) had their own limited specialties. The Cantonese concentrated on urban general stores, restaurants, groceries, butcher shops, and other aspects of the food trade; the clothing and cloth business; construction and wood products; Chinese hotels and theaters; beauty salons; and mechanics. The Teochiu worked mainly in the tea business, wholesale and retail, but also in fish (from both the Mekong Delta and Cambodia) and their products, Chinese medicinal herbs, metalworking, and trucking. The Teochiu also had the most extensive international contacts and hence foreign trade and banking. The Hokkien, for their part, had a role far greater than their numbers. This group controlled the rice trade, with its shipping and milling, as well as the secondhand, hardware, and junkyard businesses. Living and intermarrying in the countryside, the Hokkien shopkeepers provided the key economic link between the mass of the Vietnamese population and the urban Chinese merchants. Through this link came rice and scrap iron, the products of agriculture and war, to the international market. The last two groups, Hakka and Hainanese, restricted themselves to limited and well-defined specialties: medicinal herbs, baked goods, leather products, textiles, plastics, ceramics, and rubber goods for the Hakka, who were much more involved in artisanry and industry than the other groups; European-style cooking—with its restaurant and cafe trade—Western films, and pepper growing for the Hainanese.

In Cambodia, Willmott (1970) shows the Teochiu, rather than the Cantonese and the Hokkien, to be dominant in number and through the countryside as the shopkeepers who handled local commerce and the rice trade. As in Vietnam, the Teochiu handled import–export but here were more widely involved in dry goods and groceries as well as pharmacies, vegetable farming, and street peddling. The Cantonese lived mainly in Phnom Penh, Battembang, and Kampong Cham and, with their great diversity of businesses, served as extensions of the commercial interests of Cholon. Occupations of specialization were construction, transportation, carpentry, mechanics, and wine. The Hokkien focused on banking, import–export, foodstuffs, and, as in Vietnam, hardware. The Hakka and Hainanese were like their fellows in Vietnam. The former worked in bakeries, medicinal herbs, and leather, and the latter concentrated on restaurants and hotels. Here the Hainanese also included textile products, however.

REFERENCES

Barton, Clifton A.
1984   Trust and Credit: Some Observations Regarding Business Strategies of Overseas Chinese Traders in South Vietnam. In *The Chinese in Southeast Asia*, Vol. 1, *Ethnicity and Economic Activity*. Edited by L.Y.C. Lim and L.A.P. Gosling. Singapore: Maruzen Asia.

Benoit, Charles
1981   Vietnam's "Boat People." In *The Third Indochina Conflict*. Edited by D.W.P. Elliot. Boulder, Colorado: Westview Press. Pages 139–162.

Caplan, N., J. K. Whitmore, and Quang L. Bui
1984   *Economic Self-sufficiency Among Southeast Asian Refugees. Report to the Office of Refugee Resettlement*. Ann Arbor, Michigan: Institute for Social Research.

de Poncins, Gontran
1957   *From a Chinese City*. Garden City, New York: Doubleday.

Dunning, Bruce B.
1982   *A Systematic Survey of the Social, Psychological and Economic Adaptation of Vietnamese Refugees Representing Five Entry Cohorts, 1975-1979*. Washington, D.C.: Bureau of Social Science Research.

Fall, Bernard B.
1959   Commentary. In *Vietnam, The First Five Years*. Edited by R. W. Lindholm. East Lansing: Michigan State University Press. Pages 111–117.

Grant, Bruce, and others
1979   *The Boat People: An Age Investigation*. New York: Penguin Books.

Ky Luong Nhi
1963   The Chinese in Vietnam. Doctoral dissertation, University of Michigan, Ann Arbor.

Lim, L.Y.C.
1984   Chinese Activity in Southeast Asia: An Introductory Review. In *The Chinese in Southeast Asia*. Edited by L.Y.C. Lim and L.A.P. Gosling. Singapore: Maruzen Asia. Pages 1–29.

Murray, Martin J.
1980   *The Development of Capitalism in Colonial Indochina, 1870-1940*. Berkeley: University of California Press.

Mydans, Seth
1984   Chinese Refugees from Vietnam Thrive in Chinatown. *New York Times*, 11 February, 29, 32.

Ngo Vinh Long
1971   Use of the Chinese by the French in Cochinchina, 1886-1910. Harvard University *Papers on China* 24:125–145.

Nguyen Hoi Chan
1971   Some Aspects of the Chinese Community in Vietnam, 1650-1850. Harvard University *Papers on China* 24:104–124.

Peters, H., B. Schieffelin, L. Sexton, and D. A. Feingold
1983   Who Are the Sino-Vietnamese? Culture, Ethnicity, and Social Categories. Philadelphia, Pennsylvania: Institute for the Study of Human Issues.

Skinner, G. William
1951   *Report on the Chinese in Southeast Asia*. Ithaca, New York: Cornell University, Southeast Asia Program.
Tsai Maw-kuey
1968   *Les Chinois au Sud-Vietnam*. Paris: Bibliothèque Nationale.
Tsung To Way
1959   A Survey of Chinese Occupations. In *Vietnam, The First Five Years*. Edited by R. W. Lindholm. East Lansing: Michigan State University Press. Pages 118–125.
Whitmore, John K.
1983   Vietnam and the Monetary Flow of Eastern Asia, Thirteenth to Eighteenth Centuries. In *Precious Metals in the Later Medieval and Early Modern Worlds*. Edited by J. F. Richards. Durham, North Carolina: Carolina Academic Press. Pages 363–393.
Willmott, William E.
1967   *The Chinese in Cambodia*. Vancouver: University of British Columbia.
1970   *The Political Structure of the Chinese Community in Cambodia*. New York: Humanities Press.
Woodside, Alexander B.
1971   *Vietnam and the Chinese Model*. Cambridge, Massachusetts: Harvard University Press.

Cubans

According to most accounts, Cuban emigration to the United States began with the victory of revolutionary forces in 1959. Thousands fled the island in search of personal security as the revolution extended its control over each new sector of Cuban society. By 1984 twenty-five years of socialist transformation had resulted in the flight of roughly one million Cubans to the United States. Received for the most part with widespread popular and official support, the Cuban-Americans became a truly enviable story of immigrant success.

Such conventional accounts obscure as much as they enlighten. Although the recovery of the Cuban-American community has indeed been remarkable, this success has not been shared by all its members. Nor are the steps it has taken to advance economically and socially necessarily of direct relevance to other immigrant and refugee groups. Conventional wisdom masks the complexity and heterogeneity of both the historical antecedents to the refugee exodus and the personal and social experiences of those who left. In place of detailed accounts these more typical explanations consist of judgmental "worms or heroes" theses, leaning either toward supporters of the revolution or in favor of those "anti-Fidelistas" who applaud the exiles as freedom fighters.

The victory of the revolution in 1959 did not suddenly give birth to a new species in Cuba, one that took flight from the island in search of more hospitable grounds. Rather, the origins of the emigration belong in the panorama of pre-revolutionary history, for it was in this history that the dimensions of the Cuban social structure that would become the targets of revolutionary reform were initially established and continuously defended. It was this prerevolutionary society, for example, that Fidel Castro attacked in his famous Moncada speech of July 26, 1953. In this address, he identified clearly the patterns of prerevolutionary development that were to be changed by the revolution. Among other goals, the revolution would seek to improve the status of those who were discarded or subordinated by more than a century of capitalist development. Included were the unemployed, farm laborers, industrial laborers and stevedores, small farmers without land, and disaffected professionals. Excluded from the list of beneficiaries from this early period were the bourgeoisie, landowners, bankers, and industrialists. This list was a simplistic accounting of the aims of the revolution, and later exiles would come from both included and excluded groups. Still, the revolution and the exiles it created owe their origins and complex motivations to the organization of prerevolutionary Cuban society.

History also did not stop with the triumphant occupation of Havana in 1959. The revolution has not produced a single set of forces that generates refugees. Although there are shared, long-term pressures to emigration from Cuba, the refugee exodus has developed through successive waves or outflows, each with a distinctive set of pressures and a distinguishable social composition. Indeed, one reason each new wave rekindles the political and intellectual problems of Cuban emigration is that the differences among the outflows are not easily explained by existing perceptions and charges. The latest incident in 1980, the Mariel exodus, once again challenged conventional explanations and reopened questions about the origins and resettlement experiences of the Cuban-American community.

PREREVOLUTIONARY ORIGINS

Pre-1959 Migration to the United States

Even before Cuba became a republic, emigration to the United States had been established as a familiar feature of its political history. Numerous political leaders, including Jose Marti, the major figure of the Cuban independence movement, endured a spell of exile in the United States before resuming power on the island. Decades later, both Batista and Castro would also spend time in the United States organizing for an effective return.

In the early years, political turmoil sent sufficient numbers to the north that they were able to establish significant Cuban-American communities. The Ten Years War (1868-78) exiled hundreds of Cuban separatists, as well as others forced out by wartime conditions. The exiles resettled in New York, Key West, and New Orleans. The 1870 census reported that as many as 5,000 persons who had been born in Cuba were now residing in the United States (Boswell 1982). Indeed, by the mid-1870s, the population of Key West comprised a large number of Cuban emigrants.

Political leaders and activists, however, formed only part of the exodus. Throughout the later half of the nineteenth century the struggle for national independence combined with severe economic fluctuations to forge an increasing outflow of Cubans to the United States. As early as the mid-nineteenth century, significant sectors of the Cuban economy had become dependent on U.S. conditions (Jorge and Moncarz n.d.). The economic panic of 1857 led to U.S. tariffs on items manufactured abroad being raised; these duties were further increased during the Civil War. In Havana, the cigar industry buckled immediately. Factories closed or faced bankruptcy. Partly in response to these tariffs, some Cuban cigar manufacturers left Havana, resettling inside the tariff barriers in Tampa and New York. In Tampa, the Cuban-owned cigar industry founded a largely successful Cuban-American community that still thrives, despite the closing of the cigar factories.

New York City dominated the incipient Cuban-American resettlement network in these early years. It served as the center for political activities of many anticolonial groups, including Marti's Cuban Revolutionary Party. After the exodus from the 1930s revolution against Gerardo Machado in Cuba, New York held 45.4 percent of the nearly 34,000 Cubans living in the United States; Florida contained only 27 percent. Miami began its ascension to the center of Cuban-American life in the 1930s, and on the eve of the 1959 revolution only a modest percentage of the estimated 40,000 Cubans residing in the United States were living there.

Pre-1959 Cuban Society and Economy

By Latin American standards, Cuba in the 1950s had achieved enviable levels of aggregate economic development. Cubans owned more television sets, automobiles, and telephones per capita than did other Latin Americans. There was an established, domestic business class and a large government bureaucracy with relatively well-paid white-collar employees. In many sectors wages and salaries approached those found in Western European and North American countries. And a significant percentage of the work force was unionized.

In the midst of this prosperity, however, considerable disparities existed throughout the population, and in some locations poverty was particularly acute. But the primary characteristic of prerevolutionary Cuba that helps to explain the heterogeneous origins of the post-1959 refugee exodus was the pervasive foreign domination of nearly all the major economic sectors. As one observer characterized the situation, "The Cuban economy was so wedded to the U.S. economy that the country was in many ways an appendage of it—though without enjoying (the benefits) a poor state in the United States does" (Seers 1964:4). With the exception of Puerto Rico, U.S. economic, political, and cultural relations with Cuba were more intimate than with any other major country. O'Connor (1970:1) has described these connections as follows:

Coca-Cola, baseball, Standard Oil, American tourists, abstract-expressionist painting, United Fruit, and Madison Avenue advertising techniques seemed to have submerged the once powerful social and political force of Cuban nationalism. . . . In Havana, at least, a unique Cuban identity and mode of life was filed away in the memories of a few Cuban anthropologists and historians.

The quantitative dimensions of U.S. involvement were equally impressive. In the mid-1950s, U.S. capital controlled 40 percent of raw sugar production, 50 percent of the public railways, and 90 percent of public services, such as telephone and electricity. The United States also ran the popular tourist attractions in Havana, entertaining roughly 200,000 U.S. visitors annually.

This U.S. domination had significant effects on class relations in Cuba and, as a result, on the social composition of those who left after 1959 (Portes and Bach 1984). Above all, Cuban dependence on sugar exports to the North American market inhibited industrialization. For decades sugar was the Cuban economy: *Sin azucar, no hay pais*; without sugar, there is no country. U.S. investment in Cuban sugar production began before independence and was virtually unchecked after the war of independence. Indeed, rather than transforming the structure of the economy, the war merely broke Cuba loose of Spanish mercantilist policies that restrained full realization of the organic affair between fertile Cuban soil and sugar cane. The subsequent growth of sugar production not only increased U.S. investment, but also generated a significant influx of immigration from the West Indies and Spain. The result was that agriculture, developed in part by foreign capital and shaped for export, dominated the Cuban labor force. Industry was able to employ only about 20 percent of the nation's workers, significantly less than half the percentage engaged in agriculture. Foreign capital's dominance over both the agricultural and industrial sectors meant that domestic Cuban capital moved easily only into real estate and investment abroad.

Another aspect of foreign domination consisted of the extent to which U.S. life-styles had permeated Cuban social life, especially the wealthier groups in Havana. This influence was perhaps even greater than indicated in the O'Conner quote. Two Cuban-American authors, for example, have suggested that this cultural penetration was so extensive that large segments of the Cuban population had become psychologically dependent on the United States (Jorge and Moncarz n.d.).

Against this historical, economic, and cultural backdrop, a full appreciation of the Cuban revolution and the exiles it created is possible. The goals set by the revolutionary leadership encompassed enormous changes. The aims were to transform a foreign-dominated, capitalist society into a socialist state in which there was accelerated economic growth along with material guarantees to all sectors of the population. In addition, the goal was to eliminate class, region, racial, and gender inequalities. The complex social origins of the successive waves of Cuban refugees emerge from the dramatic opposition and conflict between these revolutionary goals and the prerevolutionary realities.

POST-1959 REVOLUTIONARY TRANSFORMATIONS

Four major changes under the revolutionary regime account in large part for the successive waves of emigration. First, from the earliest period there was a clear and substantial effort to redistribute wealth, away from those entrenched groups that benefited from the prerevolutionary order and toward those who had been disadvantaged. In accomplishing this, a major goal was to redistribute wealth from the city to the countryside. Throughout the nation, measures were adopted to improve the conditions of the poor. Collectivized stores offered lower and guaranteed prices, rural wages were increased, and urban rents were set at 10 percent of a family's income. Each of these reforms, however, attacked the private ownership rights of landlords, large shopkeepers, and rural landowners.

Second, the ensuing battle with the United States, ending in confiscation of U.S. holdings and complete nationalization of the Batista government's domestic property, pushed more groups from supporting the new government. Indeed, these reforms probably created more opposition than the earlier redistributive policies. So many sectors of Cuban society had been tied to U.S. holdings and management that these new reforms reached far down into the Cuban social order. In addition to the wealthy owners and members of the middle class who opposed some of the earliest redistributive measures, groups affected by this confrontation with the United States included domestic businessmen, professionals, and even laborers who worked in foreign-owned enterprises (Portes and Bach 1984).

Third, during the period of relative political and military stability after 1965, the revolutionary leadership embarked on a strategy of development that emphasized expanded production of agricultural and industrial goods, while limiting the consumption of consumer items. The government initiated a pervasive rationing program that began with meat and spread to many other food items, clothing, and consumer durables. The middle class felt the pressure of redistribution even more.

The fourth major transformation that helps to explain the history and social composition of the waves of Cuban refugees involves the substantial crisis in the economy in the last years of the 1970s. Failure to reach an overly ambitious sugar production quota, declining world prices for its major exports, agricultural diseases, and a series of self-recognized management mistakes threw the Cuban economy into a sea of difficulties. Starving for foreign exchange, the Cuban government agreed to a program of family visits from Cuban-Americans. In 1978 and 1979, more than 100,000 Cuban-Americans visited their relatives on the island. Family ties were reestablished at all levels of the social order. Perhaps more important, however, was the clear demonstration to Cubans of the consumer possibilities in the United States. Relatives from abroad carried with them a diverse range of consumption and luxury items against which the realities of rationing and consumption limitations appeared dismal. The result was, once again, a source of disenchantment that reached far into the Cuban population.

Waves of Cuban Emigration

In the most general terms, the social composition of the Cuban refugees after 1959 can be characterized by declining social status. Both average educational backgrounds and the percentage of professionals and white-collar workers decreased as the revolution aged (Casal and Hernandez 1975). Political motivations as the sole or overwhelming reason for leaving have also weakened with time

(Amaro and Portes 1972). Part of these changing motivations, however, was a result of the increasing importance of family reunion as the reason for emigration. As each wave separated larger numbers of family members, sorting desires to reunite with family from political disaffection became increasingly difficult. In addition, as the government consolidated its control of all sectors of the society and economy, the differences between economic and political motivations became virtually impossible to disentangle, if ever they could be.

For the first year of the revolution, emigration was unrestricted. However, only those who had substantial wealth or who had been members of the inner circle of the Batista government left during this time. The large-scale exodus began primarily in 1960, after a series of urban land and legal reforms initiated the redistribution of national wealth. The initial trickle of exiles resembled the historical pattern of political emigration, in which it was a matter of expectation that the groups who had low power would leave the country. But this emigration soon took a dramatically different course when, instead of simply replacing one group of leaders for another—as was the result of the war of independence— the revolution of 1959 targeted its efforts to a total transformation of the economy and society.

Even the earliest waves of emigrants, however, defy any simplistic explanation of their reasons for emigration based solely on former class positions or overt political opposition. For example, more than 14,000 children were sent out of the country by their parents in response to widespread rumors that the state would usurp parental authority. Overwhelmingly, however, the social class origins of the earliest wave mirrored the top layers of prerevolutionary society. Fagen, Brody, and O'Leary (1968) report that those who resettled in Miami between 1959 and 1962 overrepresented the professional, managerial, and middle classes of the Cuban population. Thirty-one percent of the exiles were professional, technical, and managerial workers, compared with 9.2 percent of the 1953 Cuban population. Similarly, 33 percent of the exiles were clerical and sales workers; 13.7 percent of the source population worked in these jobs.

The extent to which both U.S. activities and the revolutionary reforms had penetrated the Cuban social structure was also evident in this highly selective first wave. Although much underrepresented in comparison with the total Cuban population, 8 percent of this early wave laborered in semiskilled and unskilled sectors of the work force, 7 percent were employed in service jobs, and even 4 percent worked in agriculture and fishing.

According to the same study, these early "Golden Exiles," as they would come to be known in the United States, also possessed a much higher level of education than did the general Cuban population. Only 4 percent of the refugees had less than a fourth-grade education, compared with 52 percent of the island's population (Fagen, Brody, and O'Leary 1968). A large percentage of the refugees (36%) had completed high school or some college. The comparable figure for the Cuban population was only 4 percent.

The first wave of exiles was certainly heterogeneous but constituted a group that vastly overrepresented the higher status, wealthier strata of prerevolutionary society. As most also lived in Havana at the time, the first wave represented a severe loss of resources and talent to Cuban society, a veritable ''brain drain'' of unparalleled proportions elsewhere in the hemisphere. The same social group came to the United States with its own resources and social connections and reestablished itself within a relatively short period.

The first wave was halted abruptly by the missile crisis of 1962 and the U.S. blockade. Despite the official termination of the flow, more than 50,000 persons are reported to have made the trip (Boswell 1982). A fraction, perhaps 12 percent, escaped in boats and a few airplanes. One thousand political prisoners from the Bay of Pigs fiasco were exchanged for vital medical supplies, food, and cash. Another 5,000 family members traveled with them. Others left through third countries.

The second major wave of emigration began in September 1965, when the Cuban government announced that those with families in the United States would be allowed to emigrate in October. Departures began in the small port town of Camarioca, as hundreds of boatloads of Cuban-Americans from Florida arrived to pick up relatives. The United States and Cuba agreed within a month to an orderly departure program, establishing an airlift between Miami and Varadero. These ''freedom flights'' were restricted primarily to the reunification of family members. When the airlift ended, in 1973, 2,800 flights had carried more than a quarter of a million persons to Miami (Pedraza-Bailey 1982).

A significant feature of this orderly departure program was that it allowed for controlled, prior screening of who would leave for the United States. The Cuban government restricted from departure young men of military age (fifteen to twenty-six) and those whose talents and scarce skills might disrupt national production and service. For its part, the United States was able to enforce the priorities of its own immigration law. Relatives of people already living in the United States were given preference according to the following ranking: spouses, parents, and then siblings. Throughout this period the proportion of refugees who had relatives already living in the United States was consistently above 90 percent.

Partly as a result of the Cuban exit restrictions, and largely as a consequence of continuing advances in revolutionary reforms, the social class backgrounds of the exiles shifted dramatically. The proportion of professionals, managers, and technical workers among the refugees dropped from 31 percent in the 1959-to-1962 wave to 18 percent in 1967 (Fagen, Brody, and O'Leary 1968). Skilled workers, however, increased their proportions. By the late 1960s the revolutionary government moved to consolidate its control over the smaller sectors of the economy that, until this time, had remained fairly independent. The move to socialize these sectors pushed higher the number of merchants, artisans, and small shopkeepers who joined the outflow (Portes, Clark, and Bach 1977).

Many Cubans who wanted to leave during this period of the ''aerial bridge'' were unable to gain passage. Registration to leave was a difficult step, frequently resulting in periods of "voluntary labor" in the countryside, possibly for as long as two years. Many chose to leave Cuba and go to Spain, hoping they could enter the United States later under normal visa eligibility requirements. In October 1973, they were allowed to enter the United States under a special parolee status. A study of this group conducted in 1973-74 showed yet another change in the occupational origins of Cuban refugees (Portes, Clark, and Bach 1977). In contrast to the earlier waves, the proportion of men in the 1973-74 arrival group who worked in the service sector rose from 7 percent to 10 percent in the earlier years to 26 percent. The exile-generating capacity of the revolution had reached further into the lower ranks of the social order and had grabbed cooks, gardeners, domestic servants, street vendors, bootblacks, barbers, hairdressers, taxi drivers, and small retail merchants.

A lull fell on the Cuban flow between 1973 and 1979, a period when only 38,000 Cubans arrived in the United States. Most of these trickled in through third countries. But with a thaw in relations with Cuba initiated by the Carter administration and the opening of an informal "dialogue" between seventy-five representatives of the Cuban community in exile and the Cuban government, a new wave of emigration began. In October 1978, the Cuban government announced its intentions to release 3,000 political prisoners and 600 others who had been caught trying to escape the island. Although not all the prisoners would leave immediately for the United States, those who did were accompanied by their families. Together, they formed a small wave of between 10,000 and 14,000 exiles. As noted previously, nearly 100,000 relatives from the United States traveled to Cuba. Both the family visits and the release of political prisoners, however, ended abruptly in March 1980.

Soon after this abrupt halt, the next major wave of emigration occurred. Mariel: The word itself has come to symbolize months of chaos, drama, and antagonisms created by the exodus of 125,000 Cubans between April and September 1980. Unlike the earlier boatlift from Camarioca in 1965, no orderly departure agreement was reached by the two governments in 1980. As a result, neither government had complete control over who left and who was admitted. And as a tragic consequence, the social composition of those who left and the character of the reception in the United States became more a matter of highly charged political antagonisms than in any of the previous waves.

The pressures and motivations underlying the Mariel exodus are also perhaps more complex than those of the preceding outflows. Although family reunion again played a major role in this exodus, the heterogeneous backgrounds point to other factors. One particularly startling feature was the age composition of the Mariel flow. Its average age was young enough that many of the exiles had been raised under the revolution. For this group, prerevolutionary experiences and memories had only an indirect effect, influencing them through either the older generations in their families or historical lessons in school. Undoubtedly, the economic crises in the last years of the 1970s, combined with a "demonstration effect" of consumption possibilities in the United States, as told by visiting Cuban-Americans, created an independent source of emigration pressure. The years 1978 and 1979 were also years of increasing political dissent over austerity measures in Cuba.

The beginning of the Mariel exodus is difficult to establish with precision. As early as January 1980, several Cubans had sought political asylum by entering the Peruvian and Venezuelan embassies. Negotiations on the asylum issue were progressing between Cuba and several Latin American countries. In addition, discussions between Cuban and U.S. authorities on the possibilities of enlarging the normalized emigrant flow had stalled, largely because the United States had to await the outcome of Congressional attempts to pass new legislation, the Refugee Act of 1980.

On April 1, 1980, an incident occurred that sparked the five-month boatlift. After several similar incidents a group of asylum seekers crashed a bus through the gates of the Peruvian Embassy in Havana. In defense, Cuban security guards opened fire. During an exchange of gunfire a Cuban security officer was killed. Three days later the Cuban government withdrew all its guards from the embassy compound, allowing anyone who wanted to leave the island to enter the grounds unmolested. Within days, nearly 11,000 persons from a wide spectrum of Cuban society had taken advantage of the opening. Problems created by such a large number of persons in such a small compound and the public spectacle that the entire event was generating moved the Cuban government to announce on April 21 that the port of Mariel was open to anyone wishing to leave the country.

The response from Miami was overwhelming. Within hours of the announcement, thousands of boats were on their way to Mariel to pick up relatives. Without a bilateral, orderly departure agreement the United States could not stop the boatlift, and the Cuban government was free to allow or encourage anyone to join the flow. As a result, the social backgrounds of the Mariel Cubans became a question of international politics and a weapon of both governments in their reheated confrontation.

Despite the chaos and political manipulations, the overwhelming majority of the Mariel Cubans were similar in their occupational and educational backgrounds to the last groups in the series of freedom flights in the early 1970s (Bach 1980). Of course, compared with the high-status backgrounds and the inflated image of the "Golden Exiles" of the 1960s, the Mariel Cubans fared poorly. According to the best available data, the latest wave had an average level of education of approximately eight to nine years, similar to the arrivals in the 1970s and still higher than the average education of the Cuban population. The former occupations of this wave were also comparable to those of earlier arrivals, although they reinforced the general trend toward a declining social status with each successive wave of exiles. The proportion of professionals and managers dropped only slightly, representing around 10 percent of the total, and there was an increase in the share of working-class occupations, including craftworkers, operatives, and laborers.

An alarming feature of the group that fueled a generally negative reaction to this uncontrolled influx was the number of former criminals, mental patients, and social deviants who were placed by Cuban authorities on the boats in Mariel. The exact number and social character of this subgroup will never be known, as much from the problems of definition as from the lack of information. From a study of the U.S. Immigration and Naturalization Service records of those who were initially sent to one of four military camps for processing, the estimate of the proportion who had spent time in jail in Cuba was 16 percent (Bach, Bach, and Triplett 1982). The reasons for incarceration varied considerably, ranging from stealing a chicken to feed one's family to violent assault and murder. Political prisoners, who were part of a group that the United States had continually expressed a willingness to admit throughout the 1970s, were also included in this group.

At least two additional social background characteristics of these exiles caused public alarm. Unlike previous waves, this group had a considerable sex imbalance, with men outnumbering women by more than two to one. Previous waves had managed to bring families or had restricted the exodus of young men. The Mariel group contained a significant share of single men, many of whom did not have close relatives in the United States. In addition, a surprising number of women arrived who were also single and without direct family ties in the new land.

The latest wave also contained a large share of black Cubans, apparently much more than did previous waves. Although U.S. definitions are inadequate to capture accurately the racial composition of Cuban society, most data show a significant increase in the proportion who are black. From levels estimated at approximately 90 percent white among the earlier waves, roughly 50 percent of the Mariel Cubans were believed to be black. One consequence of this change in racial composition was a new perception for the general U.S. population of what the Cuban-American community represented.

Successive waves of refugee flows from Cuba have carried to the United States a virtual cross section of prerevolutionary Cuban society. From the professionals, landowners, and businessmen of the early 1960s, through the family groups leaving by way of the "aerial bridge," to the working-class populations of the Mariel exodus, this twenty-five-year refugee flow has transplanted a sizable and socially significant segment of the Cuban population onto U.S. soil. The Mariel exodus has even brought its share of the social outcasts that exist in all societies. Looking back on this transplanted population in the United States, many of the dimensions of social organization that stand out in the predominant Miami and New Jersey Cuban communities, including the social and economic inequalities, recall the social order of Havana in the 1950s.

INCORPORATION INTO AMERICAN SOCIETY

As Cuban refugees landed in the United States, the economic and cultural antecedents forged from a long history of periodic migration provided a basis for a positive reception. Existing Cuban-American communities were relatively small, but their presence was important. Cuban refugees were also aided by the first large-scale, federally financed refugee program. Over the course of roughly twenty years, and excluding the costs of the resettlement of the Mariel flow, nearly $1.6 billion has been spent on the Cuban Refugee Program to aid the reception and resettlement of these newcomers. Most important, however, each new wave of Cuban refugees contributed on its own to the reconstruction of a community in which family and ethnic obligations forged connections that assisted in economic growth and cooperation.

Legal History

The program of federal assistance for the resettlement of Cuban refugees was initiated by President Eisenhower in December 1960. Its original form involved the creation of the Cuban Refugee Emergency Center in Miami, whose purpose was to provide initial relief in terms of food, clothing, and health care and to begin a program of assisting employable refugees to find jobs. President Kennedy enlarged this commitment in April 1961, establishing the Cuban Refugee Program as part of the Department of Health, Education and Welfare. Initial funds were provided by presidential discretion, but in 1962 the Migration and Refugee Assistance Act established permanent authority for the relief program. Early amounts of aid allocated by President Kennedy totaled $4 million. But from 1961 to 1973 the amount increased substantially: The total expenditure during these years was roughly $867 million, or $67 million per year. A large proportion of these funds went to the Dade County public school system to absorb the impact of non-English-speaking students. The majority, however, went to welfare assistance, including health services. In 1961, for instance, 56 percent of that year's $4.1 million budget was spent on public assistance. By 1972 that proportion had risen to 82.7 percent, and the total annual budget had climbed to $136.7 million (Prohias and Casal 1974).

Such substantial amounts of aid followed a clear legal definition of Cuban exiles as refugees. The Cuban Adjustment Act of 1966 consolidated former executive and legislative temporary authorities to provide a stable framework for Cubans to be admitted to the United States and, in time, become permanent resident aliens and naturalized citizens. Although special parole authority had to be used for the group of Cuban exiles allowed to enter in 1973 from Spain, the legal framework for the Cuban program was firmly established in the 1960s.

The Mariel exodus in 1980, however, followed by only a month the adoption of a new comprehensive refugee law. The Refugee Act of 1980 accepted the U.N. definition of a refugee as a means of standardizing U.S. policy and treatment of the increasingly diverse worldwide movements of refugees. Although the Act did not supercede the Cuban Adjustment Act of 1966 or terminate the Cuban Refugee Program, it did render federal reimbursement of resettlement costs conditional on declaration of refugee status. In the face of the drama and chaos of the uncontrolled Mariel boatlift, and in a context of mounting domestic pressure against immigration and expensive public assistance programs, the Carter administration decided not to extend to the Mariel Cubans full refugee status. Instead, a special category of "entrant-status pending" was created as a temporary measure. It recognized the inevitability of the newcomers' presence in south Florida and tried to limit the costs of their resettlement. As it turned out, the magnitude and problems of the resettlement effort resulted in huge fiscal expenditures that continue to accumulate yearly. As of late 1984, the debate continued over whether these Mariel "entrants" should have their ambiguous status changed to put them in a legal path to eventually become U.S. citizens.

Economy

Before the arrival of the Mariel group, the Cuban-American community had rebounded well from its exile experiences. Overall, Cuban-Americans had attained levels of economic well-being that were higher than those of other Spanish-origin groups, although still lower than the non-Spanish-origin population. In 1979, Cuban-Americans had a median family income of $17,538, compared with $14,569 for other Spanish-origin groups and $19,965 for non-Spanish-origin groups. Cuban-Americans had also achieved an "intermediate level" of occupational status. In 1980, 23.4 percent were employed as professional or technical workers, managers, or administrators. Among the total Spanish-origin work force, only 15.1 percent had been hired in these higher-status jobs. In contrast, these occupations represented 28 percent of non-Spanish-origin workers (U.S. Bureau of the Census 1981).

One of the confounding features of the Cuban-American's employment profile is that as a group they are older than most other U.S. workers. Median ages for the three groups discussed here are as follows: Cuban-Americans, 33.5 years; Spanish-origin, 22.1 years; and non-Spanish-origin, 30.7 years. This age difference accounts for part of the perceived economic success of the Cuban-American community. For example, partly reflecting their demographic concentration in the most productive ages, Cuban-Americans have a lower unemployment rate than both the Spanish-origin and non-Spanish-origin populations. Their rate of labor force participation for both men and women is also higher (U.S. Bureau of the Census 1981).

An outstanding feature of the Cuban-American economic progress involves the social and organizational consequences of the successive waves of arrivals, each with a significantly different class background. The result of these sequential, complementary influxes has been the construction of an economic enclave in Miami, in which class and ethnicity have intertwined to form a rare resettlement experience (Wilson and Portes 1980). This enclave consists of a highly differentiated, vertically integrated set of economic activities, constructed on the basis of an initial wave of entrepreneurs with sufficient capital and experience to establish a diverse set of vital enterprises (Portes and Bach 1984). These entrepreneurs, in turn, use ethnic loyalty and kinship obligations to hire each sub-sequent wave of Cuban refugees. In exchange for the new arrivals' loyalty, which is often expressed through an acceptance of low wages and no union representation, the Cuban-American entrepreneurs offer many the opportunity to find jobs soon after arrival. It is also possible to advance within these ethnic firms without waiting to acquire the skills typically expected of new immigrants. For example, within the enclave, low proficiency in English is not necessarily a problem, as virtually everyone is fluent in Spanish.

The ability of some of the earliest waves of Cubans to bring capital with them or gain access to it quickly in the United States is a major reason for the vitality of the Miami enclave. Federal and private business loans assisted others, and some U.S. employers who had branches in Cuba before the revolution rehired their former employees. Of course, not everyone, or even the majority, was that fortunate. Most Cubans in the first waves experienced downward social mo-bility—a characteristic common to newly arrived refugees and immigrants. Al-though many took whatever jobs were available, professionals experienced licensing problems, forcing many to accept jobs that were far below their skill levels. For these early arrivals, subsequent upward status mobility, which gave this group the image of uncommon resourcefulness and success, was primarily a recovery of their temporarily lost social positions.

Still, the strength of the Cuban-American enclave in Miami is considerable. In Dade County, Cuban-Americans occupy a prominent role in promoting the resurgent financial and commercial links between Miami and Latin America. In 1980, Cuban-Americans accounted for sixteen out of sixty-two bank presidents in Dade County and an equally impressive number of vice-presidents and bank officers. Approximately one-third of the businesses in Miami are Cuban owned or operated. And in certain large sectors of the Miami economy, Cuban-Amer-icans compose a substantial majority of the workers (Bach 1980).

The unique advantages of the enclave, as well as the related disadvantages of paternal economic relations, are not shared by all Cuban-Americans. Even in Miami a recent study shows that among a sample of 1973-74 arrivals, only around half found work in the enclave (Portes and Bach 1984). Enclave em-ployment is defined as being employed by a Cuban-American or working along-side fellow employees the majority of whom are Cuban exiles. Many enclave workers were small subcontractors whose jobs were particularly well suited to reciprocal ethnic loyalties and obligations. The other half of the workers in the sample were employed in the general Miami labor market. Most had Anglo employers and worked alongside other minorities. In these jobs, many of the "protections" of the enclave were not evident. Proficiency in English language, for example, was more important in the general labor market than in the enclave, as were other individual skills. Ethnic competition and antagonisms were also more apparent.

The Cuban-American community outside south Florida faces different em-ployment conditions. In their second largest urban concentration, Cubans in the

Union City–West New York metropolitan area in New Jersey have filled jobs largely in blue-collar sectors. Light industry, including garment work among Cuban women, warehousing, and transportation provide employment for most of this community (Rogg 1974). Significantly, this area has not generated the type of entrepreneurial success on a large scale that is so evident among the Miami settlers. Except for relatively small shopkeepers and an expected professional service class, the Cuban-American community in New Jersey is primarily a working-class settlement (Rogg and Cooney 1980).

Cuban-American women have played an important role in the transition to the U.S. labor market and an Anglo-dominated society. In the earliest years of the migration, Cuban women often found jobs more quickly than did their spouses, and others joined the U.S. labor force out of economic necessity. In 1980, roughly half the eligible Cuban-American female population was either employed or actively seeking work. This rate approximates the behavior of non-Spanish-origin women. This labor force participation is particularly striking, however, in that only one-fourth of these women worked in Cuba before leaving for the United States.

In addition to the increased active participation of women in the labor force, the Cuban-American family has also responded to the realities of American life. One mechanism has been through maintaining relatively large households. Cuban-American households are roughly twice as likely as non-Spanish-origin households to contain relatives other than the immediate nuclear family relations. Nine percent of Cuban households contain additional members, compared to 6 percent among other Spanish-origin groups and only 4 percent among those without Spanish backgrounds (Boswell 1982).

Relations Outside the Community

Three characteristics of Cuban-Americans' relationships to the outside, primarily Anglo community are noteworthy. First, Cuban-Americans have established a comparatively high incidence of marriage outside their ethnic group. Fitzpatrick and Gurak (1979) have shown that among U.S.-born second-generation Cuban women, 46 percent have married husbands without Spanish origins. Thirty-three percent of Puerto Rican women and 16 percent of Mexican women have married outside their groups. Part of these differences, however, are due to the demographic and socioeconomic composition of each group. People with higher social status and those who are older at the time of their first marriage are, in general, more likely than others to marry outside their respective groups. The relative economic success of the Cubans in the earliest waves—who are the ones that have had sufficient time to see their U.S.-born children marry—and the significantly older age of the Cuban-American population contribute to this apparently surprising level of outgroup marriage.

Second, the political activity of Cuban-Americans is influenced by a wide range of factors that do not necessarily affect other immigrant groups. Foremost is the proximity, both geographical and political, of the Cuban government. No other immigrant group to the United States, for instance, has participated in a large, if ill-fated, invasion of their former homeland, nor has any other group been able to use as effectively its opposition to the new government to influence U.S. foreign policy (Casal 1979).

In terms of domestic U.S. politics, Cuban-Americans overwhelmingly have already become U.S. citizens or, projecting their eligibility, have decided to adjust their status. As citizens, they register to vote and exercise that option at levels much higher than the average U.S. population. The anti-Castro feeling among the Cuban-American population is such that it dominates the political behavior of the majority of the community. Nearly three of every four Cubans in Miami, for example, are registered as Republicans. They tend to support generally conservative issues. The Cuban-American community, however, is not without its significant liberal advocates, including those who favor normalized relations with Cuba. Frequently, portraits of the Cuban-American community ignore two basic attributes of its political position: the general conservative politics of most immigrant and refugee groups, and the special antagonisms created by the continually recharged opposition to the Cuban government.

Third, Cuban-Americans primarily speak Spanish in everyday activities, largely because they live in a social context that supports its use. Language use, however, is influenced by many factors. For those Cuban-Americans who work outside the enclave in Miami, proficient use of English is an important tool in their economic competition. Cuban-Americans who marry outside their groups certainly face multiple pressures to substitute English for their native Spanish. And, in general, those who move into Anglo-dominated, higher-status business and social circles will find the use of English a necessary skill.

Nevertheless, an important, frequently neglected pressure on the maintenance of the use of Spanish within this community is the extent to which bilingualism is officially and institutionally rewarded. Bilingualism has become a serious political issue in Miami, as elsewhere in the United States. In the early 1970s, the compatible use of Spanish and English was generally recognized in Dade County, Florida, as a positive contribution to the region's economic success and cultural vitality. Soon after the Mariel exodus, however, voters in the county rejected the planned use of public funds to promote bilingualism. But this defeat was only a temporary setback for proponents of bilingualism. Future political battles and tests are already planned. Their outcomes will influence whether or not and to what extent the Cuban community reinforces its Spanish-language tradition.

Future Prospects

After twenty-five years of the latest and largest move of Cubans from the island to the United States, it is unlikely that the migration has ended. The historical relationships formed between Cuba and the United States over at least the past century, and intensified so dramatically since 1959, make emigration across the Florida Straits a reasonable future alternative to all kinds of disenchantments and desires. Although the sources of the emigration will continue to change, the revolutionary government is unlikely to overcome these profound historical and personal connections with the United States.

The future course of the Cuban-American community will depend fundamentally on whether new waves of immigrants arrive. The Mariel episode dramatically transformed the social composition of a settled Cuban-American community and altered fundamentally its place in the larger American society. Adjustments within the community to the Mariel entrants are still too new to anticipate their future direction. After an initial outpouring of support, the older, established community withdrew and sometimes opposed the incorporation of these newcomers into their own ranks. By 1983, however, the Cuban-American leadership began to rally its resources and followers, realizing that the Mariel population was both numerically and socio-demographically important to the community's future.

Unfortunately, the future prospects of Cuban refugees are all too frequently debated in terms of the contrasting options of full assimilation or complete ethnic separation. No immigrant group in U.S. history has achieved either of these ideal typical adjustments, nor do any have a chance. The experiences of the Cuban-Americans suggest that, like most immigrant groups, they have succumbed to some pressures of living in an Anglo-dominated society and in other ways have carved out novel responses to existing conditions. The most important questions about the future are probably those that seek to know how the Cuban-Americans project their own progress and whether, as they organize themselves to achieve these goals, they will choose to call it assimilation or separation. As significant will be how longer-resident and established groups outside the immigrant community respond to the Cuban-American community. In that rich, partially unpredictable interaction lies the future of Cuban refugees in the United States.

REFERENCES

Amaro, Nelson, and Alejandro Portes
1972   Una Sociologia del Exilio: Situacion de los Grupos Cubanos en los Estados Unidos. *Aportes* 23:6–24.
Bach, Robert L.
1980   The New Cuban Immigrants: Their Background and Prospects. *Monthly Labor Review* October:39–46.
Bach, Robert L., Jennifer B. Bach, and Timothy Triplett
1982   The Flotilla "Entrants": Latest and Most Controversial. *Cuban Studies/Estudios Cubanos* 11(2)/12(1):29–48.
Boswell, Thomas D.
1982   Cuban-Americans. In *Ethnic Minorities in the United States*. Edited by Jesse O. McKee. Dubuque, Iowa: Kendall/Hunt Publishing Co.

Casal, Lourdes
1979   Cubans in the United States: Their Impact on U.S.–Cuban Relations. In *Revolutionary Cuba in the World Arena*. Edited by Martin Weinstein. Philadelphia, Pennsylvania: ISHI.
Casal, Lourdes, and Andres R. Hernandez
1975   Cubans in the U.S.: A Survey of the Literature. *Cuban Studies/Estudios Cubanos* 5(7):25–51.
Fagen, Richard R., Richard A. Brody, and Thomas J. O'Leary
1968   *Cubans in Exile: Disaffection and the Revolution*. Stanford, California: Stanford University Press.
Fitzpatrick, Joseph P., and Douglas T. Gurak
1979   *Hispanic Intermarriage in New York City: 1975*. Bronx, New York: Fordham University Press.
Jorge, Antonio, and Raul Moncarz
n.d.   Cubans in South Florida: A Social Science Approach. Miami: Florida International University.
O'Connor, James
1970   *The Origins of Socialism*. Ithaca, New York: Cornell University Press.
Pedraza-Bailey, Silvia
1982   Portrait of the Cuban Exiles: Waves of Migration. Paper presented at the Tenth National Meeting of the Latin American Studies Association, Washington, D.C., March 4–6.
Portes, Alejandro, Juan M. Clark, and Robert L. Bach
1977   The New Wave: A Statistical Profile of Recent Cuban Exiles to the U.S. *Cuban Studies/Estudios Cubanos* 1(January):1–32.
Portes, Alejandro, and Robert L. Bach
1984   *Latin Journey: Mexican and Cuban Immigrants in the United States*. Berkeley: University of California Press.
Prohias, Rafael J., and Lourdes Casal
1974   *The Cuban Minority in the U.S.: Preliminary Report on Need Identification and Program Evaluation*. Washington, D.C.: Cuban National Planning Council.
Seers, Dudley, Ed.
1964   *Cuba: The Economic and Social Revolution*. Chapel Hill: University of North Carolina Press.
Rogg, Eleanor M.
1974   *The Assimilation of Cuban Exiles: The Role of Community and Class*. New York: Aberdeen Press.
Rogg, Eleanor M., and Rosemary Santana Cooney
1980   *Adaptation and Adjustment of Cubans: West New York, New Jersey*. Bronx, New York: Fordham University Press.
U.S. Bureau of the Census
1981   Persons of Spanish Origin in the United States: March 1980 (Advance Report). *Current Population Reports* May:5.
Wilson, Kenneth L., and Alejandro Portes
1980   Immigrant Enclaves: An Analysis of the Labor Market Experiences of Cubans in Miami. *American Journal of Sociology* 86(2):295–319.

6

FREDERICK J. CONWAY AND SUSAN HUELSEBUSCH BUCHANAN

Haitians

The Haitians stand in contrast to the other refugees discussed in this volume in a number of ways. First, their very claim to being refugees has been continually challenged, partly because they come from a nation with a "friendly" government, neither Communist-controlled nor war torn, and partly because they are poor, black, and carry a particular stigma attached to being Haitian.

Second, the Haitian boat people bring a special poignancy to U.S. shores. They remind Americans that only 700 miles off the U.S. coast—much closer than Puerto Rico, not to mention far-off Southeast Asia—lies a nation whose people are pressured to risk everything to seek freedom and survival in the United States. Their voyages and the bureaucratic heavy-handedness with which they have been singled out force Americans to confront once again the noble words inscribed on the base of the Statue of Liberty. The fact that the U.S. Coast Guard, with the cooperation of the Duvalier government, patrols Haitian shores to keep the people from leaving only heightens the poignancy.

Finally, Haitian immigrants are preceded by a notoriety whose origins have been forgotten. The Haitian peasant has long been portrayed as a savage cannibal; the folk religion, vodoun, has received a Hollywood reputation far out of proportion to reality; the name of Papa Doc is better known than those of more influential despots; and more recently, Haitians were quick to be branded as the carriers of acquired immune deficiency syndrome (AIDS). How did such a small country become such an important symbol of evil? To find the answer, we must go back to Haiti's origin as a nation. At the turn of the nineteenth century, Haitian slaves overthrew the brutal French colonial plantation system and established an independent republic. The events have largely been forgotten, but at the time, Haiti was the greatest threat to the slavery systems of the Americas and the wealth they produced from Boston to Brazil. It was not enough to isolate

The views expressed in this chapter are solely those of the authors and do not necessarily represent the view of the Department of Justice or other employing agencies.

the country and its revolutionary fervor; generations of writers needed to prove that a free Haitian people could never become a viable nation. In this sense, the challenges that Haitian refugees face in the United States have a long history.

Haitians have been emigrating to the United States for several decades, some in quest of primarily economic opportunities and others seeking political asylum, especially during the Duvalier period. Haitian immigration became a crisis in the late 1970s and early 1980s with the arrival of thousands of boat people, which peaked around the same time as the Cuban Mariel exodus, in 1980. The conjuncture of these two flows of people from the Caribbean and the contrasting treatment accorded them served to publicize the Haitian dilemma. Even though the U.S. ''interdiction'' of Haitian maritime traffic has slowed the arrival of boat people, the earlier crisis remains an important chapter in the definition of refugee status and in the history of the Haitian community in the United States. For these reasons, this chapter concentrates on the influx of boat people and its aftermath.

Because Haiti is little known, the background section sketches Haiti's political and cultural history as it relates to the recent exodus and provides some indicators of social and economic trends. The chapter ends with some comments about the question of whether these people should be considered refugees within the meaning of U.S. law.

BACKGROUND

Origins

Haiti is a singular country by almost any criterion. Physically, it is dramatic; steep, rugged mountain ranges cover three-fourths of its surface. One of the best-known Haitian proverbs says, ''Behind mountains there are mountains.'' The nation's history is no less dramatic. Haiti is the second oldest republic in the western hemisphere, dating from January 1, 1804, when an army of former slaves drove out Napoleon's army. Today Haiti stands out as the poorest country in the hemisphere.

Columbus discovered the island of Hispaniola, of which Haiti is the western third, on his first voyage. (The rest of the island is the Dominican Republic). By the mid-sixteenth century, the indigenous Tainos had been almost exterminated and the importation of African slaves by the Spanish was well under way. The French took possession of Saint-Domingue, as colonial Haiti was called, at the end of the seventeenth century. The French brought in many more slaves to work their plantations of sugar cane, coffee, cotton, and indigo. By the middle of the eighteenth century, Saint-Domingue had become the most profitable colony in the world. It was far more valuable to France than were the thirteen North American colonies to Britain.

The wealth of Saint-Domingue was produced by slaves who worked in one of the most brutal plantation systems in the history of the Americas. In the decade before the start of the Haitian revolution, the slave population nearly doubled, not from childbirth, but through the importation of 338,000 West Africans (Curtin 1969:79). These statistics are witness to the horrendous treatment of the slaves, whose life expectancy in Saint-Domingue was less than ten years. In the 1790 census, the 452,000 slaves constituted 87 percent of the population (Leyburn 1966:18).

The Haitian revolution was the only permanently successful slave insurrection in the Americas. Thirteen years of intermittent warfare destroyed most of the infrastructure of the hated plantations. Early Haitian governments under Dessalines, Christophe, and Pétion sought to reestablish the plantation system to restore export-oriented agriculture. But the former slaves had no interest in providing income to their rulers at the expense of their freedom. They left the plantations, taking up land given by the government or simply removing themselves to the uninhabited mountains.

These new peasants oriented agriculture toward subsistence and the local market, which required neither the capital nor the harsh labor exacted by such exports as sugar. Land was worked by extended families that lived together. Land was plentiful, owned by individuals, and passed on to their children, both sons and daughters, equally. In the first fifty years after independence, Haitian land was transformed into a system of small holdings owned by individual peasants. This is truer today than ever before, in that population increase has resulted in smaller parcels being inherited by more individuals. Data from 1970 indicate that 85 percent of agricultural holdings are less than five hectares (about twelve acres) each and almost 50 percent are less than one hectare (Wilkie and Haber 1983:56). Haiti is a country in which the peasantry is desperately poor but still owns most of its land. Ties to land are thus far more than merely sentimental, and Haitian peasants leave their land only under the direst circumstances. In contrast to other Latin American countries, there is not a mass of landless peons working for an elite who owns the land. Conflicting class interests in Haiti are more disguised.

Aside from temporary work groups, the extended family was the largest social organization in rural areas. There were no communitywide organizations, either social or political. The relationship of a local area to the state was channeled through the local *chef de section*, a military appointee. The direction of control and communication was entirely from the top down. With some embellishments, the same system operates today.

The ruling group consisted of two elements: a mulatto elite, which had been partially free and often owners of slaves during the colonial period; and the military leadership, largely black former slaves. With the abandonment of the plantations, this group lost its chance to retain (or acquire) dominance through the control of land and agriculture. Only three sources of income remained available: the professions (for a few), commerce, and—most important—the national treasury. Politics soon became a struggle to gain control of government finances and patronage, removed from the agricultural base on which all depended. The peasant majority became simply irrelevant to the political process, and no government in the past 150 years has made a significant investment in agriculture.

Culture and Language

The ruling group, and especially the educated elite, were oriented toward the French cultural models of the colonial period. They sought to contrast themselves as sharply as possible with the peasantry, who were oriented toward their own cultural patterns forged from Haitian and African experiences. Thus Haiti developed two cultures, one indigenous and the other ambiguous in its identification, but which served to "delegitimize" the first.

The use of language in Haiti is the best example of this, since language even more than color has been a class marker in Haiti. Creole is the language shared by all Haitians. Its lexicon is largely derived from French, but its syntax is distinct, making the two languages mutually unintelligible. Historically, 5 percent to 10 percent of the population has also spoken French. French is the official language, the medium of law, of oration, of literature, of all proper formality. Creole is the mostly unwritten language of intimacy, humor, and, through its proverbs, the wisdom of the lower class.

With attitudes that pertain to all Haitian culture, both the monolingual Creole speaker and the bilingual Creole/French speaker are ambivalent toward the two languages. The elite are both sentimental toward Creole and disdainful of it. At the same time, there is an artificiality to Haitian French; it is a language without slang. French symbolizes social dominance, but French utterances often lack substance. The monolingual Creole speaker shares many of these attitudes. Creole is seen both as the truly Haitian form of expression and as a kind of baby talk without a grammar. Creole marks a person as "dumb." On the other hand, the Creole phrase *pale franse* ("to speak French") means "to be a hypocrite."

French does more than symbolize social dominance; it helps to reproduce it. Creole speakers who wish to become educated must do so in French; literacy must be acquired in a foreign language. The government secretary or the lawyer who insists on speaking French to a peasant even though both could use Creole continues the linguistic exploitation.

Creole is not the only aspect of Haitian peasant culture that is denied legitimacy. The folk religion, vodoun, is perceived by the elite as powerful, even a necessary resort at times, but a threat to their status in Western civilization. Common-law marriage (*plasaj*), however long-standing, must be ratified in an expensive church ceremony to receive respectability. The physical features of the masses are despised and feared by many of their lighter-skinned compatriots. These characteristics of Haitian culture are the heritage of the colonial period, which ended formally more than 180 years ago.

Political History

After independence, neither France nor the United States gave Haiti diplomatic recognition for some time. France waited twenty-five years before recognizing Haitian sovereignty—and then only at the crippling price of sixty million francs in "indemnities." The United States did not recognize Haiti until the U.S. civil war. Even the Vatican considered Haiti to be "schismatic" until 1860.

Beginning with the need to pay the French indemnity, and subsequently to finance both government activities and "revolutions" against the group currently in power, Haitians began to borrow heavily from French, American, and German sources. The late nineteenth and early twentieth centuries were marked by increased political and financial instability, as one group after another grabbed the presidency. This period climaxed in 1915, when the U.S. marines invaded Haiti, ostensibly because of political chaos, but principally to gain control of Haiti's finances at a time when German influence in Haiti was ascendant. The gold in the national treasury was removed to a bank in New York, and the Haitian currency, the gourde, was tied to the U.S. dollar by treaty.

The U.S. marines remained in control of Haiti until 1934. American financial control did not end until 1946. The marines established political stability through elections that gave the presidency to the mulatto elite. The marines regularized and trained the Haitian army. They substantially improved the road system. They attempted to reorient the classical French educational system. None of these actions permanently changed Haiti's political or economic structure, however. The lasting legacy of the occupation was rather the intellectual and ideological ferment caused by the shock to Haitian sovereignty and pride. The occupation confirmed that the United States, and not France, was to be the metropolis for Haiti in the twentieth century.

The orientation of the François Duvalier government (1957-71) was in part a reaction against the hegemony of the mulatto elite that the marines had tried to assure. Duvalier's main program, however, came to be the establishment of absolute personal power. A period of political tension and terror in the early 1960s resulted in the departure of many professionals and business people, as well as in the alienation of foreign governments and in a sharp reduction in foreign aid and investments. The road system all but disappeared and many economic ventures halted. In 1964, François Duvalier had himself declared president for life. He maintained power through a reshuffled army and his own militia, commonly known as the Tonton Macoutes. Duvalier did what only one other Haitian president had done before him: He died a natural death in the National Palace and passed on the reins of power to his chosen successor.

The thirteen years since François Duvalier's son, Jean-Claude, became president for life have been ones of change for Haiti. Politically, there has been a reduction in terror, as most of the government's opponents in the country have been subdued. Foreign aid has soared, resulting notably in reconstruction of the road system and improvements in the capital, Port-au-Prince. Investments have created an important light industry sector, with foreign companies taking advantage of Haiti's low wages. Remittances from Haitians abroad have been an increasingly important element in the economy.

Ideologically, the Jean-Claude Duvalier government has been more diffuse than its predecessor. *Jean-Claudisme*'s most succinct slogan, *la revolution au pouvoir*, states simply that the government is in power. Duvalier's marriage in 1980 to the daughter of a light-skinned businessman symbolized a modus vivendi with the business elite. In the late 1970s (in large part owing to "human rights" pressures from the Carter administration), there was a period of relatively relaxed controls on the radio and press. This period came to an abrupt halt a few days after the American elections in November 1980. Many journalists and radio announcers were exiled and incipient alternative political parties were crushed. Strict control over political activities in both urban and rural areas remains in effect. Municipal and legislative elections were arranged in 1983 and 1984, in part to fulfill the U.S. administration's need to demonstrate "democratization" in Haiti to the U.S. Congress.

Recent Trends

Despite increased investments and massive foreign aid, Haiti remains the poorest country in the western hemisphere. A review of statistical data about Haiti is grim. At birth, the Haitian's life expectancy is fifty-one years, the lowest in Latin America, and infant mortality is by far the highest (World Bank 1980:444, 451). Daily caloric intake and protein consumption are the lowest in the hemisphere, with the lowest rate of increase between 1965 and 1980. The literacy rate is only 23 percent, again the lowest in the hemisphere and complicated by Haiti's linguistic situation (Wilkie and Haber 1983:6–7). The gross domestic product per capita was only $267 in 1980, less than half that of the next poorest country (Bolivia) and only one-sixth of the Latin American average (Wilkie and Haber 1983:12). Rural per capita income was significantly lower than this figure.

In the Duvalier period, the long-term decline in the country's agricultural base has become evident. Population increase, decreasing soil fertility, and greater needs for cash have driven Haitian peasants to cut the tree cover off steep mountain slopes in order to plant crops. The result has been a great increase in soil erosion, as rainwater rushes down the denuded slopes carrying away soil nutrients and leaving no residual moisture. The mountain plots are soon exhausted and the peasant is driven farther uphill. It is not unheard of for peasants to be injured when they "fall off" their gardens. In the rainy season, Haiti's rivers send long tongues of mud into the sea. It has been estimated that the amount of arable land in Haiti decreased by almost half between 1938 and 1970, whereas the population rose by more than 70 percent (Lundahl 1979:212; USAID 1981:9). This trend has worsened from the 1970s to the 1980s. The peasants are too poor to buy fertilizer and other inputs that would increase production. Without massive assistance directed to peasant holdings, the prognosis for Haiti's agriculture is poor—in a country in which 75 percent of the population is rural.

A final trend in Haiti to be noted is its increased orientation toward the United States. Migration to the United States since the occupation, and especially the flight of many of the elite group in the 1960s, has familiarized Haitians with American opportunities. An American, rather than a French, education is now desired and English has rapidly become the "chic" language to use. More important, funds sent by relatives abroad have made a profound impression on many Haitian families. The increase in U.S. investment in Haiti, especially in the industrial sector in Port-au-Prince, has provided in-country examples of American economic opportunities. In rural areas, the more widespread use of Creole in radio programs has increased awareness of the outside world. The impact of American Protestant missionaries should not be underestimated. American fundamentalist denominations have permeated even the most isolated valleys in Haiti, conveying a beneficial image of the United States as a generous country whose wealth is based on its righteousness. All these factors have helped to make the United States a strong pole of attraction for Haitians pressed by political abuse and economic devastation.

THE HAITIAN "REFUGEES"

Patterns of Haitian Emigration

Given the conditions described above, it is not surprising that one million Haitians have emigrated since the 1950s (Allman 1981). An estimated 400,000 to 500,000 Haitians have settled in the United States, with major communities in the metropolitan areas of New York, Miami, Boston, Chicago, and Philadelphia.

The history of Haitian emigration reflects a long-standing relationship with the United States. In the eighteenth century, French colonists with their slaves and free mulattoes fled Saint-Domingue for safe havens in Charleston, Philadelphia, and New York. During the 1920s and 1930s, Haitian students pursued their education at Teachers College, Columbia University, in cultural exchanges developed during the U.S. occupation. By the late 1930s, Haitians in New York formed a colony of about 500. Many of them participated in the cultural and political movement of the Harlem Renaissance (Reid 1939).

Large-scale emigration to the United States began in the late 1950s as many middle- and upper-class Haitians, including military personnel, civil servants, and political opponents, fled the early terrors of the Duvalier period and entered the United States legally. As economic and political conditions deteriorated during the 1960s, poorer, less educated Haitians joined the migrant stream. More than half the Haitians who are legal U.S. residents have entered since 1968. The introduction of preference categories, numerical quotas, and labor certification requirements by the Immigration and Nationality Act of 1965, however, created a backlog of Haitians waiting to emigrate to the United States legally. Entering the United States on a tourist or commercial visa soon became more attractive than the two-year wait for a permanent resident visa. Thousands of Haitians entered the United States during the late 1960s and 1970s with valid nonimmigrant visas. Visas were often obtained through travel agencies in Haiti, for many at the price of hundreds and even thousands of dollars. Many of the Haitians simply overstayed their allotted time in the United States or violated the conditions of entry by accepting employment and thus joined the ranks of the undocumented. Emigration has generally been a family affair, a chain migration through which split domestic units are reunited over a long period as one family member after another rejoins kin in the United States.

The 1970s and 1980s witnessed the arrival of Haitians from the most disenfranchised and impoverished sector of Haitian society—the urban poor and the peasantry. Called boat people in the press, these Haitians preferred to risk their lives at sea rather than face intolerably bleak conditions in Haiti. The first known boatload of Haitians swept ashore in Florida on December 12, 1972, having sailed directly from Haiti.

For a number of years, the Bahamas had served as a focus of emigration for Haitian peasants. (Considerable migration to the Dominican Republic still takes place, especially during the cane-cutting season; the same was true of Cuba until 1959.) By the mid-1970s, however, the Bahamians showed less tolerance for Haitian workers as tourism waned and the economy declined. In 1978, when the Bahamian government threatened to deport illegal Haitians, many of them chose to continue their search for a better life in Miami rather than return to Haiti. The movement to Miami had begun.

As the Bahamas became less attractive and as smuggling operations from Haiti became more sophisticated (and commercialized), the outflow of people from Haiti to Florida increased. In addition, requirements for obtaining entry visas from the U.S. consulate in Haiti stiffened, making it more difficult than ever to travel to the United States legally. A series of favorable court rulings (see below) for Haitians seeking asylum in the United States, which included work authorization on release from detention, added impetus to the movement. Many Haitians who were determined to leave Haiti, but who could not afford documents or an airplane ticket, sold their meager assets to pay for the trip by sea or joined with others to build boats for the 700-mile voyage. Unknown numbers of Haitians have died in their attempt to reach the United States, as craft designed for coastal traffic foundered on the high seas or dishonorable captains abandoned their human cargo to their fate.

Most Haitians were unable to make the voyage in a single crossing. They had to stop at Cuba or islands in the Bahamas to replenish supplies or make repairs. The Cubans generally provided the Haitians assistance and towed them back into the Gulf Stream to continue their voyage. The Bahamian reception was less than congenial and sometimes inhumane, as witnessed by the Cayo Lobos incident in early 1981, when the Bahamian government refused to rescue shipwrecked Haitians from a deserted, waterless island. Those Haitians who did make the voyage directly to Florida often spent ten to fourteen days at sea and staggered ashore dehydrated, famished, and ill.

Although the majority of Haitians arrived in Florida by boat during this period, commercial airlines also brought undocumented Haitians directly from Port-au-Prince to Miami. Well-organized commercial ventures that routed Haitians through the Dominican Republic, Jamaica, and Curaçao often ended with sadly disappointed Haitians who discovered that their costly visas were not valid for the United States.

Prior to 1977, approximately 7,000 boat people were recorded by the U.S. Immigration and Naturalization Service (INS). In 1978, 3,916 entries were recorded and the figure for 1979 was 4,449. The greatest influx occurred in 1980, with approximately 25,000 arrivals, a dramatic increase. Another 15,000 Haitians entered during the first six months of 1981 (Cuban-Haitian Task Force 1981). The INS estimates that between 40 percent and 50 percent of the arrivals may have escaped detection, so these figures may record only half of the actual arrivals.

Characteristics and Adaptation of the Haitian Boat People

Haitians seeking asylum in the United States are generally young men and women who, if they had remained in Haiti and had been employed, would have formed part of the primary sector of the labor force and the country's hope for the future. Cuban-Haitian Task Force (1981) statistics indicate that approximately 30 percent of the 1980-81 arrivals were female and 70 percent, male. Less than 10 percent were minors under the age of eighteen. Fifty-five percent to 60 percent were between eighteen and twenty-nine years old, and 25 percent to 30 percent were between thirty and forty-four. Approximately 5 percent were over forty-five.

A Cuban-Haitian Task Force (1981) sample showed that although the majority of the Haitians were illiterate, many possessed rudimentary reading and writing skills, usually in French. Occupational data show that male arrivals had most frequently been engaged in unskilled work, primarily field-crop farming, with a minority possessing such skills as tailoring and mechanical repair work. Haitian women arrivals had work experiences as seamstresses, domestics, vendors, farmers, and factory workers. (The majority of the Haitian arrivals listed themselves as single, but these data are difficult to interpret, as common-law marriages may not have been included in responses and because the question was also misinterpreted as asking whether they had arrived in the United States alone.)

Unlike Haitians arriving in southern Florida in the 1970s, most who arrived during the 1980-81 influx had embarked from Haiti (and not the Bahamas), pouring out from all areas of the country. The main areas of departure were from the northern and northwestern coasts of Haiti. The Department of the North was most frequently listed as the place of origin by arriving Haitians. The

Department of the West, including Port-au-Prince, was the second largest sending area. (Many of the Haitians arriving from this region entered by airplane and were stopped at Miami International Airport. The "Boeing people," as they were called, were more often from the more educated working and middle classes than were the arrivals by sea.) The third major area of outflow was the Artibonite Valley, where large-scale thefts of peasant land have been alleged. The number of recorded arrivals listing southern regions as their origin was the smallest. However, a series of droughts and the devastation of Hurricane Allen in 1980, as well as the repression of human smuggling on the northern coast, have increased the percentage of arrivals from the south of Haiti.

A large percentage of the Haitian boat people, approximately 85 percent, settled in southern Florida, primarily in the Miami area. New York and New Jersey received most of the remaining 15 percent of the arriving Haitians. Secondary migration has occurred among these areas since 1981, as Haitians have become discouraged by employment and housing problems in Florida or find the northern winters too harsh.

The main problems of the Haitians are their unresolved legal status, underemployment, and substandard housing. Employment poses the most persistent problem for new arrivals, especially as they are unskilled, do not speak English or Spanish, and sometimes are illiterate. Employment is often seasonal or temporary and low paying with few benefits. Haitian men and women find work in service industries, factories, construction or as domestics. They must compete with other immigrant groups, especially with Spanish-speakers, whose language is an advantage in Miami. Although statistics are not available, lack of employment has forced many Haitians to become agricultural migrant laborers, traveling along the eastern seaboard to pick crops. Others have opted for a grueling life of cutting sugar cane in Belle Glade or Immokalee, Florida; they are the poorest of the Haitian immigrants. Haitians also compete for agricultural jobs in Homestead, south of Miami, and in Broward County, to the north. Opportunities for exploiting these Haitians abound.

In Miami itself, most of the Haitians have settled in the Edison–Little River section, now known as "Little Haiti." (Details about conditions in Little Haiti can be found in Behavioral Science Research Institute 1983). A poverty-stricken zone with substandard housing, the area is the center for Haitian business, social, cultural, and religious activities in Miami. Up to a dozen individuals, related or not, find themselves living together in houses built for single families. The housing is expensive, despite its dilapidated state. Rats and other vermin create environmental and health problems. The Haitians have formed a highly mobile population, individuals moving from one residence to another as required by circumstances. Often only a few members of a household are employed; their wages support the others who are less fortunate.

Social, educational, and health services struggle to meet the needs of the Haitians and south Florida but are frustrated by lack of Creole interpreters and knowledge about Haitian cultural beliefs and social patterns. Among the problems they face are emotional difficulties stemming from separation from families in Haiti, prolonged detention, and adjustment to the American system. These problems are aggravated by the fact that these Haitians' status in the United States has not yet been resolved.

Despite these problems, many of the Haitian boat people have the advantage of preexisting networks of kin and friends in the United States who have eased the transition and adaptation process. A recent study showed that these Haitians have a remarkably positive outlook about their circumstances and prospects in the United States, are anxious to learn English and obtain an education, and are not isolated from non-Haitians either at work or in the community (Stepick and others 1982). Haitians have made a positive impression on south Floridians who discover their fundamentally friendly nature and strong work ethic. They bring many other strengths from the Haitian cultural heritage: fortitude, perserverance in the most arduous circumstances, deep religious faith, high self-respect, reliance on the extended family, and a tradition of sharing. These characteristics have enabled them to make a new life in the United States despite their problems and in the face of a welcome that has been less than open-armed.

The Federal Response and Its Aftermath

The most consistent aspect of the U.S. federal government's response to the Haitian boat people is the view that they are not collectively entitled to be designated as refugees, as individuals who fear returning to their own countries because they fear persecution on the basis of race, color, national origin, religion, social group, or political opinion. In the view of the U.S. Department of State and the INS, Haitians are "economic" rather than "political" refugees; that is, their motivation to enter the United States stems from the desire for employment rather than from fear of persecution or from actual persecution. Thus throughout the 1970s and 1980s, Haitians' claims for asylum as refugees have been almost uniformly rejected, despite evidence that human and civil rights are regularly violated in Haiti and that persecution for political opinions occurs there. Opposition to this stance has taken two directions: first, that Haitians should be considered legal refugees, and second, that in any case their claims should be accorded due process.

Haitians and their advocates have fought an unparalleled series of legal battles to assure that claimants receive due process of law; fair treatment, including access to Creole interpreters and attorneys at INS hearings; and work authorization on release from INS detention. (See Stepick 1982a and 1982b for a complete discussion of these issues.) In 1978, a flagrant violation of Haitians' rights occurred when the INS attempted to clear a backload of Haitian asylum cases by processing 150 per day and by revoking work authorizations. Haitian advocates took the INS to court. In June 1980, Judge James King, ruling in *Haitian Refugee Center vs. Civiletti*, ordered new INS asylum hearings for approximately 5,000 Haitians and rebuked the federal government for intentional discrimination and racism.

The Cuban Mariel exodus of April 1980 greatly complicated matters. Faced with the prospect of providing refugee status to 125,000 Cubans and pressured by the Haitian dilemma, the Carter administration equivocated, creating the ambiguous legal category of "Cuban/Haitian Entrant (status pending)." The category included undocumented Haitians and Cubans who arrived in the United States before October 10, 1980. Cubans and Haitians entering the United States without documentation after that date are subject to exclusion and deportation by the INS, although they are eligible for the same social service benefits as entrants while they are in the United States. By late 1984, the U.S. Congress had still not decided on a permanent legal status for the Haitians, and their rights to legal processes were still being contested in the courts as they lived in a legal limbo.

Faced with the Mariel crisis, the Carter administration assigned the Federal Emergency Management Agency to handle the immediate problems of shelter, food, and other necessities for the arriving Cubans and later for the Haitians. In June 1980, the Cuban-Haitian Task Force, a special interagency unit, attempted to institute a method for processing and resettling the entrants. Expecting to begin a new life in Miami, arriving Haitians who were encountered by the INS found themselves transported to the Krome South camp and later to the Krome North camp, parts of a former Nike missile base in the Everglades swamp. The camp was initially plagued with numerous problems: inadequate staff, especially Creole interpreters; lack of running water, sanitation, and supplies; lack of telephones and other means of communication for the Haitians; and lack of shelters other than tents and hangars. By the end of 1980, the government had begun to build permanent structures, including dormitories.

Anxiety, confusion, and plain fear marked the faces of Haitians who did not understand the chaotic resettlement process, were unsure of their fate, and tried their best to wait out the boredom of each day. Concertina wire atop the camp fence grimly reinforced the notion that the United States might not be the friendly haven the Haitians had sought.

In cooperation with voluntary agencies, such as the United States Catholic Conference, the Lutheran Immigration and Refugee Service, Church World Service, World Relief, and HIAS (Hebrew Immigrant Aid Society), the Cuban-Haitian Task Force developed a more systematic, responsible resettlement approach requiring verified sponsors and reducing time spent in the camp. The Fascell–Stone Amendment to the Refugee Assistance Act of 1980 provided Haitians and Cubans with a limited range of federal benefits and made states eligible for 100 percent reimbursement for cash and medical assistance to them. Thus funds became available to assist Haitians with their immediate financial needs and with longer-term social service needs.

Growing numbers of Haitian minors posed special problems during this period, as they often entered in the company of siblings, unrelated adults, or kin whose relationship could not be verified immediately, rather than with their parents. Many of these minors were declared to be "unaccompanied," in some cases according to a narrow American definition of kinship rather than the more extensive Haitian system. Thus some minors were unnecessarily separated from bona fide relatives or adoptive parents. Unaccompanied minors were placed in a separate facility at Krome South until care and sponsorship were developed by the Office of Refugee Resettlement, which was responsible for them. The Haitian minors were gradually transferred to Greer Woodycrest, a facility in Millbrook, New York, where they received care and educational opportunities until appropriate placements were made. Krome South closed in July 1981, and all the minors were resettled out of Greer Woodycrest by January 1982.

By May 1981, the new Reagan administration, seeing the flow of Haitians unabated, directed the INS to halt resettlement of arriving undocumented Haitians and to detain them. The detention policy instituted a regrettable and sad chapter in the U.S. treatment of those seeking haven on its shores. By July 1981, Krome North had changed from a temporary, short-term holding facility into a permanent detention camp filled to overflowing with confused and worried Haitians. As numbers grew, five federal prisons, the INS processing center in Brooklyn, and the former military base at Fort Allen, Puerto Rico, were pressed into service. Except for those released on humanitarian parole, nearly 1,800 Haitians spent fifteen months in bleak despair. In July 1982, Judge Eugene Spellman ordered the detained Haitians released, rebuking the INS for its failure to follow proper administrative procedures. Advocates appealed because the rebuke did not include condemnation of the INS's discriminatory treatment of Haitians, the only aliens incarcerated in this fashion at the time. A federal District Court of Appeals agreed and rebuked the federal government for discrimination and racism. In October 1982, a similar decision by Judge Carter released forty-eight Haitians confined in the INS Special Processing Center in Brooklyn.

At the same time as it ordered the detention of the Haitians, the Reagan administration pressured the Haitian government to reduce the smuggling operations on the north and northwestern coasts of the country. In September 1981, a U.S. Coast Guard cutter began patroling the Haitian coasts for the purpose of "interdicting" Haitian vessels on the high seas, determining whether their passengers have a legitimate claim to political asylum in the United States, and turning them back. The Haitian government concurred in this policy, although its legality under international law has been questioned.

The outflow from Haiti has been greatly reduced since mid-1981, with an occasional boat still landing in full view of sunbathers basking on south Florida beaches. (Haitian community leaders claim that several hundred Haitians arrive each week but are not detected by the INS.) Although the newly arrived Haitians are no longer singled out for incarceration—Krome North now resembles a small United Nations with aliens of many nationalities confined there—this fact does not make the detention easier to bear as their claims for asylum are decided.

The Refugee Question

Cubans and Haitians arriving before October 10, 1980, were assigned the status of "Cuban/Haitian Entrant (status pending)." This was an ambiguous legal category that allowed them to remain in the United States without granting them either refugee status or collective political asylum. The "entrant" status enabled the federal government to avoid either defining the issues involved or dealing with them in a decisive manner. Four years later the entrants still awaited a decision by the U.S. Congress about their permanent legal status.

Haitians arriving after October 10, 1980, are not given "Cuban/Haitian Entrant" status but are considered undocumented aliens who are excludable or deportable. Many of these Haitians have elected to claim political asylum in the United States and await decisions on their claims. Most of these claims will probably be rejected.

The U.S. State Department and the INS maintain that Haitians do not have legitimate claims to political asylum or refugee status. These federal agencies make the assumption that because Haiti is a poor but "friendly" country, people leave for strictly economic reasons. This position can be questioned on several levels. The economic conditions of a population and the political system to which they are subject are not so easily separated. This is as true of Haiti as it is of Communist countries. Interviews with Haitians have shown that political and economic factors are often intertwined in decisions to leave Haiti. In some cases, the abuse of a local authority pushed the individual to leave; in others, political abuses were part of a broader situation that made life intolerable. (Buchanan 1981 discusses these issues more completely). In the case of many Haitians, the fear of persecution for political opinions on return is not so much based on formal opposition to the central government as on problems with the arbitrary actions of local officials, for example, in the militia. Most Haitians are much too frightened to express an opinion that is contrary to the policies of the central Haitian government. This does not mean either that there is universal approval of the government or that individuals do not have severe political problems at other levels.

Finally, the U.S. State Department maintains that deported Haitians are not persecuted on their return. These claims are difficult to verify, however. Even the most conscientious U.S. foreign service personnel find it difficult to obtain accurate information about events in rural areas. Even without an official Haitian policy of action against returnees, abuses can occur on an individual level. Therefore, it is difficult to say definitively that Haitian claimants for asylum would not suffer persecution on return.

The acceptance of claims for asylum has been rare and the disposition of the Haitian boat people remains unresolved. The exodus of Haitians and Cubans in the 1970s and 1980s has challenged the United States as the country of first asylum for the first time in a generation. The response has been a continuing equivocation.

REFERENCES

Allman, James
1981   Haitian Migration: Thirty Years Assessed. *Migration Today* 10(1):7–12.
Behavioral Science Research Institute
1983   *Demography, Social Status, Housing and Social Needs of the Haitian Population of Edison–Little River*. Coral Gables, Florida.
Buchanan, Susan Huelsebusch
1981   Haitian Immigration: The Perspective from South Florida and the Island. Unpublished report to USAID Mission to Haiti.
Cuban Haitian Task Force
1981   Entrant Data Report (May 31). Washington, D.C.
Curtin, Philip D.
1969   *The Atlantic Slave Trade*. Madison: University of Wisconsin Press.
Leyburn, James G.
1966   *The Haitian People*. New Haven, Connecticut: Yale University Press (orig. 1941).
Lundahl, Mats
1979   *Peasants and Poverty: A Study of Haiti*. London: Croon Helm.
Reid, Ira de A.
1939   *The Negro Immigrant: His Background, Characteristics and Social Adjustment*. New York: Columbia University Press.
Stepick, Alex
1982a   Haitian Refugees in the United States. *Minority Rights Group Report* No. 52.
1982b   Haitian Boat People: A Study in the Conflicting Forces Shaping U.S. Immigration. *Law and Contemporary Problems* 45(2):163–196.
Stepick, Alex, and others
1982   Haitians in Miami: An Assessment of Their Backgrounds and Potential. Unpublished paper, Florida International University, Miami.
USAID (U.S. Agency for International Development)
1981   Haiti: Project Paper: Agroforestry Outreach. Washington, D.C.: U.S. Department of State.
Wilkie, James W., and Stephen Haber, Eds.
1983   *Statistical Abstract of Latin America*, Vol. 22. Los Angeles: UCLA Latin America Center Publications.
World Bank
1980   *World Tables: The Second Edition*. Baltimore, Maryland: Johns Hopkins University Press.

7

TIMOTHY DUNNIGAN
                    AND DOUGLAS P. OLNEY

Hmong

The Hmong were relatively unknown to the American public when they began arriving in the United States from Thailand refugee camps during the spring of 1976. In news reports about the rather obscure conflict in Laos at the time of the Vietnam War, this Laotian ethnic minority had been called the Meo, a Vietnamese name rejected by the Hmong. As the Meo, they were described as a primitive hill tribe who fought fiercely and effectively on the side of the democratically elected government of Laos against communist insurgents called the Pathet Lao. The tragic results of Hmong involvement with the U.S. Central Intelligence Agency, a connection dating back to the early 1960s, did not fully come to light until after the Pathet Lao and North Vietnamese took over the country in 1975. Partly as a result of Hmong efforts to establish contacts with American citizens willing to publicize how the Hmong had supported U.S. interests in Laos, the media began paying special attention to this new refugee group. Descriptions of the plight of these former allies fostered a sense of indebtedness toward the Hmong and stimulated concern for the refugees. Unfortunately, media exposure also created some misleading images of Hmong society.

Articles and news stories about Hmong refugees in America have tended to emphasize factors that impede satisfactory adjustment. Often mentioned are Hmong illiteracy, ignorance of spoken English, and technologically simple agrarian traditions. Also implicated are the large corporate kin groups of the Hmong that seem so out of place in an industrial society. Because the Hmong have undergone a traumatic transplantation from rural Laos to urban America, adjustment problems undoubtedly will be severe and protracted. As a migratory ethnic minority of Southeast Asia, they have already adjusted many times to extremely complex and shifting cultural environments. In the United States they are handling many of their problems of adjustment by using established strategies of accommodation. It should not be assumed that the need for change will force the American Hmong to abandon or radically alter the essentials of their social organization.

Throughout the chapter we highlight those aspects of the Southeast Asian experience that affect how the Hmong define and manage the present challenges of resettlement in the United States. We begin by reviewing the Hmong role in Laotian politics, the exodus from Laos after 1975, camp life in Thailand, and resettlement to third countries. Next, we compare pre- and postresettlement differences in Hmong employment, education, and housing. Kinship, religion, internal politics, and ethnicity are the themes of the last sections. Kinship is particularly important because connections based on descent and marriage exert a pervasive influence on the social relationships of Hmong refugees.

HISTORICAL BACKGROUND

The Laotian population is composed of many ethnic groups representing a number of language families. The politically dominant Lao (Laotian Thai) are concentrated primarily in the alluvial plains of the Mekong River. Related Thai groups inhabit the mountain valleys of central and northern Laos. Living on the mountain slopes are various Mon-Khmer–speaking groups. The Hmong and the Mien (Yao), who speak Sino-Tibetan languages, occupy the highest elevations. As LeBar and Suddard (1960:2) point out, "to the elite—virtually all Lao—the history of Laos is the story of the Lao." This is true despite estimates (Hickey 1955) that the minorities total half the population. This bias is reflected in most historical and cultural surveys of Laos. Relatively little coverage is given the ethnic minorities, and their importance in recent history is still to be assessed.

The Hmong are relative newcomers to Laos, having migrated from China and Vietnam in the first part of the nineteenth century. The area of greatest settlement was the province of Xieng Khouang. Significant numbers also moved into the adjacent provinces of Sam Neua, Luang Prabang, and Phong Saly. This concentrated the Hmong in northeast Laos, near the border with Vietnam, an area that became strategically important during the Vietnam War. Adequate documentation of early Hmong history is lacking (Savina 1924; Dreyer 1976; Weins 1967; Larteguy 1979), and the main source of information continues to be oral tradition.

Observers writing in the 1950s and 1960s describe Hmong political organization as being generally limited to the village (Hickey 1955; Halpern 1964; LeBar and Suddard 1960; LeBar and others 1964). Mention is made of former Hmong "kings" in China and Vietnam who, for fairly brief periods, controlled large areas and dominated neighboring groups, situations that are called "unusual" (Hickey 1955:310). Actually, the Hmong have repeatedly shown an ability to unify into supralocal organizations when their collective welfare is threatened.

In the course of their long history, the Hmong have accommodated to a variety of political systems in China and Southeast Asia. Their solidarity did not give them complete independence from the dominant nationalities, but they often enjoyed considerable autonomy because of the way they were integrated into

national structures. For instance, LeBar and others (1964:70) describe the following situation in sixteenth-century Kweichow, China:

Tribal chieftains, including Miao [Hmong] chieftains, were appointed to hereditary administrative positions, adopting Chinese surnames and entering into a kind of feudatory
arrangement with the imperial government on behalf of the tribesmen within their
jurisdiction.

The Hmong sought similar arrangements with French colonial administrators
and various Lao political leaders. The strategy was to maximize Hmong autonomy by supporting established authorities or emerging powers. The rewards were
increased control over their own affairs at the local level and a sharing in the
benefits of national development. In areas where they were numerically and
politically weak, the alternative was discrimination and exploitation by other
ethnic groups. The struggle for a measure of self-governance in Laos before
1975 has been interpreted by some critics of U.S. involvement with the Hmong
(e.g., Adams and McCoy 1970) as a secessionist movement. By 1975, however,
Hmong integration into the political, military, economic, and educational institutions of Laos had progressed to a point where ethnic separatism would have
been extremely unlikely had the royalist government prevailed.

The Hmong are perceived throughout Southeast Asia as politically suspect
because of their cultural distinctiveness, independence, and ethnic loyalty. On
a number of occasions the Hmong have rebelled against the exactions of hostile
governments. One of the most serious uprisings in this century lasted four years
(1918-22) and spread through parts of northeast Laos and northwest Tonkin
(North Vietnam). Because the principal leader was a shaman, Pa Chay, who
prophesied the destruction of the Lao and French oppressors by supernatural
means, French historians have denigrated the rebellion as "the crazy man's war"
(Larteguy 1979:91–105).

Chao Fa, a Lao term meaning "Lord of the Sky," is a more recent militaristic
revitalization movement similar to the one of Pa Chay. It arose in the Laotian
province of Xieng Khouang during the mid-1960s, when fighting between right
and left political factions in Laos destroyed many Hmong villages. The Chao
Fa movement continues both within Laos and in the Thailand refugee camps.
Its adherents, a small but undefined portion of the Laotian Hmong, are the
implacable enemies of the Pathet Lao and Vietnamese. Consequently, Chao Fa
settlements are still priority military targets in Laos.

Notwithstanding these episodic revolts, the Hmong assiduously cultivated
alliances with outside groups. The choosing of certain allies by Hmong leaders
caused deep internal divisions. Two powerful lineages belonging to different
clans began in the 1930s to compete for official French recognition in the Nong
Het area of Xieng Khouang. The rivalry led to the formation of pro- and anti-
French factions and eventually drew many Hmong into the Indochinese wars as
combatants on both sides (Lee 1982). The Hmong who achieved political as-

cendancy during the late colonial period transferred their allegiance to the French-supported constitutional monarchy established in 1949. These same Hmong became allies of the United States as the latter replaced the French as the military backers of rightist elements in the Royal Laotian Government. A much smaller group of Hmong joined with the Lao Issara in agitating for an independent Laos, free from French influence. After independence, the disaffected Hmong became part of the Pathet Lao movement.

Lee (1982:203) describes the situation of the Hmong after more than a decade of war in Laos:

By 1973, the Hmong formed 32 per cent of the 370,000 refugees on government support in Laos, and 70 per cent of 155,474 in Xieng Khouang—the biggest ethnic group affected by the war. About 12,000 are believed to have died fighting against the Pathet Lao from 1962 to 1975. This heavy toll was partly the result of the military draft introduced by the RLG [Royal Lao Government] in its offensive against the PL and North Vietnamese forces. . . . An American refugee relief worker in Xieng Khouang established that 20 per cent of Hmong civilians died in the early 1960s as a result of sickness or enemy attacks during their flight to refugee camps.

The Hmong had become refugees in their own country long before it became necessary for many of them to seek sanctuary in Thailand.

The present status of the Hmong in Laos is difficult to ascertain. A Hmong resistance movement continues, possibly with the covert help of China, Thailand, and the United States. The stronghold of the Chao Fa in the mountainous and forested region of Phou Bia, near the Plain of Jars, has been under attack for some time, and the vitality of the resistance movement in that area is in doubt. The Lao People's Democratic Republic claims to have instituted programs of reconciliation and development for the Hmong. We do not have objective information about these programs, but Hmong families are still crossing the Mekong River into Thailand and few are returning to Laos (Lee 1982).

Since 1976, refugees have been accusing the Pathet Lao and their Vietnamese allies of carrying out lethal ''gas'' attacks against both resistance fighters and noncombatant Hmong in Laos. A Canadian research team who conducted a small-scale epidemiological study on Hmong and Khmer subjects, the latter from Kampuchea, concluded that chemical/biological warfare was being waged in Southeast Asia, and they surmised that the principal agents were mycotoxins (Humphreys and Dow 1982; Shiefer 1982). This is also the position of the U.S. State Department (Haig 1982; Schultz 1982). Strong denials have been issued by the governments of Laos, Vietnam, and the Soviet Union. Evans (1983) dismisses the claims of chemical/biological warfare as fabrications. Scientific evidence indicates that some Hmong have been exposed to unusually large amounts of mycotoxins, but researchers are still debating the source of these poisons.

Table 7.1. Hilltribe Movement to Thailand

1975	44,659
1976	7,266
1977	3,873
1978	8,013
1979	23,943
1980	14,801
1981	4,356
1982	1,816
1983 (May)	1,785
Total	110,512

Source: U.N. Commission for Refugees, 1983 Monthly Statistics, Bangkok, Thailand.

THE EXODUS FROM LAOS

When the Pathet Lao came to power in 1975, the United States abruptly ceased aiding its Laotian allies. Most Hmong who had sided with the Royalists believed that their position was untenable. General Vang Pao, chief military leader of the Hmong, departed by air from Laos for asylum in Thailand on May 14. He was accompanied by his family and a group of officers. Soon afterward, many Hmong began fleeing overland to Thailand. By the end of the year, 44,659 Lao hill people, the majority of whom were Hmong, had arrived in Thailand refugee camps (UNHCR 1983). The flow of Hmong refugees out of Laos lessened considerably during 1976 and 1977 but again increased to rather high levels in 1979-80. Subsequently, there has been a decline in the rate at which Hmong refugees are arriving in Thailand. These trends are summarized in Table 7.1.

Initially, the Hmong who arrived in Thailand were given temporary asylum at Nong Khai and Nam Phong. The Thai government began in 1979 to consolidate the camps by ethnic group, and Ban Vinai became the main Hmong camp. Other camps housing Hmong are Chiang Khong, Ban Nam Yao, Sop Thuang, and Chiang Kham, as well as the Phanat Nikhom and other transit centers for those about to move to a third country. In the summer of 1983, Hmong refugees in the United States were told by relatives that recent arrivals from Laos were being held at Nong Khai for possible return to Laos.

Since 1980, the number of Laotian Hmong in camps seeking third-country refuge dropped to the point where the total Hmong refugee population in Thailand has stabilized at around 55,000 (DeVecchi 1982:23). Published figures, in Table 7.2, for individual camps pertain to the hilltribes, including small numbers of Mien, Khmu, Thai Dam, and other groups.

The Thai Ministry of the Interior has assumed responsibility for setting up the refugee camps and managing basic services, such as food, shelter, and sanitation. The U.N. High Commissioner for Refugees funds camp operation, and a number

Table 7.2. Refugee Camp Populations

Ban Vinai	32,683
Ban Nam Yao	11,612
Chiang Khoung	5,408
Sop Thuang	3,765
Phanat Nikhom	971
Transit centers	276
Chiang Kham	109
Total	54,824

Source: Refugee Reports, Special Issue of December 17, 1983.

of voluntary agencies, or VOLAGS, a total of seventeen at Ban Vinai, provide additional services in Thailand, ranging from medical care to educational programs (CCSDPT 1982:3).

A refugee camp has several levels of organization, official and unofficial. Ban Vinai, which opened in December 1975, is administered by a Thai camp commander, and directly under him is a Hmong camp commander. Ban Vinai is divided into seven residential areas, each having its own Hmong leader. A residential area is further divided into three subareas, each of which contains a number of large, ten-room dwellings encircled by smaller units. Each subarea and large dwelling has its own head. Hmong leaders at the various levels in this hierarchy are elected by their constituents. The role of the leader is to assign labor tasks, oversee the fair distribution of food, and ensure that information is disseminated properly (Smalley n.d.; CCSDPT 1982). In contrast to Ban Vinai, Sop Thuang is divided into twelve areas, according to ethnic group distinctions. The houses are clustered in ways similar to those found in the villages in the refugees' home provinces (CCSDPT 1982:52).

The unofficial camp organization at Ban Vinai is nicely summarized by Smalley (n.d.:19):

The deeper cultural and emotional life of the Hmong refugees was not lived only within these loosely superimposed hierarchies. It was lived also within traditional families, lineages, sub-clans and other social relationships which people brought with them as they migrated. Some families had been shredded, with members lost in war and escape, others still back in Laos. But the intricate and extensive ways which Hmong have of relating people to people were brought with them. A lineage head might be in another section of camp, but even so that was closer than the half day's walk or more distance that he might have been in Laos. The members of a village might be scattered all over Ban Vinai, but those who were there still looked to their village headman from Laos or some other leader they had known.... Decisions were made within the traditional frameworks, marriages were made within the traditional patterns, ceremonies were performed within traditional groupings. All this was constrained by the camp situations of course. Adaptations had

Table 7.3. Hilltribe Resettlement to the United States

1975	301
1976	3,058
1977	1,655
1978	3,873
1979	11,301
1980	27,242
1981	3,704
1982	2,511
1983 (May)	300
Total	53,945

Source: U.N. High Commission for Refugees, 1983 Monthly Statistics, Bangkok, Thailand.

to be made. But these fundamental parts of Hmong life went on in camp, and on that level the Thai, international, and even the Hmong camp hierarchy was relatively irrelevant.

MOVEMENT TO THIRD COUNTRIES

The magnitude of the Indochina refugee problem and its potential for political destabilization throughout Southeast Asia was not immediately appreciated in the international community. Only 12,300 Laotian hill people were resettled in third countries from 1976 through 1978. International concern for the refugees increased markedly with the fall of the Pol Pot regime in Kampuchea and the advent of the Vietnamese boat people crisis. As a result, more Hmong, along with other refugees, were received by third countries. The figures pertaining to Laotian hill people for 1979 and 1980 were 13,000 and 29,000, respectively. After 1980, the Hmong showed less interest in moving to third countries. Only 8,000 were resettled between January 1981 and May 1983 (UNHCR 1983).

By May 1983, the United States had received about 50,000 Hmong, France 7,000, French Guyane 1,200, Canada 800, Australia 300, Argentina 200, and various other nations, including China and Japan, 300 or so (UNHCR 1983). The resettlement experience has been different for the Hmong in each country, ranging from an extensive agricultural experiment in French Guyane involving the creation of two self-sufficient Hmong villages in the jungle to a bewildering number of programs offered in the context of urban America. Table 7.3 summarizes the history of resettlement to the United States.

The mid-1983 Hmong population in the United States was believed to be more than 61,000, including 10,000 to 12,000 persons born in the United States, a reflection of the high Hmong birthrate. The Hmong were widely scattered in over seventy communities, most of which had 300 or more members. The majority of the Hmong were living in seven major centers: Minneapolis–St. Paul,

Minnesota (9,000); Orange County, California (3,000); Providence, Rhode Island (2,500); and several cities in the central valley of California, namely, Fresno (10,000), Merced (4,500), Stockton (4,000), and Sacramento (2,500) (ORR 1983; NWREL 1984).

The current distribution of the Hmong is more a reflection of secondary migration than of initial resettlement. A majority of families have moved from locations where they were originally sponsored in order to be with relatives in areas that offered employment, education, and social services.

EMPLOYMENT, EDUCATION, AND HOUSING

The main occupation of the Hmong in Laos was swidden agriculture. Forest growth had to be cut and burned on the land that was cultivated. A variety of crops were planted for three or four years on average until soil exhaustion required the development of new plots. Old fields were sometimes replanted after a long period of fallow. Hmong strategies of field rotation, crop sequencing, soil selection, fertilization, and so on were quite sophisticated and productive, although long-term effects of slash-and-burn methods on highland slopes and valleys have been criticized.[1] Hmong who had access to fertile areas with permanent sources of irrigation water practiced intensive agriculture. The Hmong also raised horses, pigs, cattle, and chickens.

Besides planting varieties of rice, corn, and many types of vegetables, the Hmong cultivated opium poppies as a cash crop. They were one of the many ethnic groups producing raw opium, but relatively few Hmong participated as traders in an opium market that had de facto legitimacy in Laos. Hmong who did trade opium usually collected from the producers for resale to higher-level distributors. Because the Hmong used opium as a broadly useful medicine and depended on its sale for cash income, it has been difficult to convince some of the older Hmong to cease using opium entirely.[2] A small number of refugees in the United States have received raw opium in the mail from relatives in Thailand, sometimes in repayment for financial support provided by the former. Opium confiscations by U.S. postal authorities have caused some police officials to worry about a potential opium trafficking problem in the United States.[3] Hmong political leaders have sternly warned against the use of opium for any purpose. These warnings, together with the perceived threat of deportation for drug-related crimes, appear to have convinced the Hmong to give up one of their most powerful home remedies, even when alternative treatments are more costly.

When hostilities escalated after 1960 in northeastern Laos, more and more Hmong were prevented from supporting themselves by farming. Families that congregated in large refugee settlements in north central Laos at least tried to maintain gardens. Later, in Thailand, some of the Hmong were initially allowed to plant on land close to the camps. Just before the second harvest, the fields were taken over by local Thai.

Middle-aged and older Hmong would like to practice farming in the United

States. Families have formed groups to plant large vegetable gardens for home consumption and commercial sale through farmers' markets. Young Hmong men and women are also participating in these gardening partnerships as a way of earning income. The refugees have shown considerable interest in publicly and privately funded farming projects that have the objective of training the Hmong in current methods of agricultural production and marketing. The attraction of farming for the Hmong is apparent in the large migration to the central valley of California. Although it is difficult to become an established grower, a number of families have been able to lease land in the vicinity of Fresno and raise labor-intensive commercial crops, such as pea pods and tomatoes.

The Hmong Resettlement Study (NWREL 1984) shows marked variations in Hmong employment characteristics in different parts of the country. In such cities as Dallas, Texas, and Fort Smith, Arkansas, Hmong adults were reported as being almost fully employed. The situation was much worse in Fresno, California, where as few as 10 percent of the Hmong adults found steady work. Employment levels for Hmong heads of household in Minneapolis–St. Paul were between 20 percent and 30 percent, and as many as 85 percent of the families were receiving some sort of public assistance. In all areas in which employment opportunities for the Hmong are scarce, there is heavy reliance on public assistance.

In a survey conducted in Minneapolis–St. Paul in 1982 (Olney 1983), it was found that approximately 74 percent of the Hmong received no education before they came to the United States, although 3 percent received ten or more years of formal education in Laos and, in some cases, attended college in France or the United States. Hmong refugee leaders have always stressed the need for vocational training, and a great many Hmong have entered programs at vocational/technical institutes. It has been discouraging for the Hmong to discover that, even when they graduate with a certified skill, employment is hard to find. Many Hmong who began skilled jobs were laid off in times of recession, and this experience has caused some of them to look for other kinds of work for security.

In 1983, significant numbers of young Hmong men and women were in the early stages of academic study at American colleges and universities. Most of the already educated Hmong who speak English have tended to accept positions that allow them to work with their own people. The social and medical services employ many of these individuals. Others hold supervisory positions within special development projects. A group of Hmong men in Minneapolis–St. Paul have been recruited to sell insurance nationally, which enables them to act as financial consultants to Hmong in many parts of the country.

According to the Hmong, their biggest problems are their limited knowledge of spoken English and the lack of literacy skills, which bar them from many types of employment. Twenty-six percent of those surveyed reported that they speak English well or very well and 31 percent said they do not speak English at all (Olney 1983).

Most Hmong live in public housing or substandard units within deteriorating parts of the inner cities. The tendency for the Hmong to cluster in certain areas appears to be determined by both the availability of housing and a strong desire on the part of the Hmong to reside near relatives. In some cases, the Hmong have slowly taken over whole apartment buildings by filling all available vacancies.

Initially, the disadvantaged minorities who had established themselves in neighborhoods with relatively cheap housing stock strongly resented the influx of Hmong refugees. The resentment was sometimes expressed in vandalism and physical violence. Such attacks on the Hmong have gradually lessened, and much of the earlier fear felt by the Hmong has subsided.

KINSHIP

Barney (1967:275–276) describes the essential Meo, that is, Hmong, social categories and groups that are based on descent through the male line:

The patrilineal clan system of the Meo dominates their social organization, serving as a primary focus for their culture as a whole by tying together social, political, economic, and religious aspects of behavior. The basic unit of the Meo social structure is the "household" or patrilineal extended family, meaning not only those who live under one roof, but also including all those under the authority of one household head. Thus a single household could include a man's unmarried daughters, his sons and their wives and children, and possibly his sons' sons' children and might also include a few other feeble or otherwise dependent relatives. All members of the household carry the clan name of the household head in addition to their given name. The clan name refers to descent from a mythical ancestor, and common membership in a clan serves as a bond of kinship and friendship between people who would otherwise be strangers. Members of the same lineage, who can trace their common descent from a known ancestor, refer to their lineage mates by a common term meaning "my olders and youngers" [kwv tij].

As an enclaved minority in Laos practicing swidden agriculture, the Hmong developed patterns of kin group formation that have helped them survive as refugees in Thailand and other countries of asylum.[4] Members of the extended family were sometimes forced to separate in order to find sufficient agricultural land in the Laotian highlands. They remained in contact with one another and made every effort to reunify in an area that would support the entire group. When families became fragmented during the flight from Laos to Thailand, and again in the course of permanent resettlement, the Hmong placed greater reliance on lineage and even clan ties as a basis for close cooperation. For most Hmong, solidarity among one's patrilineal relatives still provides the greatest security.

In the 1960s and early 1970s, some Hmong extended families and lineage groups were able to prepare for the future through occupational diversification. In addition to farmers, their memberships included soldiers, traders, students, various kinds of technicians attached to the military and development missions, and other people with special knowledge who served their respective kinship groups as circumstances changed. The expectation of mutual assistance among family and lineage members remains strong. Status and wealth differences do exist between nuclear families that make up the patrilineal group, but the general goal is to advance the socioeconomic position of all members.

Linkage through marriage entails additional reciprocity. On marriage, women customarily leave their patrikin and become fully integrated into the families of their husbands. This establishes an alliance of lineages belonging to different clans. Should there be marital discord, the wife's consanguineal relatives try to help arrange a reconciliation. A divorced woman returns to her group until she remarries. The children ordinarily remain with their father's group.

Married couples sometimes choose to live with the wife's patrikin. This is most likely to happen when the wife's relatives are better able to help the new couple. The husband's descendants will try to maintain understandings of mutual obligation with both the affiliated lineage and their own patrikin. The option of emphasizing relations of descent or marriage at different times, depending on circumstances, further enhances the security of individuals and small family units.

RELIGION

In Laos, most Hmong believed that many types of spirits occurred in nature. Some of the spirits resided in such objects as trees, springs, and rock formations. A number of dangerous demons roamed the forest. Certain spirits had the power to possess people or capture souls and cause a variety of illnesses. The souls of ancestors were also powerful and had to be properly honored. To these animistic beliefs were added the philosophies and practices of Taoism, Confucianism, Buddhism, and, beginning in the early 1950s, Christianity. A relatively small number of the Laotian Hmong were converted to Catholicism and Protestant fundamentalism, but about half the refugees claim a form of Christianity as their religion. Hmong Christian congregations elect their own lay leaders and tend to separate themselves from non-Hmong for worship and socializing. Religiously trained Hmong have little difficulty gaining a following from among their own people.

The Hmong strongly desire religious consensus with the kinship group. The conversion of key leaders quickly spreads to other members. Lineage organizations have sometimes directly addressed the problem of achieving religious unity and have chosen either to accept a particular form of Christianity or return to an earlier set of beliefs. In part, the continued attraction of the pre-Christian religion can be attributed to the fact that sacred rituals help to define the boundaries of the kinship group. Shared funerary practices and rites of ancestor worship can be used to establish lineage ties even when genealogical connections are unclear. Moreover, many Hmong continue to use native spirit curers, a practice that strict Hmong Christians condemn. Fortunately, religious differences have not prevented interlineage cooperation. Tensions that occasionally exist between animist and Christian groups related by marriage are usually managed without overt conflict.

POLITICS

A Hmong-sponsored conference on resettlement in the United States was held in St. Paul, Minnesota, on June 17-20, 1981. Hmong representatives came from communities located throughout the country. One of the best-attended sessions focused on the ''effective development of leadership.'' The participants were concerned that the leadership structure responsible for holding the Hmong together was being ignored by American authorities, and that this would lead to disunity and weakness. The speakers recalled that the Hmong had not advanced materially until their leaders attained positions in the government above the village level. As district officials, judges, military officers, legislative representatives, and department ministers, these leaders were able to mobilize support for national aims and bring back to the Hmong some of the economic and educational advantages enjoyed by dominant Lao.

Early in the resettlement process, the Hmong refugees began exerting pressure on the various service agencies to hire certain bilinguals. Some service directors may have seen this as an attempt on the part of formerly powerful people or emerging leaders to selfishly promote themselves and their relatives, but many agencies understood the advantages of recruiting respected members of the client community to help solve difficult problems. The Hmong also formed a national organization with regional branches that could provide services directly to refugees. The competition for government funding created some tensions between the Hmong and established agencies.

So long as almost all the kinship groups were struggling to adjust to life in a new land, the appeal of a national mutual assistance association was strong. Divisions based on kinship, regional loyalty, dialect, and political alliance could be bridged by a leadership coalition headed by General Vang Pao. As the more advantaged kinship groups improved their situation, they became less interested in national issues and turned their attention to local and lineage-level concerns. Rather than being merely symptomatic of a kind of ethnic community breakup experienced by other immigrant populations, these changes are indicative of a recurring cycle of alliance building in the face of a common threat, followed by segmentation when the need for general cooperation subsides. A significant number of Hmong families will require a great deal of help for some time to come, and Hmong leaders are working to maintain the vitality of mutual assistance associations in as many communities as possible. The national Hmong leaders would like to see all segments of the Hmong refugee population prosper. They worry that eventual socioeconomic stratification will destroy a historically important asset of the Hmong—the ability to unify in times of crisis.

AN ENDURING PEOPLE

The successive traumas of war, persecution, internment, and resettlement have affected each Hmong age-group somewhat differently. The elderly frequently express the hope that they can someday return to a more congenial cultural setting. They worry in particular that some of the Americanized, younger Hmong will avoid the responsibility of personally caring for aging parents and honoring them with the proper funeral rites. The unemployed middle-aged are struggling with the loss of status that comes with economic dependence. Some in this group also think about the possibility of going back to Laos if the political situation changes. The majority of Hmong who are committed to a new life in the United States closely follow developments in Southeast Asia and financially support the international political activities of Hmong leaders who are trying to help the refugees in Thailand. Except for the relatively few who received advanced academic or technical training in Laos, the young adults have difficulty finding permanent jobs that pay enough to support a large family. Parents are concerned about the children who suffered physical privation during the exodus and then languished for years in refugee camps. All grieve the death of close relatives.[5]

Despite these demoralizing problems, the Hmong are adjusting to the values of this society while retaining their separate identity. Most parents have accepted the idea that their children, both boys and girls, should stay in school and try to complete some kind of postsecondary training that will allow them to undertake satisfying careers. High school students are being strongly urged to abandon the former custom of teenage marriage and wait until they have greater financial security before starting a family. Indeed, the concept of family planning is gaining in popularity with the Hmong. Women are taking jobs in industry and forming their own support groups. Although these and many other changes are occurring, kinship continues to be a cohesive force. The extended patrilineal group shows no sign of weakening. Ethnic group endogamy is still preferred, and with few exceptions, the first language of the children continues to be Hmong.

In his study of the Yaqui people, a Mexican Indian tribe that endured difficulties similar to those survived by the Hmong, Edward Spicer (1980:360) observed the following:

In their sense of identity every people molds a vessel into which they pour from generation to generation the meanings of their historical experiences. Each such creation is for every enduring people a summation of the meaning and purpose of life. The spirit of a people cannot be known through a mere recitation of their customs; in such a listing the vital dimension is not present. This dimension is the people's feeling about the way they have performed and the values they have stood for in the course of their life history as a people. Such associations with real events in which people have suffered and triumphed are poured into the mold of identity and some come to have significance.

The Hmong are quite conscious of the need to transmit a sense of collective experience from generation to generation. They are not entirely confident that

124

Timothy Dunnigan and Douglas P. Olney

they can give the newest generation growing up in America an adequate appreciation of what it has meant historically to be Hmong. A positive sign of cultural vitality, however, is the interest shown by young Hmong adults in preserving the histories of their lineages, going all the way back to their China origins. We cannot predict the future shape of Hmong identity. As Spicer (1971:798) points out, "the continuity of a people is a phenomenon distinct from the persistence of a particular set of cultural traits." The Hmong will retain their ethnic distinctiveness by both maintaining and gradually reformulating their unique system of identity symbols expressing the main theme of kinship.

NOTES

1. See Geddes (1976) for a general discussion of Hmong ecology in Thailand.
2. See Westermeyer (1982) for a discussion of opium use in Laos.
3. Meier (1983) provides a good illustration of community reaction to stories about Hmong opium use in the United States.
4. See Dunnigan (1982) for a more complete description of Hmong kinship in an urban community.
5. Studies of the psychological adjustment of Hmong refugees in a U.S. urban community are reported in Westermeyer, Vang, and Lyfong (1983); Westermeyer, Vang, and Neider (1983a, 1983b, 1983c); and Williams and Westermeyer (1983). Westermeyer, Vang, and Neider (1984) report a high rate of depression among Hmong refugees, with 40 percent achieving "depressive" scores on the Zung Depression Scale. They found some improvement over time, but lack of employment and English proficiency is associated with the high rates of depression.

REFERENCES

Adams, Nina S., and Alfred W. McCoy
1970   *Laos: War and Revolution*. New York: Harper & Row.
Barney, Linwood
1967   The Meo of Xieng Khouang Province, Laos. In *Southeast Asian Tribes, Minorities, and Nations*. Edited by Peter Kunstadter. Princeton: Princeton University Press. Pages 271–294.
CCSDPT (Committee for the Coordination of Services to Displaced Persons in Thailand)
1982   *CCSDPT Handbook: Refugee Services in Thailand*. Bangkok: Du Maurier Associates for the Committee for the Coordination of Services to Displaced Persons in Thailand.
DeVecchi, Robert
1982   Politics and Policies of "First Asylum" in Thailand. *World Refugee Survey, 1982*. Edited by Rosemary Tripp. New York: American Council for Nationalities Service. Pages 20–24.
Dreyer, June
1976   *China's Forty Millions: Minority Nationalities and National Integration in the People's Republic of China*. Cambridge, Massachusetts: Harvard University Press.

Dunnigan, Timothy
1982   Segmentary Kinship in an Urban Society: The Hmong of St. Paul–Minneapolis. *Anthropological Quarterly* 55(3):126–136.
Evans, Grant
1983   *The Yellow Rainmakers: Are the Soviets Using Chemical Weapons in Southeast Asia?* London: Verso Editions and NLB.
Geddes, William R.
1976   *Migrants of the Mountains*. Oxford, England: Clarendon Press.
Haig, Alexander M., Jr.
1982   *Chemical Warfare in Southeast Asian and Afghanistan*. Special Report No. 98. Washington, D.C.: U.S. Department of State.
Halpern, Joel
1964   *Economy and Society of Laos: A Brief Survey*. New Haven, Connecticut: Yale University Southeast Asia Studies Monograph Series No. 5.
Hickey, Gerald C.
1955   The Ethnic Minorities of Laos. In *Area Handbook on Laos*. Edited by Gerald C. Hickey. Chicago: University of Chicago Press.
Humphreys, G. R., and J. Dow
1982   *Report of the Medical Team's Epidemiological Investigation of Alleged CW/ BW Incidents in Laos and Cambodia*. Ottawa, Canada.
Larteguy, Jean
1979   *La fabuleuse aventure du peuple de l'opium*. Paris: Presses de la Cite.
LeBar, Frank M., and Adrienne Suddard
1960   *Laos: Its People, Its Society, Its Culture*. New Haven, Connecticut: Human Relations Area Files Press.
LeBar, Frank, and others
1964   *Ethnic Groups of Mainland Southeast Asia*. New Haven, Connecticut: Human Relations Area Files Press.
Lee, Gary Yia
1982   National Minority Policies and the Hmong. In *Contemporary Laos*. Edited by Martin Stuart-Fox. New York: St. Martin's Press. Pages 199–219.
Meier, Peg
1983   Hmong, Opium: A Culture Clash. *Minneapolis Star and Tribune*. (October 1.)
NWREL (Northwest Regional Educational Laboratory)
1984   The Hmong Resettlement Study. Unpublished.
Olney, Douglas P.
1983   Hmong Community Survey, Minneapolis–St. Paul. Unpublished.
ORR (Office of Refugee Resettlement)
1983   Recommendations of the Hmong/Highland Lao Workgroup.
Refugee Reports
1982   Special Issue of December 17, 1982. New York, N.Y.: American Council for Nationalities Service.
Savina, F. M.
1924   *Histoire des Miao*. Hong Kong: Imprimerie de la Societe des Missions-Etrangeres.
Schiefer, H. B.
1982   *Study of the Possible Use of Chemical Warfare Agents in Southeast Asia*. A Report to the Department of External Affairs. Ottawa, Canada.

Schultz, George P.
1982   *Chemical Warfare in Southeast Asia and Afghanistan: An Update.* Special
        Report No. 104. Washington, D.C.: U.S. Department of State, Bureau of Public
        Affairs.
Smalley, William A.
n.d.   From Laos to the United States. In *Tradition and Adaptation: The Hmong in
        America.* Edited by T. Dunnigan, B. Downing, and W. Smalley. In preparation.
Spicer, Edward
1971   Persistent Cultural Systems: A Comparative Study of Identity Systems That
        Can Adapt to Contrasting Environments. *Science* 174:795–800.
1980   *The Yaqui: A Cultural History.* Tucson: University of Arizona Press.
UNHCR (U.N. High Commission for Refugees)
1983   Monthly Statistics. Bangkok, Thailand.
Weins, Harold J.
1967   *Han Chinese Expansion in South China.* Hamden, Connecticut: Shoe String
        Press.
Westermeyer, Joseph
1982   *Poppies, Pipes and People: Opium and Its Use in Laos.* Berkeley: University
        of California Press.
Westermeyer, Joseph, Tou Fu Vang, and Gaohli Lyfong
1983   Hmong Refugees in Minnesota: Characteristics and Self Perceptions. *Minnesota
        Medicine* 66:431–439.
Westermeyer, Joseph, Tou Fu Vang, and John Neider
1983a   A Comparison of Refugees Using and Not Using a Psychiatric Service: An
        Analysis of DSM-111 Criteria and Self Rating Scales in Cross Cultural Context.
        Journal of Operational Psychiatry 14(1):36–40.
1983b   Refugees Who Do and Do Not Seek Psychiatric Care: An Analysis of Premi-
        gratory and Postmigratory Characteristics. *Journal of Nervous and Mental Dis-
        ease* 171(2):86–91.
1983c   Migration and Mental Health Among Hmong Refugees: Association of Pre-
        and Post-migration Factors with Self Rating Scales. *Journal of Nervous and
        Mental Disease* 171(2):92–96.
1984   Acculturation and Mental Health: A Study of Hmong Refugees at 1.5 and 3.5
        Years Postmigration. *Social Science Medicine* 18(1):87–93.
Williams, Caroline, and Joseph Westermeyer
1983   Psychiatric Problems Among Adolescent Southeast Asian Refugees: A De-
        scriptive Study. *Journal of Nervous and Mental Disease* 171(2):79–83.

Khmer

The name Khmer designates the ethnically dominant inhabitants (and their language) of ancient and modern Cambodia, also known since 1975 as Kampuchea.[1] The Khmer were dominant in two senses: Ruling power was in their hands, and they constituted the numerical majority of the country's population, which included other ethnic groups, such as Chinese, Vietnamese, Chams, and hill tribes. Thus, although "Cambodian" or "Kampuchean" refers to any national from that country, one should recognize that ethnic/cultural differences existed within the population. This chapter focuses specifically on the Khmer, although passing reference is made to other groups.

The Khmer possess a long and illustrious history. Their ancestors at one time forged a vast empire that spread over much of mainland Southeast Asia and built the renowned edifices of Angkor Wat. More recently, however, Cambodia has suffered exceptionally troubled and traumatic times that led large numbers of its people to flee to other countries. This exodus has created, for the first time, a sizable population of Khmer in the United States.

Before the Indochinese conflict, most Americans knew next to nothing about Cambodia, except perhaps that it was the site of Angkor. Even now—despite the fact that the war in Indochina, the Pol Pot regime, and the famine of 1978-79 brought Cambodia onto television screens and the front pages of newspapers—there is still little knowledge of who the Khmer are and what their distinctive historical and cultural background is. The following discussion attempts to provide some answers to these questions by offering, in the first two sections, an overview of Cambodia's past and present, in particular the political changes of the 1970s and early 1980s that precipitated several waves of refugees out of Cambodia and, ultimately, into the United States. The third section and conclusion consider aspects of Khmer adjustment to American society and Khmer prospects for the future.

HISTORICAL AND SOCIAL BACKGROUND

Ancient and Pre-Modern History

The earliest history of the ancestral Khmer is not clear, but it is thought that they may have moved into the general region of what is now Cambodia during protohistoric times, coming possibly from somewhere to the north or west. In the early centuries of the Christian era, a number of polities, often referred to as kingdoms, emerged on the Southeast mainland: Funan, Champa, Mon, and Chenla, the latter often identified with the Khmer. Chenla gained dominance over Funan in the mid-sixth century, and during the ninth century the Khmer kingdom became known as Kambujadesa. During this early period, cultural influences from the neighboring civilizations of India and China, particularly the former, merged with indigenous Khmer culture to produce an increasingly complex and powerful polity. The Khmer reached a height of particular brilliance during the so-called Angkor or Kambuja period (A.D. 802-1431). During this time, the Khmer had an elaborate sociopolitical organization with divine kingship, wielded extensive political power, and produced magnificent art and architecture.

After this florescence, however, Cambodia entered a period of vacillating and weakening power during the sixteenth to eighteenth centuries. Although the Khmer polity continued to exist, its hegemony shrank to a region that approximates present-day Cambodia, and it was subject to repeated encroachments from the neighboring Thai on the west and the Vietnamese to the east. Caught between these pincers, the embattled Khmer turned for aid to France, which was establishing a colonial outpost in Southeast Asia.

In 1863, Cambodia became a French "protectorate"; and in 1887, Cambodia, Laos, and Vietnam were combined to form the Union of French Indochina. French colonial rule brought various changes, notably to aspects of the national economy and political administration. A number of basic features of Khmer culture (such as Buddhism and peasant agriculture) continued, although other aspects of life at both the local and national levels were inevitably altered by the colonial situation.

Prerevolutionary Modern Cambodia

French control was interrupted by World War II and occupation of Cambodia by Japanese forces. After the war, increasing feelings of nationalism led to efforts to acquire independence from France. This was achieved in 1954, when the kingdom of Cambodia (Royaume du Cambodge) was established as an autonomous country. The new government was headed by Norodom Sihanouk, who continued to dominate national politics for some sixteen years until increasing difficulties led to a coup in 1970, in which Lon Nol became head of state.

Lon Nol's newly renamed Republic of Kampuchea was sorely troubled and short-lived, to be overthrown in its turn by revolutionary forces in 1975.

In the decade or so after independence, Cambodia was relatively stable and peaceful. It was a fundamentally agrarian society with limited industrialization, although it was involved in a national and international capitalistic market system. There was limited urbanization as well; perhaps only Phnom Penh would fit our image of a true city, whereas provincial capitals were more in the nature of towns. The majority of the population lived in rural villages as peasant cultivators of rice, fruits, and vegetables; as fishermen along rivers and Lake Tonle Sap; and as craftsmen producing cloth, pottery, and metal objects.[2] Most peasants were small-scale cultivators, owning limited amounts of farmland (the national average was about four acres per household) on which crops were grown for family subsistence and, in some cases, for sale on the market.

The Khmer constituted some 85 percent to 90 percent of the population in the 1950s and 1960s, composing most of the top and bottom levels of society as government and military officials, aristocrats, Buddhist monks, and other elite, as well as peasants, artisans, and urban laborers. A middle stratum of merchants, white-collar workers, and professionals was relatively small and composed mainly (if not exclusively) of Chinese and Vietnamese, who together made up about 10 percent of the population (about 5 percent each).[3] Although there tended to be general enmity toward the Vietnamese as historic ''enemies'' of Cambodia, the Chinese were regarded more tolerantly. Through time, there was a fair amount of Khmer intermarriage with Chinese (especially at the upper levels of society); the Sino-Khmer descendants of such marriages did not constitute a distinct group but were generally absorbed into either the Khmer or Chinese ethnic groups.

Until the 1970 coup, Cambodia was a constitutional monarchy with a figure-head king and real political authority vested in a prime minister, cabinet, and legislative assembly. After Lon Nol deposed Sihanouk, the government became a republic, but apart from the demise of the monarchy, there were no major changes in governmental structure. However, from the late 1960s into the early 1970s, the fabric of Cambodian life began to be torn apart by a number of serious political and economic problems: widespread corruption, alienation between the government and people, a weakening economy, the increasing organization and militancy of Communist revolutionaries (often referred to as the Khmer Rouge), and repercussions from the heated conflict in neighboring Vietnam. Although the Communist left had been relatively insignificant in national politics and few in numbers at the time of the 1970 coup, the Khmer Rouge grew with remarkable rapidity during the next few years and expanded its control over much of Cambodia. Much of the countryside suffered terrible disruption and destruction in the fighting between Lon Nol government troops and the Communist insurgents, as well as from the Nixon–Kissinger policy of ''strategic bombing'' that was presumably meant to destroy Communist enclaves in Cambodia but which also dropped a staggering amount of bombs (more tonnage than was used on Japan during all of World War II) on ordinary people as well (Shawcross 1979). Phnom Penh became swollen with refugees fleeing the turmoil in the countryside, while those remaining in their villages gradually came, voluntarily or involuntarily, under Communist control even before 1975.[4]

Democratic Kampuchea, 1975-78

In April 1975, the Khmer Rouge marched into Phnom Penh and instituted a new polity, named Democratic Kampuchea (DK), that was to become one of the most startling and traumatic periods in Khmer history. Pol Pot and other DK leaders (who had been exposed to Marxism during student days in Paris) sought to construct a revolutionary new society that would be freed from class exploitation of the poor by the rich and from domination by "colonialist–imperialist" foreign powers. In the early days of the Communist movement, such idealistic goals attracted people from various walks of life, from intellectuals to peasants. But ironically and tragically, as time went on, DK became a highly oppressive state as it sought to enforce radically new forms of organization, ideology, and behavior. It is important to recognize that living conditions varied through time and in different regions of Kampuchea. At the outset of DK, some areas were controlled by factions of the Kampuchean Communist Party that were more moderate than Pol Pot, and these regions experienced tolerable living conditions in terms of work loads, availability of food, and so on. However, after 1977-78, when Pol Pot gained ascendancy over the other factions, harsher circumstances and measures came to prevail virtually everywhere. Among the most dramatic transformations of life were the following:

(1) Collectivization of the economy. DK's aim to reconstruct the war-torn economy, achieve relative economic self-sufficiency, and maximize agricultural production—as well as to create an egalitarian society—led to turning virtually the entire population into peasants and workers. The inhabitants of Phnom Penh and other urban centers were evacuated into the countryside, and social classes were abolished.[5] People were organized into cooperatives with communal ownership of property (land, draft animals, tools, etc.) and communal distribution of goods and produce (although after 1977-78, the state appropriated increasing amounts of food and left the populace with meager rations). The work team (*krom*), composed of ten to fifteen "families," became the basic building block for organizing larger labor units of varying size. The latter were mobilized for agricultural work and construction projects, especially the building (mainly by hand) of large-scale irrigation projects that were meant to improve food production.

(2) Dissolution of the family. In traditional Khmer culture, the family—whether nuclear or extended—was a basic and critical socioeconomic unit. Members of a household were held together by deep emotional bonds, cooperative efforts in work, sharing of resources, and mutual aid; and similar sentiments and obligations extended outward to relatives on both sides of the family. All

this was subverted in DK as the work team superceded the family in economic activities and as various measures physically separated family members and undermined customary domestic life. Youngsters past the age of six or seven were taken from their parents to live and work in separate children's labor teams; adolescents (and sometimes married men) were put into mobile work groups and sent away to various parts of the country; family meals were replaced by communal dining halls; and in some regions, there were forced marriages arranged by local officials. Young people were a particular target for political indoctrination into revolutionary ideology and were drawn into youth associations, the army, and mobile work teams. Parents were seen rarely, if at all, and were replaced as authority figures by political officials. The "family" as a residential unit came to consist of only a couple and very young children; even then, husbands and wives spent most of their time laboring in separate men's and women's work teams.

(3) Suppression of religion. Theravada Buddhism was the state religion of prerevolutionary Cambodia and a fundamental part of Khmer culture. The Buddhist temple had served as a sacred, moral, social, and educational center; monks were given the highest respect as exemplars of Buddhist doctrine; many Khmer men became monks for a temporary period some time during their lives (since monkhood did not entail a lifelong commitment); and Buddhist norms of conduct were important guides for daily behavior (Ebihara 1966). However, DK defined Buddhism as exploitative and feudalistic because temples and monks were supported by donations from the laity. Therefore, it was to be eliminated. Temples were destroyed or desecrated; some monks were killed outright, and others were forced to give up their robes or were put into separate work teams.

Buddhist doctrine was replaced by secular political ideology that propounded new "revolutionary" values and codes of conduct, disseminated through political meetings and associations. DK rules of behavior encompassed details of daily life, such as prescribing simple black clothing, short haircuts for women, and humble demeanor. Obedience and discipline were expected in all areas of behavior, and infractions of rules were met with various punishments, such as criticism sessions, hard labor, beatings, imprisonment, and even execution. Large-scale executions also occurred as a result of the factional disputes within the Kampuchean Communist Party; as the Pol Pot group rose to power, there were widespread purges of both high officials and ordinary people defined as being on the wrong side. These account for part of the enormous death toll that occurred in DK, with various estimates ranging from one to three million deaths out of an original population of some seven million in 1975 (cf. Hawk 1982). The exact number of deaths will never be known. Probably the lower figure is more likely, but it is nonetheless substantial and includes high mortality owing to malnutrition, debilitation, illness, and battle wounds and deaths of soldiers. Such deaths also affected the living in terms of psychological trauma and the loss of family, relatives, and friends.

People's Republic of Kampuchea (1979-Present)

The relationship between the Kampuchean and Vietnamese Communists was, through time, vacillating and ambivalent. At various points the Vietnamese had been sources of aid and support, but the highly chauvinistic Pol Pot group became hostile toward their neighbor. Battles broke out along the border region between the two countries; fighting escalated and eventuated in the Vietnamese moving into Kampuchea in late 1978 and capturing Phnom Penh in January 1979. Pol Pot's forces retreated to the mountains bordering Thailand, leaving most of the country under Vietnamese occupation and a new regime named the People's Republic of Kampuchea (PRK). The new administration is composed of Khmer officials, but there is some debate among observers as to whether (or to what degree) PRK is essentially under the control of Vietnam, or if Vietnamese officials and troops are present only in an advisory and peace-keeping capacity.

The overthrow of Pol Pot created, once again, a period of considerable upheaval and plight for the Kampuchean people. The fighting between DK and Vietnamese forces disrupted or destroyed most of the rice harvest that would normally have been gathered at the end of 1978, thus creating the famine conditions of 1978-79 that drew international attention and relief efforts. Once DK controls were lifted and cooperatives dissolved, there was also a great deal of population movement, as people went in search of food, looked for relatives, returned to their home communities, or fled Kampuchea altogether for refuge in other countries.

As conditions stabilized in the early 1980s, PRK became an interesting combination of both "traditional" and socialist features. Phnom Penh was repopulated; villages were reconstituted or rebuilt; family and kin networks were reestablished as best possible; and Buddhism has been revived. In its effort to reconstruct the economy, the PRK government has instituted a semisocialist system in which there is both some collectivization and some private enterprise. Markets are flourishing once again, with brisk trade in foods and consumer goods. There is some controversy, however, as to the general quality of life in PRK. Some observers believe that the Vietnamese-sponsored PRK administration has been benign and that, despite some problems, living conditions have been greatly ameliorated. Others, however, are less sanguine about the Vietnamese presence and see various difficulties (such as the reemergence of socioeconomic strata) within the society.

At this point, Kampuchea's political future is uncertain. Resistance to the Vietnamese occupation is currently being mounted by a coalition combining remnants of DK forces under Pol Pot, Sihanouk loyalists, and followers of Son Sann, a former official in prerevolutionary Cambodia. These three elements are quite diverse in terms of their political ideologies and supporters and are united only by their mutual desire to oust the Vietnamese and hold "free elections" for a coalition government. Although there continues to be periodic fighting between the Vietnamese and the resistance forces that are based primarily along the Thai border, at present the latter are so limited in strength and numbers that there is little likelihood of their success—or that the Vietnamese would voluntarily leave Kampuchea. The feelings of the ordinary Kampucheans are probably mixed: Although most people were initially grateful for deliverance from the Pol Pot regime, and many see the continued Vietnamese presence as necessary to prevent the return of DK forces, there is also some ambivalence toward the Vietnamese and concern for reestablishing an independent Kampuchean state. Given the unpredictability of events in Southeast Asia and international power politics, it is impossible to say what further developments may occur in Kampuchea.[6]

EXODUS AND TRANSIT

These political upheavals of the 1970s generated several major waves of Cambodian refugees who fled the country during different periods of turmoil (Stein 1982; Hamilton 1982). Subsequently, there were also distinct flows of Khmer leaving refugee centers for resettlement in the United States. It is useful to distinguish these waves because they differed with regard to the numbers of people involved, their socioeconomic backgrounds, and their experiences in both Cambodia and the refugee centers.

Exodus from Cambodia/Kampuchea

The first large exodus of refugees took place in 1975, when the Democratic Kampuchean revolutionaries overthrew the Lon Nol government. Some 35,000 to 40,000 persons fled to Thailand, and another 150,000 or so went in the opposite direction, to Vietnam. This first wave included Lon Nol government officials, professionals, and others in higher socioeconomic strata who obviously would have had antipathies toward (and fears of retribution from) a Communist state. There were also, however, townspeople and rural peasants from regions near the western border who fled into Thailand. (In addition to Khmer, many Cambodian Chinese were included in this group, going either to Thailand or Vietnam [Willmott 1980.]) In the next three years, almost all the refugees in Thailand were eventually resettled elsewhere, going primarily to France, the United States, Australia, and Canada.[7] During the same period, there was only a light flow of new refugees into Thailand because the tight controls of the Pol Pot regime made escape difficult.

The second influx into Thailand occurred during the unsettled conditions generated during and after the Vietnamese invasion of Kampuchea in December 1978. With the breakdown and withdrawal of DK control, almost 100,000 persons fled to the Thai border region, propelled by desire to escape the rigors of the previous few years, starvation conditions owing to disruption of the harvest, and fears of Vietnamese rule. These refugees had varied socioeconomic backgrounds: Khmer Rouge cadre and army, former urban professional and business people who had managed to survive DK hostility toward those from higher social strata, and rural peasants.

The Thai government was disturbed by this enormous influx. It raised administrative and economic problems of coping with a mass of homeless and hungry refugees suddenly camped on Thailand's doorstep, and there were also political anxieties that a depopulated Kampuchea would enable Vietnamese troops to move easily westward and threaten both the remnant DK forces and Thailand itself. Such concerns led the Thai, at one point, to force more than 40,000 refugees (said to be "illegal immigrants") quite literally over a precipice, back into Kampuchea. Many died in the mine fields, and of illness and starvation, and the incident precipitated an international outcry. The U.N. High Commissioner for Refugees (UNHCR) prevailed on Thailand to offer asylum to the Kampucheans and set up holding centers from which the refugees could be resettled or voluntarily repatriated.

Another major flow came later, from the summer and fall of 1979 into early 1980, owing to severe famine conditions and a Vietnamese offensive against insurgents in western Kampuchea. Some 500,000 entered either holding centers (e.g., Khao I Dang and Sakaeo, set up in the fall of 1979, and others, such as Kamput and Mai Rut, established in the spring of 1980) or settled in "village-camps" that sprang up in the "political no-man's land" along the border (Hamilton 1982:5). Both types of settlements were important centers for receiving food and other supplies from international relief efforts. The composition of this third wave of refugees was similar to that of the preceding exodus.

By June 1980, there were more than 150,000 Kampuchean refugees in UNHCR holding centers in Thailand, and several hundred thousand more were to be found in the village-camps along the border (Hamilton 1982:6). Subsequently, the flow of refugees diminished as conditions inside Kampuchea improved and as the major centers of Khao I Dang, Kamput, and Sakaeo were technically closed to further influx. In addition to shelter and food, the holding centers also eventually established (with the aid of various governmental and private agencies) educational, medical, and processing services. Even though refugees were provided with basic necessities for survival, their lives were not easy as they coped with the aftermaths of their ordeals and existed in a limbo of uncertainty about their futures. Some border settlements were (and still are) subject to periodic battles, displacement, casualties, and deaths, when Vietnamese troops launch offensives against the various resistance forces in the region.

Movement to the United States

Just as there were several major flows of refugees into Thailand, so were there three main waves of Khmer *leaving* the Thai centers for resettlement in the United States. The latter, however, do not neatly coincide with the former.

From 1975 to 1978, some 6,299 Khmer came to the United States. Because those people with "connections to the U.S. or to the war effort in Cambodia" were more apt to be selected for settlement, this first group of Khmer refugees "tended to be more educated and more urban than was typical of subsequent groups" (Stein 1982:5). (Another 12,500 or so of the refugees who had fled at the time of the DK takeover went to other countries, especially France, between 1975 and 1979 [Stein 1982:5].)

In 1979, the general plight of Indochinese refugees drew worldwide attention and led the United States to increase its admissions quota for all Indochinese to 168,000 per year and to ease its selection criteria to include people without connections to the United States. Some 10,000 Khmer—primarily rural people who had been left in the Thai centers since 1975—entered the United States under the new policy (Stein ibid.). Although these people had not been subject to the Pol Pot regime, they had nonetheless endured several years of existence in refugee centers in which there was little preparation for resettlement in an alien society. Given their rural backgrounds as peasants, fishermen, and artisans, these refugees (in contrast to the preceding group) would have experienced considerable culture shock on arrival here.

The third and most massive influx of some 60,000 Khmer entered the United States between January 1, 1980, and August 31, 1982. This wave (representing about three-fifths of the total number of Khmer refugees in the country) consisted of those people who fled Kampuchea during the turmoil of the Vietnamese invasion and famine conditions, after having survived the Pol Pot period. These people, therefore, have been subject to exceptionally difficult experiences. However, because of adjustment problems suffered by earlier Indochinese refugees, greater efforts were made to prepare this third group for resettlement. Transit to the United States involved an intermediate step: Most people went from the Thai centers to Indochinese Refugee Processing Centers at Bataan or Galang in the Pacific for fourteen weeks of instruction in English as a second language (a minimum of 216 hours) and cultural orientation (100 hours) before arrival in the United States (Stein 1982:7; HHS 1983:29). Furthermore, once in the United States, a number of the refugees were settled in "clusters" of Khmer as a further attempt to ease transition to a new society.

By March 1984, some 98,000 Cambodians had journeyed to the United States, representing one-seventh of the total Southeast Asian refugee population. The heaviest concentrations of Khmer are in California (especially the Long Beach area of southern California, which has the largest number of Khmer in the United States), Washington state, Oregon, Texas, and the Washington, D.C., area, although there are also Khmer in other parts of the country (Stein 1982:20). In an effort to minimize further influx into cities already heavily impacted by refugees, the Office of Refugee Resettlement devised the "Khmer Cluster Resettlement Project," which placed groups of Khmer in twelve selected locations: Atlanta, Boston, Chicago, Cincinnati, Columbus, Dallas, Houston, Jacksonville, New York City, Phoenix, Richmond, and Rochester (see Granville [1982] for an overview and assessment of this project).

It may be useful to note here some demographic features of the Khmer refugees. The Indochinese refugees are, in general, a young population with a median age of twenty on arrival, about 30 percent school-age children, and few elderly (HHS 1983:3). Although figures specifically on the Khmer are not available, they probably approximate this profile, and the relative youthfulness of the population may have implications for future adjustment. However, the Khmer are also distinctive compared with other Indochinese refugees in certain respects. First, they have a relatively high proportion of "free cases" without close relatives, or any kin whatsoever, in the United States. This reflects the fact that few Khmer were here before the turmoils of the 1970s in Cambodia. Second, there are a number of "unaccompanied minors" and female-headed households.[8] The orphans and widows, as well as some of the free cases, are clearly a product of the high mortality in Cambodia during a decade of adversity that included warfare preceding the Communist revolution, the conditions of the Pol Pot years, famine, and the Vietnamese invasion. It has been suggested that male mortality was especially high not only because men were soldiers, but also because in DK, men were more often the targets of execution and less able to withstand starvation and other severe conditions than were women (Boua 1982).

ADJUSTMENT

Khmer refugees have faced a number of problems, some of which are common to immigrants generally and others emerging out of the particular cultural and historical circumstances of Cambodia. It is further important to recognize, as noted earlier, that Khmer refugees do not constitute a homogeneous group, but include people with diverse backgrounds and experiences. Thus the particular kinds and severity of difficulties encountered by individual refugees would vary according to such factors as previous socioeconomic level, amount of education, date of leaving Cambodia, age, sex, and other attributes, such as being widowed or orphaned.

Economic Adjustment

"Adaptation" to a new society has many facets, but the U.S. government conceives of it primarily in terms of attaining economic self-sufficiency (HHS 1983:22; Haines 1982:10). This involves several interrelated factors that are frequently noted in the literature as constituting major problems and toward which concerted efforts have been directed: English competency, occupational training, and employment.

Knowledge of English is obviously critical to sociocultural adjustment in general and employment in particular. One source cites competence in English as the "major characteristic" influencing "successful involvement in the labor force," noting that there is a higher level of employment among those who are fluent in English (HHS 1983:24; see also Haines 1982, Ima and others 1983). Thus English-as-a-second-language (ESL) classes have been a major concern of refugee assistance programs. According to government-funded surveys, the general level of English fluency among Khmer refugees is low (cited in Stein 1982). But differences within the population should be kept in mind: Khmer from upper or middle social strata generally had varying degrees of familiarity with French or English, whereas peasants had little or no knowledge of western languages and, in the case of older women, often had limited literacy in Khmer itself. Furthermore, young people who grew up in DK, where schooling was minimal or nonexistent, also might be illiterate in Khmer (although some education was available in Thai refugee centers).

However, even given literacy in Khmer, there are a number of differences between Khmer and English, such that there is no easy transfer from one language to the other. For example, the Khmer language is written in a script derived from India that is radically different from the English alphabet. Khmer does not have verb tenses; a sense of time is conveyed by phrases (such as "last year" or "tomorrow"), indicating past or future action. It also has a somewhat different system of phonemes, or meaningful sounds: For example, *v* and *w* are distinguished as different sounds in English but not in Khmer. Hence, it is not easy for an English-speaker to learn Khmer or for Khmer refugees to learn English.

Prior education and occupational experience play a role in job training and placement, although the relationship among these factors is complex. Urban middle- or upper-strata Khmer usually had secondary school (*lycée*) and often college or postgraduate education, and in Cambodia, they had government, professional, and white-collar occupations. However, many refugees—especially those who were peasants, workers, or raised in DK—may have limited education and job skills suited to this society. Because the latter constituted a large proportion of recent Khmer refugees, it is not surprising that one survey indicated almost three-quarters of Khmer had junior high school or less education, and of this number, 37 percent had no schooling whatsoever (Stein 1982:11).[9]

Limited education combines with other circumstances to limit access to jobs (HHS 1983; Stein 1982; Granville 1982; Ima and others 1983). First, the largest number of Khmer arrived during an economic recession and faced competition from other ethnic groups for existing work in a tight job market. In some instances, they have also encountered employer prejudice against hiring people with "dark skins." Second, although most refugees were productive workers in their homeland, their skills may not be transferable to the United States. This is particularly true for peasants and unskilled laborers (and during DK, most of the population was engaged in farming and construction), who would have little or no experience of urban industrial occupations, such as factory jobs. Former artisans may find no demand for expertise in such crafts as weaving and stone carving (see, e.g., one case in Ima and others [1983]). Even those people who held professional, governmental, or business positions in Cambodia often have difficulty moving into comparable occupations in the United States, such that a former high-ranking official may end up working as a busboy in a restaurant. Third, the Khmer often lack capital, expertise, and contacts to establish enterprises in the United States, even though some of them were self-employed, small-scale entrepreneurs in their homeland (see cases in Ima and others [1983]). Many come from poor backgrounds or, if once prosperous, lost their wealth during the DK period. Moreover, for the early wave of refugees, there were few existing Khmer communitites in the United States to provide business connections, and there are no established economic niches for Khmer to move into, as has been the case with some immigrant groups.[10]

Job training and placement have been a priority of refugee aid programs. But the rate of unemployment is still relatively high, owing to factors just noted as well as to other circumstances. For instance, the Khmer have been here a relatively short time; many refugees did not seek employment during the months of cash assistance after arrival because of need for preliminary ESL instruction and job training; some people, such as widows with families or those with health problems, cannot work; young people may seek above all to acquire an education; and so on (HHS 1983; Ima and others 1983; Stein 1982). Nonetheless, another important statistic to note is that rate of employment rises with length of residence in the United States (see Chaper 2).

Sociocultural Adjustment

Adjustment involves much more in the way of accommodation to a new culture than achievement of economic self-sufficiency. It is obvious but nonetheless critical to emphasize that the Khmer come from a cultural setting that differs from American society in a host of both conspicuous and subtle ways. Although processing centers have instituted cultural orientation sessions, refugees encounter differences in climate, language, foods, technology, family patterns, religion, values, styles of interpersonal interaction, and numerous other aspects of life that present problems of adjustment for the refugees as well as misunderstandings by people in the host society (see also Ebihara [1980], Proum [1980], Van Esterik [1980], Ima and others [1983], Haines [1982], Stein [1982]). Although it is impossible to offer here a full discussion of such cultural differences, a few examples might be noted.

People from rural areas and those who grew up in the spartan conditions of DK may be unfamiliar with many basic items of Western technology (the village I studied had no electricity, running water, bathrooms, refrigerators, clocks, cars, etc.), although refugees would find various material goods desirable and quickly assimilate them into their lives. These same people would be unused to a strictly monetary economy in which one works for wages that constitute one's sole means of support, and in which there are such things as banks, savings accounts, and checks.

More subtle are differences between the Khmer and Americans in modes of interaction. Several points that struck me while living in a Khmer village were that face-to-face confrontations and open conflict between individuals were avoided (anger was expressed only to third parties); aggressive and competitive behavior was shunned; and villagers were accustomed to docile acceptance of orders from above and deference to those of superior status. Even when caught in troublesome situations, Khmer generally do not assert themselves, complain, or "fight for one's rights," as Americans might do. Thus they are apt to appear compliant and passive in the face of various difficulties, although in fact they may feel considerable distress, frustration, or hostility inside.

Compounding the problem of cultural differences is the fact that refugees in some areas encounter prejudice against "Asians" who are perceived to receive benefits at the expense of other minority or disadvantaged groups. Moreover, in some cities, refugees were settled in poor neighborhoods (because of the availability of low-cost housing), where they became vulnerable targets of brutal assaults and robberies.[11] There can also be other difficulties, such as that encountered by a refugee placed in a largely Hispanic section of New York City who said plaintively that he had been taught some English in the refugee center, but now he also had to learn Spanish in order to survive in his neighborhood.

Both economic and sociocultural adjustment may also be affected by problems of mental and physical health. These are particularly apt to occur among those who endured severe and traumatic circumstances in DK, such as malnutrition, stringent work and living conditions, lack of medical care, separation and loss of family members, witnessing violence, dangerous treks to freedom, and other experiences that are almost beyond our ken (see, e.g., descriptions of life in DK in Kiernan and Boua 1982 and some cases in Ima and others 1983). Even those who left Cambodia before the DK regime have suffered warfare, deaths of loved ones, and other deprivations, including, in some cases, years of languishing in refugee centers. All such experiences take their toll of physical and mental well-being. Khmer refugees suffer from various health problems, such as tuberculosis and vitamin deficiencies;[12] one survey in California indicated that 84 percent of Cambodian households reported a member under physician's care, as contrasted to 45 percent for Vietnamese, 24 percent for Hmong, and 24 percent for Lao (Ima and others 1983:47; Granville 1982:148; Haines 1982:6). Psychological problems are also expectable (Ima and others 1983:47–48; Stein 1982:16–18; Suh 1980). Information specifically on the Khmer are lacking, but studies of other groups that have undergone similar traumas show that people often suffer long-lasting psychological effects, such as depression, anxiety, paranoia, "survivor guilt," and risk-taking behavior (Stein 1982). Although risk-taking may be useful in some contexts, other psychological problems may be somatized into physical ailments or otherwise compound the general hardships of adapting to a new sociocultural setting.

Although it is important to recognize differences between the Khmer and Americans, it might also be noted that they are alike in certain respects, and some elements of Khmer culture will be useful to refugees in adapting to their new setting. Some examples of congruences between the Khmer and Americans follow.

Theravada Buddhism differs from the Judeo-Christian religious tradition in many ways, but the two also share some basic similarities. Both religions emphasize the importance of moral, harmonious, and compassionate conduct toward others. Both have "commandments" for behavior that prohibit killing, stealing, lying, and nonmarital sexual relations. Both have a round of annual holidays that are occasions for sermons, prayers, and offerings, as well as festive gatherings of relatives and friends. The Buddhist temple (of which there are now almost a dozen in the United States) resembles the church or synagogue in being both a religious and a social center for its congregants; for refugees, it is likely to acquire additional importance as a source of moral support and means of preserving cultural identity and traditions.[13]

Among both the Khmer and Americans, the family is a major focus of enduring devotion and loyalty. The parent–child bond is particularly strong, and children are the objects of great affection and attention (see also Proum 1980). Furthermore, although Buddhist ideology and the prerevolutionary Cambodian law code assigned superior status to men, in fact Khmer women enjoyed considerable authority and independence. The Khmer wife/mother played a critical role in household management and decisions, and she had complete control over the family treasury. Women owned land, houses, and other property; the peasant wife worked alongside her husband in the fields and often pursued small-scale enterprises on the side to earn extra money; adult women had freedom of movement within and outside the community (see Ebihara 1974). Khmer women are, therefore, strong and competent, accustomed to a say in things and to work. That they are often isolated in their homes here (Granville 1982:26, 172) is a pity, and it would be a mistake to underestimate their capabilities and importance.

Finally, the Khmer villagers I knew were intelligent, industrious, and enterprising people who worked hard with meager resources to make ends meet, and who endured hardships with patience and resilience. The adversities suffered by the Khmer during the 1970s were exceptionally severe and have left a legacy of problems noted earlier. But survivors of such experiences may also have qualities of great fortitude, resourcefulness, and adaptability that will serve them in good stead in the United States.

Adjustment Strategies

In the face of numerous difficulties, the Khmer utilize various adaptive strategies not unlike those found in other refugee/immigrant/poor groups. Complementing the institutionalized aid provided by governmental and private agencies, the refugees themselves help one another through exchange and sharing of material resources, information, services, advice, contacts, and so forth. Indeed, Ima and others (1983:v) see such exchanges and sharing as "invaluable" and incapable of being "duplicated by any government agency."

Mutual aid may occur, first, at the level of the household. In prerevolutionary Khmer society, extended families were as common as nuclear ones, and households might include a married child and his or her family; needy relatives, such as a widowed sister or an orphaned nephew; and sometimes a "*towaa* relative," that is, a friend who was informally adopted and treated as kin (Ebihara 1968:135ff., 177–180; Ebihara 1977). Such patterns have persisted among Khmer refugees and provide a crucial means of coping with loss of family members and straitened socioeconomic circumstances. A number of refugee households are extended families composed of miscellaneous relatives who have banded together (see cases in Ima and others 1983). Non-kin friends may also be included, evidently to a greater extent than occurs among other Indochinese refugees (Ima and others 1983:33). Single people seeking to join households rather than living alone are also highly consistent with the Khmer conception that being with other people is pleasurable, whereas living by oneself is lonely and miserable.[14] Attachment of lone individuals to families is mutually advantageous: a person is provided with companionship and shelter, and the family benefits from sharing income, expenses, and chores (or, sometimes, payments for room and board) (Ima and others 1983:34 and passim).

People beyond the family/household constitute other sources of help. Although the Khmer do not have lineages or clans as do the Vietnamese and Hmong, there is a tradition of emotional bonds and mutual aid within the bilateral kindred, that is, relatives by blood and marriage on both sides of one's family. Among the refugees, such kin continue to be important for support and exchange of food, goods, and services, such as child care, transportation, and translation (Ima and others 1983:13, 15, 38). Kin may act as sponsors for relatives, give initial aid on arrival, and maintain contacts with one another in different parts of the country. In addition, although friendship relations are not stressed over family ties, non-kin fellow Khmer may also supply mutual aid of various kinds, for example, job information, instruction (such as driving lessons), advice, and translation services, and in some locations there are rotating credit arrangements (Ima and others 1983:16 and passim). Cambodian mutual assistance associations exist in some communities, offering various services and opportunities for Khmer to interact with one another socially (Granville 1982; Indochinese Refugee Action Center 1981). Finally, American sponsors and friends may also provide both emotional and material support, as well as help in learning a new culture (Van Esterik 1981; Ima and others 1983).

Various other strategies may be used by refugees. For instance, individuals may not seek employment, instead receiving public financial aid, in order to put maximum effort into ESL and job training programs that will enhance future employment prospects; younger members of a family will get support for schooling that will do likewise; women may devise money-earning projects that can be carried out at home so that child care is not a problem. In another vein, there is the ingenuity of refugees with minimal or no knowledge of English who nonetheless manage to get driver's licenses through sheer rote memorization of correct responses on the written examination and actual driving test (Ima and others 1983:46).

142   May Ebihara

CONCLUSION: PROSPECTS FOR THE FUTURE

Because most Khmer have been in the United States for a relatively short period, it would be premature to make any definite statements as to the success of their adjustment or their prospects. At this moment, most refugees are still working through many problems noted above, and the resolution of various difficulties will doubtless continue into future years. In the meanwhile, with the help of public and private agencies, as well as mutual aid among the Khmer themselves, individuals are coping with life in a new society with varying degrees of success.

With respect to the question of achieving economic self-sufficiency, the overall prognosis seems favorable. According to one general survey of Southeast Asian refugees, increase in length of residence in the United States correlates with increase in employment, amount of weekly wages, and English language competence. Conversely, unemployment and enrollment in ESL classes decreases, although there is continuing effort to seek further education and occupational training (HHS 1983:24; see also Ima and others 1983). Certainly the refugees themselves want to be economically self-sustaining but face many difficulties, especially those less educated people in the last wave of refugees who came at a time of economic recession and cutbacks in social services (Stein 1982:19; Ima and others 1983) and those families with a large number of dependent children to support (HHS 1983:25).

The question of more general cultural and social adaptation to the United States is harder to predict. The Khmer fled terrible conditions in their homeland rather than migrating voluntarily under peaceful circumstances. If the small number of cases in one study is at all representative of the larger Khmer population, many adult refugees may have a sojourner mentality, with thoughts of possible return to Cambodia (Ima and others 1983:44–45), that might inhibit concerted efforts to adapt to a new setting. But it is likely, given Kampuchea's uncertain political future, that most Khmer (like "sojourners" in other ethnic groups) will indeed remain in the United States and that various acculturative processes will occur.

Almost one-third of Indochinese refugees are of school age, and it has classically been the case that immigrant children, with their greater facility for learning languages and exposure to the larger society through school, are the ones who become more (or most) acculturated.[15] Stein suggests that some of the older Khmer children are handicapped by having been deprived of several years of schooling during the Pol Pot period, such that "the hopes and status of the Khmer community may have to rest with an even younger generation...who were younger than 10 when they arrived in the U.S....thus delay[ing] the progress and rise in status of the Khmer" (1982:18–19). Greater acculturation of the young is, however, a double-edged sword. Another common occurrence in other immigrant groups has been tension between generations as youth acquire new modes of thought and behavior conflicting with those of their elders.

What has generally happened with other groups is that some "traditional" cultural patterns and sense of ethnic identity are maintained, but they coexist with or are modified by elements from American society. The content of this cultural synthesis and the nature of ethnic (Khmer–American) identity is just beginning to be formed, and what exact course their future development may take cannot be foreseen at this point.

NOTES

1. Some ethnic Khmer were/are also found in eastern Thailand and the Mekong Delta region of southern Vietnam. The native pronunciation of "Khmer" approximates "kuh-my."

2. For descriptions of Khmer peasant culture in two prerevolutionary villages, see Martel (1975) and Ebihara (1968), etc. My research in a Khmer rice-cultivating village was conducted in 1959-60 under the auspices of a Ford Foundation Foreign Area Training Fellowship.

3. Although some Chinese and Vietnamese had been present in Cambodia since ancient times, large numbers were brought in during the colonial period to work on plantations and in the civil service. For more information on the Chinese in Cambodia, see Willmott (1967, 1971, 1980).

4. The question of how and why the Communist revolutionaries were able to grow so rapidly is too complex to discuss here. For some perspectives on this topic, see Chandler and Kiernan (1983), and Kiernan and Boua (1982). Also, the general history of Cambodia up to 1975 is vastly more complex than the brief sketch presented. For more detail, the best general overview of Cambodian history is Chandler (1983).

5. The evacuation of Phnom Penh drew worldwide attention, as well as bewilderment as to why it occurred. There were probably a number of reasons: shortage of food and, hence, the need to get people into the countryside to plant rice when the rainy season began; the lack of adequate Khmer Rouge administrative cadre to control the enormous city population; the fear of resistance from counterrevolutionary elements in Phnom Penh; the identification of the city with corrupt, foreign, "imperialist–colonialist" oppression; and the revolutionary goal of creating a classless, communal society in which everyone would be peasant-workers.

6. The preceding sections on DK and PRK have been based on information from Chandler and Kiernan (1983), Kiernan and Boua (1982), Heder (1980a, 1980b, 1980c, 1981), Quinn–Judge (1982). For more detailed discussion of sociocultural changes in DK and PRK, see Ebihara (1984).

7. As of August 1982, there were still 4,000 or so Khmer in the Bataan and Galang processing centers awaiting entry into the United States, and another 84,568 Khmer in Thai holding centers who were eligible for resettlement (Stein 1982:1). This number had declined to about 50,000 by spring 1984. There has been some movement of Khmer refugees from the Thai centers back into Kampuchea (Hamilton 1982).

8. In 1982, about 250 unaccompanied Khmer minors entered the United States, many of whom were placed in cluster sites (HHS 1983:10). At the time of writing, a dispute had arisen regarding two unaccompanied minor teenagers who were rejected by the U.S. Immigration and Naturalization Service for admission on the grounds that they had worked for Pol Pot (*New York Times* article, 15 January 1984:3). According to State

Department guidelines outlined in 1983, no one (adult or children) associated with Pol Pot forces can enter the United States. Because adolescents were often part of execution squads in DK, the State Department fears that some might claim unaccompanied minor status to gain entry into the United States and later act as sponsors for immigration of other family members. The Joint Voluntary Agency (JVA) of the International Rescue Committee has challenged the ruling on the grounds that the two cases in dispute involve individuals who had performed only menial tasks as children during the DK period. Given the fact that in DK, children were taken from their families and were scarcely in a position to resist orders, the JVA challenge is certainly valid.

9.   Prior to the mid-1950s, education was limited largely to males. At the time of my research (1959-60), there was a widespread system of public schooling, and both male and female village children were attending primary school, acquiring literacy in Khmer and some elementary French. It seemed to me likely, however, that few village children would go on to secondary school (*lycée*, equivalent to American high school). The educational system was disrupted by warfare and bombings in the early 1970s and virtually died during DK.

10.   In this regard the Khmer contrast with the Vietnamese and Chinese. According to newspaper articles, Chinese from Vietnam generally have contacts through regional and kinship organizations that enable them to establish businesses in the United States (article by Seth Mydans, *New York Times*, 11 February 1984:29, 32); Vietnamese in southern California have established large shopping centers and other businesses (article by Jeff Wenstein, *The Village Voice*, 6 September 1983:79).

11.   See articles in the *New York Times*, 14 February 1982:50 by Laurie Johnston and 21 March 1983:B1 by Michael Norman and Dena Kleinman on the troubles of Khmer families settled in poor neighborhoods in Brooklyn, New York. Assaults became so severe that a number of families were relocated to another city.

12.   Boua's (1982:60) discussion of contemporary PRK notes that women suffer several physical problems that may also occur among refugees in the United States, for example, back and limb injuries caused by work strain or accidents during the DK period, and a large number of miscarriages and vaginal infections. She further reports a "baby boom" in PRK (ibid.), and that a similar phenomenon may be occurring here. (The Khmer women I knew in prerevolutionary Cambodia did not use contraception, although it is possible they may learn to do so in the United States.)

13.   I have heard reports of Khmer who converted to Christianity in refugee centers or who attend churches in the United States because religious groups often act as sponsors. I think it likely, however, that most Khmer remain fundamentally Buddhist.

14.   According to one survey in San Diego County, only 1 percent of Cambodians lived alone (Ima and others 1983:30). When I did research in a Cambodian village, I caused considerable amazement and consternation among my neighbors by choosing to live alone. They considered this peculiar behavior and asked constantly whether someone shouldn't move in to keep me company. Proum (1980) offers a Khmer's perceptions of American culture, and among the points that strike her as unusual are Americans' striving for freedom and independence from the family, their "love of privacy," and the emphasis on nuclear families.

15.   Ima and others mention in passing that children seem to have better command of English than do parents in the households studied (1983:32). A news item reported in several newspapers in 1983 (e.g., *New York Daily News*, 19 April 1983:22) concerned a twelve-year-old Cambodian girl who had no schooling for three years during DK and

knew no English on arrival here, but who became (after four years in the United States) a spelling bee champion in Chattanooga, Tennessee. But the process of adaptation can be socially and psychologically painful for youngsters as well as adults; for one example, see Gail Sheehy, "The Americanization of Moum Phat," *Parade Magazine*, 18 September 1983.

REFERENCES

Boua, Chanthou
1982   Women in Today's Cambodia. *New Left Review* 131:45–61.
Chandler, David
1983   *A History of Cambodia*. Boulder, Colorado: Westview Press.
Chandler, David and Ben Kiernan, Eds.
1983   *Revolution and Its Aftermath in Kampuchea: Eight Essays*. New Haven, Connecticut: Yale University Southeast Asia Studies, Monograph Series No. 25.
Ebihara, May
1966   Interrelations Between Buddhism and Social Systems in Cambodian Peasant Culture. In *Anthropological Studies in Theravada Buddhism*. Edited by Manning Nash and others. New Haven, Connecticut: Yale University Southeast Asia Studies, Cultural Report Series No. 13. Pages 175–196.
1968   *A Khmer Village in Cambodia*. Ann Arbor, Michigan: University Microfilms.
1974   Khmer Village Women in Cambodia. In *Many Sisters: Women in Cross-Cultural Perspective*. Edited by C. Matthiasson. New York: Free Press. Pages 305–348.
1977   Residence Patterns in a Khmer Peasant Village. In *Anthropology and the Climate of Opinion*. Edited by S. Freed. New York: Annals of the New York Academy of Sciences, Vol. 293. Pages 51–68.
1980   Khmers and Americans: Cultural Differences. Paper presented at a symposium on "Who Are the Cambodians? Cambodian-American Cross-Cultural Perceptions," The Asia Society, Washington, D.C.
1984   Revolution and Reformulation in Kampuchean Village Culture. In *Cambodia: People and Politics in the Interregnum*. Edited by D. Ablin and M. Hood. Armonk, New York: M. E. Sharpe.
Granville
1982   *A Preliminary Assessment of the Khmer Cluster Resettlement Project, A Final Report*. Prepared for the Office of Refugee Resettlement. Washington, D.C.: Granville Corporation
Haines, David
1982   Southeast Asian Refugees in the United States: An Overview Based on the Existing Literature. Paper presented at the meetings of the Association for Asian Studies, Chicago, Illinois.
Hamilton, J. Patrick
1982   Cambodian Refugees in Thailand: The Limits of Asylum. New York: U.S. Committee for Refugees, American Council for Nationalities Service.
Hawk, David
1982   The Killing of Cambodia. *New Republic*, 15 November 1982:17–21.

146 May Ebihara

Heder, Stephen
1980a   *Kampuchean Occupation and Resistance*. Bangkok: Chulalongkorn University, Institute of Asian Studies, Asian Studies Monograph No. 027.
1980b   From Pol Pot to Pen Sovan in the Villages. Paper prepared for the International Conference on Indochina and Problems of Security and Stability in Southeast Asia, Chulalongkorn University, Bangkok.
1980c   Kampuchea, October 1979 to August 1980, The Democratic Kampuchea Resistance, the Kampuchean Countryside, and the Sereikar. Paper prepared for the U.S. State Department.
1981   Kampuchea 1980: Anatomy of a Crisis. *Southeast Asia Chronicle* 77:3–11.
HHS (U.S. Department of Health and Human Services)
1983   *Refugee Resettlement Program, Report to Congress*. Washington, D.C.: U.S. Department of Health and Human Services, Office of Refugee Resettlement.
Ima, Kenji, Alfredo Velasco, Kota Ou, and Beverley Yip
1983   Adjustment Strategies of the Khmer Refugees in San Diego, California: Six Ethnographic Case Histories. San Diego: Union of Pan Asian Committees. Mimeo.
Indochinese Refugee Action Center
1981   *The Indochinese Mutual Assistance Associations: Characteristics, Composition, Capacity Building Needs, and Future Directions*. Washington, D.C.: Indochinese Refugee Action Center.
Kiernan, Ben, and Chanthou Boua, Eds.
1982   *Peasants and Politics in Kampuchea, 1942-1981*. Armonk, New York: M. E. Sharpe.
Martel, Gabrielle
1975   *Lovea, Village des Environs d'Angkor*. Paris: Publications d'École Française d'Extrême-Orient, Vol. XCVIII.
Proum, Sivone
1980   As Khmers See Americans. Paper presented at a symposium on "Who Are the Cambodians? Cambodian-American Cross-Cultural Perceptions," The Asia Society, Washington, D.C.
Quinn–Judge, Sophie
1982   Working for the Basics in Kampuchea. *Southeast Asia Chronicle* 87:17–25.
Shawcross, William
1979   *Sideshow: Nixon, Kissinger, and the Destruction of Cambodia*. New York: Simon & Schuster.
Stein, Barry
1982   Resettlement of Khmer Refugees in the United States. Paper prepared for a conference on "Kampuchea in the 1980s: Prospects and Problems," Woodrow Wilson School of International Affairs, Princeton University, Princeton, New Jersey.
Suh, Matthew
1980   Psychiatric Problems of Immigrants and Refugees. In *Southeast Asian Exodus: From Tradition to Resettlement*. Edited by E. Tepper. Ottawa: Canadian Asian Studies Association. Pages 207–220.
Van Esterik, Penny
1980   Cultural Factors Affecting the Adjustment of Southeast Asian Refugees. In *Southeast Asian Exodus: From Tradition to Resettlement*. Edited by E. Tepper. Ottawa: Canadian Asian Studies Association. Pages 151–172.

1981   In-Home Sponsorship for Southeast Asian Refugees. *Journal of Refugee Re-
        settlement* 1(2):18–26.
Willmott, William
1967   *The Chinese in Cambodia*. Vancouver. Publications Centre of the University
        of British Columbia.
1971   *The Political Structure of the Chinese Community in Cambodia*. London School
        of Economics, Monographs in Social Anthropology No. 42. New York: Hu-
        manities Press.
1980   The Chinese in Indochina. In *Southeast Asian Exodus: From Tradition to Re-
        settlement*. Edited by E. Tepper. Ottowa: Canadian Asian Studies Association.
        Pages 69–80.

Lao

Since 1975 more than 83,000 lowland Lao refugees have resettled in the United States (ACNS 1983). This figure represents slightly more than 5 percent of all lowland Lao presently alive. It also represents 13 percent of all Southeast Asian refugees resettled in the United States between 1975 and 1983. The public has not been as aware of lowland Lao refugees as it has been of the Vietnamese boat people, the Hmong tribesmen (also from Laos), or the Cambodian survivors of the Khmer Rouge holocaust. Yet, the sad disruption of life in Laos during the recent wars in Southeast Asia and the attempt by Lao refugees to adapt to life in the United States deserves attention.

This chapter is divided into three sections. The first gives a brief synopsis of the history of the Lao state. Besides outlining ancient, colonial, and recent history, this section introduces the relation between Buddhism and the Lao state and people. This relation is important for understanding the moral impetus to sharing among the Lao, which is discussed later in the chapter. In addition, the historical background discusses the antecedents to the presence among the Lao of geographically and socially based divisions. It also outlines the concepts of hierarchy, kinship ties, and shifting alliances so important for understanding the Lao.

The second section gives information and figures on the lowland Lao refugee experience. It is suggested that this experience was disruptive in social and psychological ways not yet fully realized. Also, life in the camps did not prepare the Lao for life in the United States, where they have attempted to re-create the social organization and cultural patterns of their homeland.

The third section outlines these social and cultural patterns as discovered in an ethnographic research project carried out in central New York state (cf. J. Van Esterik 1983). Important features of adjustment include geographic, social status, and kinship divisions and aspects of Lao life, including sharing of goods and services, hierarchical social relations, and patron and client relationships. This section draws together themes mentioned in the earlier discussions on Lao history and the refugee experience.

Finally, a summary section provides a few ideas on what may be expected in the immediate future for Lao adjustment in the United States. Reasons for being optimistic are balanced against reasons for being pessimistic. The reader is left to draw his or her own conclusions.

HISTORICAL BACKGROUND

Kingdom of Laos

The Lao nation first emerged in the fourteenth century, with the reign of King Fa Ngoun (1353-73), founder of Lan Xang (Land of a Million Elephants). At that time, most of the small states in the region were Theravada Buddhist kingdoms. Claim to legitimate rule coincided with acceptance of Theravada Buddhism by the king. Legend holds that Fa Ngoun brought Buddhism to the Lao and established the Buddhist image, *Phra Bang*, as the palladium of the Lao kingdom at Muong Swa (Luang Prabang), his capital.

The Lao state began by establishing a balanced relationship among rulers, commoners, and the upland tribal peoples. The lowland Lao are Thai-language-speakers, closely related to the Siamese Thai and the Shan of Burma. The Thai group are generally agreed to have originated in South China and were identified with the eighth century A.D. kingdom of Nan Chao in western Yunnan. The upland tribal non-Buddhist peoples of Laos were previously referred to by lowland Lao as *Kha*, or slaves. They are now called Lao Theung (Lao of the mountain slopes) and Lao Soung (Lao of the mountaintops). The Lao Theung include both Thai and Mon-Khmer language groups. Basically, they are hill-dwelling non-Buddhist tribal groups who practice swidden agriculture. The Lao Soung are Sino-Tibetan–speaking tribal groups who arrived out of China in the nineteenth century, for example, the Hmong and the Yao.

The three levels of the Lao kingdom—rulers, commoners, and the *Kha*—depended on Laotian origin myths and Buddhism for their legitimization. The origin myths and associated rituals performed in the capital by the king demonstrated the hierarchical relations between the ruler and a hereditary aristocracy, the ethnic Lao commoners, and the upland hill tribes (cf. Reynolds 1978). In the rituals and myths, the ethnic Lao gave recognition to the ancient rights that the *Kha* had in the land but asserted the reality of Lao rule. Buddhist ideology justified the relative status of rulers and commoners through the concept of *karma*. A king ruled because of good acts in his previous lives that, through karmic action, led to good results in this life. The *Kha* being non-Buddhists were naturally lower status than ethnic Lao commoners because they did not have enough good karma to participate in a Buddhist world. The Buddhist monastic order provided the underpinning to the system by an educational and religious presence in village Laos, where political control from the capital was relatively weak. In return, the king generously supported the monastic order materially, providing a model to all Buddhist Lao of the appropriate way to revere the monks. The Buddhist world order was graphically illustrated by the king's annual lustration of the *Phra Bang* Buddha image housed in a temple near the royal palace. This state palladium "stood at the ritual centre of the kingdom symbolically representing the world axis" (Stuart-Fox 1983:432) of the Buddhist universe. The king thereby displayed his subjugation to the higher Buddhist Truth and his right to rule as a Buddhist monarch.

The system had two weaknesses. First, hill peoples were less likely to accept the legitimate rule by the lowland Lao, since they did not participate in a Buddhist world order. Second, the political organization of the Lao state depended on local princes and hereditary families to swear allegiance to the king at the center. Buddhist ideology allowed for a local prince to claim the power of the center if his *karma* permitted him to expand his authority. "Shifting allegiances were seen as a natural accommodation to political circumstances" (Stuart-Fox 1983:434) by both villagers and the aristocracy.

Lan Xang, in its first 200 years, expanded over a wide area, including modern-day Laos and parts of what are now Thailand, Cambodia, Vietnam, and China. These areas were held by the Lao king, who formed tributary relations with a number of local rulers and chiefs. By the middle of the sixteenth century, Lan Xang's capital had been moved to Vientiane on the Mekong River. During this period, the Lao kingdom entered into constant conflict with Ayutthia (Siam) and Pegu (Burma) (Hall 1970:266). In the early eighteenth century, Lan Xang split into three kingdoms: Luang Prabang in the north, Vientiane in the center, and Champassak in the south. In the early nineteenth century, Vientiane was annexed at various times by both Siam and Vietnam (cf. LeBar and Suddard 1967).

This transition of Lan Xang from an important and large kingdom in the fourteenth century to a small dismembered kingdom of the nineteenth century, easily taken by the French colonialists, can be explained briefly. The landlocked kingdoms of mainland Southeast Asia some 600 years ago depended on land trade between China and India and places in between for their wealth. When the Europeans began shifting the major trade routes to the world's seas, the only nations that could grow economically and politically were those with access to the sea. Thailand, through its port capital at Bangkok, survived the European onslaught and grew in power, whereas Laos, landlocked and with its capital on a river not navigable to the sea, shrank in power and extent.

Colonial Laos

By 1893, the French had obtained control of Laos and ended Siamese claims there. Treaties between Siam and France determined the Mekong River as the border between Thailand and Laos. This resulted in a separation of the Lao on the right and left banks of the Mekong. The Lao in the region have often ignored this legal boundary, moving back and forth across the border at will. Lao visited and traded across the border until the early 1970s. However, the separation naturally weakened any effort by lowland Lao to establish strong opposition to outside control. It also meant that tribal groups in Laos were as numerous as the ethnic Lao and had to be considered in any new political order.

The French allowed the king of Luang Prabang to keep his titles and royal prerogatives. The other Lao kingdoms were demoted to provinces, and princes who were willing to recognize French authority became the governors. Vientiane, where the French resident held authority, became the administrative capital of Laos. The French held Laos with few disturbances or difficulties, except for uprisings by some tribal groups, until the beginning of the Second World War. During the French colonial period, there was a time of relative peace, but the seeds of later disruption were also laid. The French had some influence on the educational and judicial systems. They outlawed slavery and established government health and sanitation services (LeBar and Suddard 1967:17).

The greatest impact the French may have had was on the influence and role of Buddhism. As in all the Buddhist kingdoms in the region, the ruler had an intimate and crucial relationship with the Buddhist monastic order. By demoting the Lao princes and effectively taking administrative authority from the king at Luang Prabang, the French destroyed much of the meaning of ritual events and the relations between the monarchy and the Buddhist moral order (cf. Stuart-Fox 1983). This has happened to some extent among all the Theravada Buddhist countries, including Cambodia, Burma, and Thailand, as monarchies have lost their authority. The implications of this lack of power for a Buddhist-defined social order should not be underestimated, given the ideologies that eventually came to dominate Cambodia, Burma, and Laos.

The French colonialists also undermined Buddhist moral order by establishing a secular education system. Buddhist temples were the only educational centers in Laos before the arrival of the French. Although they tried to use the system already available to them, the French naturally wanted a system that was aimed at developing French-speaking Lao who would take low-level bureaucratic positions and act as interpreters. Although they attempted to build a secular education system throughout the country, few schools were actually established. The secular schools became the only avenue to desired bureaucratic employment, with monastic schools of less importance. Secondary education was poorly developed and required an extensive knowledge of French. Only a few elite members of the society obtained education outside Laos in Thailand, Vietnam, or France.

The French regarded Laos as a minor part of their colonial holdings in Southeast Asia. It had few resources, and most of the population, whether upland or lowland dwellers, were peasant farmers. Industry was almost nonexistent, sawmills and the Nam Patene tin mine being the only productive installations (LeBar and Suddard 1967:162). Laos entered the postcolonial period poor and underdeveloped with a limited educational and administrative infrastructure, its Buddhist moral order undermined by years of French rule.

Postcolonial Period

The Second World War changed relations among the countries of Southeast Asia. In 1940, the Japanese victories in Southeast Asia encouraged a group of Lao to attempt a coup against the French administration (Adams 1970:102). Although Vichy France (1940-45) controlled Laos during much of the war, real power was in the hands of the Japanese military. After the war, Laos, with the rest of Southeast Asia, welcomed the end of the Japanese occupation, but most members of the Lao elite did not want the return of French authority and many feared the growing power of the Vietnamese. The immediate postwar period was chaotic. The French were seeking to reassert control. Prince Phetsarat, who led a collection of forces united as the Lao Issara (Free Lao), and his half-brother, Prince Souphanouvong, who had the support of the Viet Minh (Ho Chi Minh's forces), were trying to establish a Lao government. After a brief period of confrontation, the French eventually took control. The Free Lao and Prince Souphanouvong's group separated while in exile. When the Geneva Convention of 1954 declared Laotian independence, the separation of these two groups set the stage for political and military conflict in Laos for the next twenty years.

Seizure of power in Laos in 1975 by the Pathet Lao should be seen in a wider context of growing Vietnamese Communist power throughout Indochina. The Pathet Lao had its beginning in the assignment by Ho Chi Minh of Vietnamese troops to assist Prince Souphanouvong and Kaysone Phomvihane in opposing French rule in postwar Laos. Under the Geneva agreements, the Pathet Lao were allowed to be based in the two northeastern provinces of Laos. This zone grew throughout the years of political and military struggle so that by 1973 it covered four-fifths of the country. In the Paris agreements of 1973 between the United States and Vietnam, it was decided that the Royal Lao Government would form a national coalition with the Lao Patriotic Front (Pathet Lao), with equal membership of Communist and non-Communist members.

During this time, the North Vietnamese had large concentrations of troops in eastern Laos available to back the Pathet Lao. Meanwhile, the United States had withdrawn from Laos, leaving right-wing Lao without support. The collapse of Saigon and Phnom Penh in April 1975 increased the Pathet Lao pressure on the coalition government. Prime Minister Souvanna Phouma was not prepared to shed blood and oppose the Pathet Lao troops, who were moving into zones that were the responsibility of the Royal Lao Army. In May, right-wing leaders and commercial interests began the flight to exile across the Mekong River, to Thailand. In Vientiane, on December 2, 1975, the Lao People's Democratic Republic was established. The prime minister of the coalition government resigned and the king of Laos abdicated. The Communists finally took control of Laos.

EXODUS

The growing power of the Pathet Lao Communists persuaded some Lao right-wing leaders and businessmen to leave Laos as early as May 1975. When the

Lao People's Democratic Republic was established, the trickle of refugees turned into a flood. Between 1975 and 1980 an estimated 300,000 left a country of three million persons (Van-es-Beeck 1982:324).

Many of the first groups out were members of Thai-speaking tribal groups who originally came from Vietnam, where they had opposed the Communists. Hmong and Yao groups also came to Thailand in the late spring and summer of 1975. At about the same time, lowland Lao who were soldiers and bureaucrats in the Royal Lao Government began to leave. The Pathet Lao began to send these officials to reeducation camps in the north of Laos. It is estimated that at least 40,000 former officials were sent to reeducation camps (Dore 1982:114 n.11), a sizable number given the relatively small population of Laos. Many Lao feared that they would never return from such camps. A number of other Lao left in the period from 1975 to 1980 for reasons connected with the deteriorating social and economic conditions in the new state. The Lao People's Democratic Republic sought to control the populace by placing limitations on the freedom of movement and the sale of produce. It imposed controlled pricing of goods and agricultural taxes, nationalized factories, and required civil servants to cultivate cooperative gardens and attend political seminars. The economy stagnated and the country was on the brink of ruin. This, combined with the loss of the benefits of United States aid, persuaded many lowland Lao to leave for Thailand.

The Thai officials regarded these people as illegal immigrants, although Thailand was forced by circumstances to set up camps for them along the Thai border at Nong Khai, Ubon, Bon Thang, and other places (Van-es-Beeck 1982:330–331). The United Nations High Commissioner for Refugees (UNHCR) recognized the Lao as refugees and therefore provided protection under international law. Furthermore, the UNHCR provided the bulk of the funding to maintain the refugee camps (Thomson 1980:128).

The size and number of camps in Thailand varied during the early 1980s. In 1980, there were two major camps for lowland Lao. Nong Khai, near the provincial capital of the same name, opened in 1976, holding 30,000 lowland Lao in 1980. The other camp, Ubon, near the provincial capital of the same name, was established in 1975, holding 20,820 Lao in 1980. There was a total of 52,820 ethnic Lao in Thailand in 1980 (UNHCR 1980). By 1982, there were still two main camps: Ubon, with 9,867 lowland or ethnic Lao, and Ban Na Pho, in Nakhon Phanom, established as a "humane deterrent" camp with minimal resources to discourage refugee flows, which held 12,186 in 1982. A total of 26,770 ethnic Lao were in Thailand in September 1982, a substantial reduction from 1980. By 1983, all the Lao were moved to one camp, Ban Na Pho. In 1984, there were slightly more than 20,000 ethnic Lao refugees in Thailand. Between 1975 and 1984 approximately 175,000 ethnic Lao arrived in the camps in Thailand.

Lao typically spend two to five years in these refugee border camps. The stresses and frustrations of camp life must influence adjustment in America. At the very least, the years spent in the camps were wasted years for many Lao. Educational programs in the border camps were limited to individual efforts, since the emphasis in the camps is on adequate diet, housing, and security for the residents. These were the unproductive, lost years for the Lao refugee. It is difficult to evaluate what effects these experiences may have on adjustment, but in general, they were poor preparation for a new life in a complex, industrialized society.

Many of the first Lao refugees who were ultimately resettled in the United States were the best educated within the Royal Lao Government—bureaucrats, interpreters, clerks, and army officers. Many of these people were the first to leave. Later, as conditions in the new Laos deteriorated, less educated and trained people left and came to the United States for resettlement. Laos thus lost some of its best trained and educated people. Only 2,397 were officially repatriated to Laos between 1980 and 1983. The United States received about half the ethnic Lao who escaped. Most of these people came to the United States in the early 1980s, after spending two or more years in the refugee camps. Although the flow from Laos has not stopped, it is much reduced from earlier years. The high point of Lao immigration to the United States has been passed. The effects of the war, flight, and camp experiences are being felt now. The Lao spent long years in a camp environment with limited educational and training experiences. Many believe that they had no choice but to leave the land they now miss greatly. It is to be expected that they will try to re-create social forms and cultural patterns that they knew in the homeland.

ADJUSTMENT

Adjustment of refugees may refer to economic self-sufficiency and personal adjustments necessary for life in a new country. Also important are "the status and potential of such core social units as the family and the ethnic community, and the longer-range economic issues of occupational mobility" (Haines 1982:4). There is a great deal of information available for the economic adjustment of refugees (cf. Bach and Bach 1980). Economic self-sufficiency has been a major concern of the federal government (cf. Refugee Act of 1980) and has received greatest attention. But the other issues in adjustment have been a concern of fewer researchers (cf. Haines and others 1981).

Adjustment among lowland Lao is beginning to be documented. Based on Office of Refugee Resettlement surveys (personal communication David Haines), it appears that the lowland Lao have a higher labor force participation (62% in 1983) than do other Southeast Asian refugee groups (from 37% to 59.7% in 1983). However, this impressive level of employment is dampened by two other survey results. One is that Lao mean weekly wages are among the lowest of any other Southeast Asian refugee group, except the Khmer. The other is that the Lao do not have as high a participation in language or other training (45.6%) as do the other groups (Vietnamese, 54%; Khmer, 66.5%; Hmong, 57%). Apparently, the lowland Lao prefer to find work immediately, even if the pay is low, and forego lengthy training in either English or vocational study. This correlates with their relatively low use of cash assistance compared with other refugee groups (35%) and perhaps with their relatively high use of food stamps (51.9%). Their low-paying jobs prevent them from receiving cash assistance but not food stamps. A study of Lao refugees in St. Louis, Missouri, found that a lack of strong sexual dichotomy with regard to household and out-of-household labor allows both husbands and wives to seek work (Rynearson and Devoe 1983:7). Similar results were found in a study of Lao in five cities, in which 59 percent of Lao women worked, 60 percent of Lao men worked, and the Lao had among the highest labor participation of all groups (personal communication Quang L. Bui; Whitmore 1984).

It may be speculated that the Lao find adjustment in immediate working situations with no concern for long-term goals. Immediate economic survival and amassing of consumer goods seem to be of high priority. These orientations are also related to the use of networks of sharing among the Lao. The ability to share goods and services is of prime importance in a Lao community. The following sections outline the process of Lao adjustment based on an ethnographic study of these networks in central New York State (J. Van Esterik 1983).

Lao Refugees as Immigrants

The distinctiveness of the lowland Lao, their language, culture, and social organization, suggests that Lao adaptation may be different from that of other refugee groups. Refugees, as a group, are distinct from immigrants, since refugees are people who have not left their homeland voluntarily with specific plans to live in a particular country (cf. Stein 1981). The Lao come to the United States without a clear idea about their new society and with a number of cultural assumptions based on their Lao experience. Because the receiving culture is radically different from the one they left, there is a great deal of room for misunderstanding. To cope with these differences, the Lao seek ways to establish social patterns they knew in Laos.

The ethnography carried out in central New York supports the concept that the Lao have retained many of their social forms. Regional differences are maintained. People tend to associate with Lao that came from the same section of Laos, that is, southern Laos versus Vientiane. People who held high office in Laos tend to become leaders in America, although expertise in English may be more important for instrumental leadership. Extended family ties often form the basis of many social networks. Ritual events and entertainments similar to temple fairs form a focus for Lao social life in the United States. The Lao themselves point out the differences between their customs and those of Americans, and value Lao social relations. A relationship found to operate in the Lao refugee community is that of patron and client. Other principles of social organization may help explain the development of Lao adjustment in the United States.

Breton (1964) outlined three sets of factors for the development of institutional completeness within ethnic communities. He demonstrated that the institutional completeness or amount of formal organization in an ethnic group strongly influenced the social integration of immigrants. The higher the institutional completeness, the more likely that the immigrant would form interpersonal networks within his or her own ethnic group. One of the three factors that he suggested developed institutional completeness was distinctive social or cultural attributes that differentiate the ethnic group from the native population. These include language, color, and religion. Another set of factors surrounds the level of resources in an ethnic group. If members of a group have few resources in skill or wealth, a "social entrepreneur" among them may try to organize something for people in need. His reward could be monetary, higher prestige, or a growing clientele for his business or organization. Finally, the number of immigrants and whether they come in large groups or as individuals can influence the development of formal organizations among the immigrants. Preliminary evidence suggests that these sets of factors can be usefully applied to an interpretation on Lao refugee adaptation in the United States.

Lao refugees are easily distinguished from the rest of the population by physical appearance, language, and religion. They have come to American communities in relatively large numbers in the past few years. Few have adequate resources to deal with their new society. According to Breton's (1964) speculations, these factors would result in some of the Lao becoming "social entrepreneurs" to meet the needs of their ethnic group. However, in addition to these social structural forces, the Lao already have the cultural categories glossed here as patron and client, which reinforce the development of these entrepreneurial leaders.

The Lao form networks to share goods and services among themselves. In conjunction with such networks they form hierarchical relations with one another. Education, age, and kinship are some of the factors that influence the nature of the hierarchical relations. For example, an older person is usually more respected than a younger person. These hierarchical patron-and-client relationships are an important element of Lao social organization. Such relationships have formed the basis of Lao social organization both in the past and at present, in Laos and now in the United States. This organization builds a way of sharing goods and skills and its strength is increased by the needs of the Lao in a new land.

Lao Social Organization

The analysis that follows is based on a seven-month study of Lao refugees in three counties of central New York State—Tompkins, Cortland, and Tioga. The Lao came to the area as part of the large refugee flows of 1979 and the early 1980s. Characteristically, most of them are poorly educated with few skills appropriate to a complex, industrialized society. The few well-educated among them have become community leaders.

The Lao community in the three counties is small, some fifty persons in all. Most families have someone employed, usually in an entry-level job, in the active and thriving service industry in Ithaca (Tompkins County), which boasts Cornell University, one of the Northeast's major institutions of higher learning. Within the American community, the Lao interact with a variety of service-provider agencies and their American sponsors, typically members of church groups. However, contacts with Americans other than service providers, sponsors, teachers, and workplace acquaintances are limited. The Lao spend a great deal of time and social energy with members of their own ethnic group both in the local community and in other major centers of central New York, like Rochester and Binghamton.

A patron-and-client relationship may be defined as a reciprocal dyadic relation of unequal statuses. Lao refugees establish these sorts of relationships soon after arrival in a community. They identify the patron as "the person who helps with everything." Patrons must be generous with time, energy, and goods. Typically a male, he must take a friendly interest in the problems voiced by a client. If he fails the client in some way, the client will seek a new patron. The relationship can be brittle. This can explain the factionalism that is common in Lao social groupings. For example, in the three-county area, there were two major patrons, each with his own clients or clique. The two patrons were themselves clients of major patrons in Rochester, where there was a major Lao population of some 1,500 persons.

In the anthropological literature on Southeast Asia, this particular type of patron-and-client relationship has been referred to as entourage (Hanks 1966). The entourage is a group of clients around a patron. Each client has a personal, one-to-one relationship with the patron, which must be maintained by some regular, personal contact. The Lao refugees maintain such contact by visiting in person or by telephone, and sending letters. The entourage concept has helped analyses of political behavior in Southeast Asia. A political party is often the result of one man's efforts and charisma. The constant shift of loyalties and policies in recent Lao political history can be related to the movement of clients among various patrons (cf. Adams 1970:100ff.). The history of the Lao kingdoms, with allegiances between the king and various princes shifting and collapsing, exhibited similar organizational principles.

Clients obviously gain from such relationships by obtaining help and goods. Lao patrons in the United States help clients with government agencies, interpreting, finding jobs, and sometimes monetary loans. The Lao refugee patron is Breton's (1964) "social entrepreneur" who seeks to help his fellow compatriot who does not speak English well and who is unfamiliar with American institutions and bureaucratic practices. People who have skills and resources are expected to help. It is obvious what clients receive, but what do patrons gain?

Patrons receive the benefits of building an entourage, a group of people who feel some obligation toward them. Along with other Lao, they also receive validation of their ethnic identity. "Lao help one another" was repeated often during fieldwork. The set of obligations established through the patron and client roles not only moved goods and skills among people, but also allowed Lao to place themselves in a moral world they could comprehend. Refugees suffer loss and deprivation. They also lose their familiar cultural referents. By forming social structures familiar to them from the homeland, they can reassert their distinctive values. This can be important in a new world in which values and structures are so radically different.

A description of the patrons and their activities in the three counties of central New York state will help readers understand important aspects of Lao refugee adjustment. One patron, a forty-year-old man, had a secondary-school education in Laos and worked for more than ten years in the Lao government as a payroll clerk. He is the best educated in the small Lao community and spoke the best English. A student at a nearby community college, he is the only Lao refugee in the community getting additional training. He spends a great deal of time helping other Lao refugees with their problems, providing interpretation services when necessary, and contacting agencies for his clients. His apartment and that of his Lao neighbor act as the hub of the social network to which Lao from as far away as sixty miles frequently gravitate for impromptu, informal parties.

The other clique in the small community is headed by a male in his early thirties. He was a soldier in a crack special anti-Communist unit when Laos fell to the Pathet Lao in 1975. Within a few months of arrival in the United States, he was speaking English well enough to act as a spokesman for a group of relatives and clients that formed a second clique in the community. He is himself a client of a well-educated Lao in a nearby town who came to the United States as a student and lived in the area for several years. Through this patron, he has an extensive network of contacts among Lao in Rochester and Binghamton. Using these networks, he held a number of formal parties for Lao and their friends over the past three years. Because he was a soldier, he found men who were members of his unit living in central New York. At one point, he represented the local community at a regional meeting of the Union of Lao Associations in America.

Both cliques are necessarily small. Each had a core group of three families. Skills and resources were not developed well enough for either patron to take on too many clients. The patrons themselves did not associate with each other. In general, clique members did not associate with one another. The only Lao that are able to move between the two groups are the young men. They sometimes visit the clients of the opposite patron. When asked about the lack of contact between the two groups, a variety of reasons may be given. Patrons claimed they did not have time to visit each other. A young man in one group claimed that the members of the other group looked down on them because they were poor. Because Lao communities can be expected to develop competing patron-and-client networks, it is suggested that their existence is not necessarily a result of particular antagonisms in a community, but rather a result of broader social and cultural factors.

Important cultural factors that inform patron-and-client networks include concepts of hierarchy, self-esteem, and moral order. These factors provide the framework for patron-and-client relationships and supply the Lao with a familiar guide for behavior in their new environment.

Hierarchy refers to the sense of relative social status that is so important in Lao interaction. As mentioned before, age is one factor in relative status; in general, the older the person, the higher the status. Status can be related to a multitude of factors, however, including, but not exclusive to, education, wealth, kinship ties, occupation, religious or ritual knowledge, political connections, and so forth. A Lao's relative status impinges on every social action in which he or she is involved. A Lao scholar describes a Lao entering a social gathering where he meets people for the first time. He says: "He is in a difficult situation, not knowing...how to behave properly...he has to explore continuously and learn the status of others" (Phommasouvanh 1983:89). Naturally, patrons are of higher relative status than are clients. Because those who hold higher relative status have more resources, skills, or knowledge than those who are lower in status, they are expected to help the less fortunate.

The less fortunate are dependent on the higher-status patrons. Yet all Lao have a need to establish their own personal integrity and self-esteem. Such esteem can be augmented by establishing contact with a patron who is confident and has high self-esteem. But a Lao patron who does not respect his client's personal integrity will quickly lose support. A Lao "learns to be considerate, share food and work, and avoid any act that will offend people" (Phommasouvanh 1983:86). Patrons who begin to impinge on others' personal integrity by excessive exercise of power or control can find their support, and therefore power, ebbing away. This means that patron entourages are necessarily limited in extent and level of control. Divisiveness and continual shifting of loyalties and coalitions are a regular feature of Lao social organization.

The factor of moral order animates the operation of the patron and client networks. Patrons are obligated to assist clients. Part of the moral imperative is contingent on kinship relations, that is, one is bound to help family members. However, the Lao family, in its broadest sense, encompasses a vast number of people, that is, all bilaterally related kin members including in-law relations (cf. Phommasouvanh [1983:85]). These obligations really extend from patrons to each and all of his clients, whether they are relatives or not. Such connections may be phrased in terms of kinship connections, of course, and the analogy between helping family and helping presumptive kin is there. However, the moral obligation and reciprocity behavior is also related to Buddhism and the normal acts of religious worship among the Lao. As noted before, the most important aspect of Lao Buddhist worship is giving to the monkhood. By this giving, the donor is assured of a store of positive karma, which will have good results either in this life or in some future lives. This religious act of giving has profound consequences for individual salvation. It also has a social analogue. Giving to any individual is a moral act and has moral consequences and obligations. In fact, Buddhist teachings hold that any act of selfless giving has good karmic results. Therefore, a patron who helps his client is acting in a moral order that is wider than the patron-to-client dyadic relationship. Giving and its reciprocal return is accomplished with a religious and social moral order that makes the establishment of patron-and-client networks of crucial significance for a Lao community.

Patron-and-client networks can be socially defined in a number of ways. One way is found in the historically significant geographical backgrounds of a network's members. All members of one local clique came from an area of southern Laos around the town of Pakse. Members of the other clique came from Vientiane and another province of central Laos. These areas generally coincide with two kingdoms in Lao history, Vientiane and Champassak. When large numbers of Lao came together at formal parties, people from the same province or region tended to sit together. A woman at one party explained that she was sitting alone because she was from Vientiane and all the other Lao at the party were southerners.

Family ties are another important feature in defining clique membership. Many of a patron's clients are part of his family. Cliques can contain a patron's in-laws and distant cousins. One Lao man took a lower-paying job to move to a city to live with relatives at a cousin's request. Another indication of the importance of kin ties is the accusation by clients that a patron is helping only his relatives. Lao knew that family loyalties can sometimes influence behavior and the claim of preference for relatives is a handy and believable weapon for Lao to use against one another in social maneuverings. Clients who do not have identifiable kin ties to the patron are concerned about the willingness of the patron to help them. This can affect their self-esteem and therefore their loyalty to the patron.

A third influence on the definition of networks is the effect of different experiences under the old regime in Laos. Different levels of education and different sets of social connections in Laos can divide refugees in the United States. The most commonly observed split is between the military and the civilian groups. Lao who were soldiers in the Royal Lao Army sometimes feel the civilians did not suffer as much in the fight against the Communist Pathet Lao. The civilians are often better educated and therefore have social reasons to separate themselves from patrons who were soldiers. Thus cliques headed by patrons who were high officials in the civilian government exist in opposition to cliques headed by patrons who were military leaders in the old regime.

To summarize, the networks of patron-and-client relationships are composed of wide-ranging chains of relatives and friends organized along the lines of common geographical, occupational, and social backgrounds. Cultural factors of status, esteem, and moral order frame the social organization of these networks. The building of these networks into more formal organizations is likely given the attributes Breton (1964) has outlined. The Lao are distinctive culturally by way of language, ceremonial and religious practices, and a host of behavioral patterns that differ from the surrounding American society. They have developed a number of leaders who may be described as "social entrepreneurs." There are a large number of Lao refugees who need help, since few speak adequate English or have the necessary skills to obtain high-paying jobs. The patron is ready to help these people seek jobs and negotiate with social agencies and to supply goods and loans. Finally, the large number of Lao refugees coming to the United States in the past few years has encouraged the development of more formal organizations. Thus there was a need for ethnic organizations to provide social contacts, goods, and services in a context that suited their cultural backgrounds and practices.

Lao Networks and the American Community

Sponsors are an important part of Lao refugee adjustment. Sponsors are groups, church committees, and concerned individuals who take on the responsibility of resettling refugees into a community. The voluntary agencies (VOLAGS), like Church World Service and the U.S. Catholic Conference, seek out these volunteer sponsors and connect them to refugee families. The VOLAGS help sponsors with technical assistance and some funds. In some large cities, Lao associations cooperate with VOLAGS to resettle refugees. Many times Lao patrons will take on the sponsorship role. But if Lao refugees have any major contacts with the American community outside of social agencies, this contact is usually with sponsors.

Both the Lao refugees and the American sponsors have expectations of each other that are based on important assumptions in each respective culture. The Americans count on the Lao eventually adjusting and adapting to life in the United States. This usually means learning to care for one's own family without the sponsor's constant help with a concomitant improvement in economic status. The Lao, in turn, apply sets of expectations to American sponsors that are similar to those that they apply to Lao patrons.

American sponsors appear to be much like patrons when the refugees first meet them. The sponsors stop in and visit the refugees from time to time. They help the refugees shop, give them rides, and help them find jobs. The Lao refugee responds as a good client by doing as the sponsor asks, joining the sponsor at church, filling out forms, and going to English class.

As time passes, the Lao may see that things are not quite the same with American sponsors as with Lao patrons (cf. P. Van Esterik 1981:23–24). A Lao patron will visit his client just to talk, joke, or share a meal. Americans seem too busy to sit and visit. They always have something to do, something to bring, or something to arrange. Often they are in a hurry.

American sponsors meanwhile are trying to develop the refugees' independence. They expect the refugees to do things without the sponsors' constant assistance. The refugees see this withdrawal of help as a breakdown in the patron-

and-client relationship. Patrons should be willing to continue the relation because of the benefits it is assumed can derive from the relationship. If an American sponsor withdraws, it is sometimes explained that the sponsor is too poor to help and has to care for his or her own family. The refugee seeks other patrons in the community to help out. This could mean other people in a sponsor group, service providers, teachers, and so forth. Eventually, the refugees will be able to find Lao patrons who can provide some services and who will be interested in establishing a patron-and-client relationship.

This suggests that eventually sponsorship relations break down and dissolve. However, this does not mean an end to patron-and-client relationships. Rather these are maintained among Lao, and in some cases, they develop into formal organizations. Such formal groups may grow into mutual assistance associations, some of which have been funded by the government. These associations can strengthen the Lao community, providing a focus for social events, political maneuvering, and ethnic identity. Eventually, these formal groups and associations may be able to mobilize Lao as an identifiable ethnic group with particular interests and concerns within an American political and social context. At the moment, such groups serve to deal with basic survival among the Lao and help buffer them from the personal and social disruptions they have experienced coming to a strange, new land.

SUMMARY

Lao refugees have suffered much and lost a great deal. Most of them have lived through chaotic and disruptive times in their homeland. Coming to resettle in the United States, they have sought to restructure their lives around social and cultural forms they find familiar.

As a result, they have reestablished a flexible and adaptable social organization. They form networks of self-help based on chains of patron-and-client relationships that are grounded in values of respective status, self-esteem, and a moral order of giving and receiving. Besides validating ethnic identity, these entourage networks can have a stabilizing effect on people who know that in a time of need they have a network of relationships to call on. To the Lao, this is natural. As they say, "Lao help each other." This system can help all members of the community. Lao youth can be absorbed into such networks, perhaps stabilizing their adjustment to American life. Lao women are respected within the family for the economic contributions they can make to the household. Outside the family, the women supply labor and organizational ability for the ritual and celebratory events that serve as foci for the networks. Lao male leaders have successfully built formal organizations, based on their entourages, some of which have received government funding as mutual assistance associations. These factors make it possible to be optimistic about Lao in the United States.

On the other hand, the legacies of regional loyalties, social and educational divisions, and the brittle nature of patron-and-client relationships can inhibit the development of self-help associations. Conflict between patrons with large entourages can split Lao communities and limit their effectiveness. Furthermore, individual adjustments are difficult when educational backgrounds are not well developed. A social organization that relies on dependency relationships between hierarchically related people who reciprocate goods and services contrasts strongly with American society, which emphasizes self-reliance and achievement-based evaluations for economic and social advancement. The contradictions between the two systems are apparent in the relationships between American sponsors and Lao refugees. The hope is that networks may develop into more formal organizations that can begin to act as an ethnic interest group in an American political and social context.

REFERENCES

Adams, Nina
1970   Patrons, Clients, and Revolutionaries: The Lao Search for Independence, 1945-
             54. In *Laos: War and Revolution*. Edited by Nina Adams and Alfred McCoy.
             New York: Harper Colophon Books.
ACNS (American Council for Nationalities Service)
1983   *Refugee Reports* 4(15–22).
1984   *Refugee Reports* 5(1).
Bach, Robert L., and Jennifer B. Bach
1980   Employment Patterns of Southeast Asian Refugees. *Monthly Labor Review*
             102(10):31–38.
Breton, Raymond
1964   Institutional Completeness of Ethnic Communities and the Personal Relations
             of Immigrants. *American Journal of Sociology* 70:193–205.
Dore, Amphay
1982   The Three Revolutions in Laos. In *Contemporary Laos: Studies in the Politics
             and Society of the Lao People's Democratic Republic*. Edited by Martin Stuart-
             Fox. New York: St. Martin's Press.
Haines, David W.
1982   Southeast Asian Refugees in the United States: An Overview Based on the
             Existing Research. Paper presented at the annual meeting of the Association
             for Asian Studies. Chicago, Illinois.
Haines, David W., Dorothy Rutherford, and Patrick Thomas
1981   Family and Community Among Vietnamese Refugees. *International Migration
             Review* 15(1):310–319.
Hall, D.G.E.
1970   *A History of South-East Asia*. New York: St. Martin's Press.
Hanks, Lucien M.
1966   The Corporation and the Entourage: A Comparison of Thai and American Social
             Organization. *Catalyst* 2:55–63.
LeBar, Frank, and Adrienne Suddard
1967   *Laos: Its People, Its Society, Its Culture*. New Haven, Connecticut: Human
             Relations Area Files Press.

Phommasouvanh, Bounlieng
1983   Aspects of Lao Family and Social Life. In *Bridging Cultures: Southeast Asian Refugees in America*. Los Angeles, California: Special Service for Groups.

Reynolds, Frank E.
1978   Ritual and Social Hierarchy: An Aspect of Traditional Religion in Buddhist Laos. In *Religion and Legitimation of Power in Thailand, Laos, and Burma*. Edited by Bardwell L. Smith. Chambersburg, Pennsylvania: ANIMA Books.

Rynearson, Ann M., and Pamela A. Devoe
1983   Off Center Stage: The Role of Women in Community Formation for Laotian Refugees in the U.S. Paper presented at the annual meetings of the American Anthropological Association, Chicago, Illinois.

Stein, Barry N.
1981   The Refugee Experience: Defining the Parameters of a Field of Study. *International Migration Review* 15(1-2):320–330.

Stuart-Fox, Martin
1983   Marxism and Theravada Buddhism: The Legitimation of Political Authority in Laos. *Pacific Affairs* 56(3):428–454.

Thomson, Suteera
1980   Refugees in Thailand: Relief, Development and Integration. In *Southeast Asian Exodus: From Tradition to Resettlement*. Edited by Elliot L. Tepper. Ottawa: Canadian Asian Studies Association.

UNHCR (U.N. High Commissioner for Refugees)
1980   *Indochinese Refugees in Thailand*. Geneva: UNHCR.

Van-es-Beeck, Bernard J.
1982   Refugees from Laos, 1975-1979. In *Contemporary Laos: Studies in the Politics and Society of the Lao People's Democratic Republic*. Edited by Martin Stuart-Fox. New York: St. Martin's Press.

Van Esterik, John
1983   Final Report: The Individual, Social, and Cultural Characteristics of Adjustment and Refugee Program Use of Laotian Refugees. Prepared for the Office of Refugee Resettlement, U.S. Department of Health and Human Services.

Van Esterik, Penny
1981   In-home Sponsorship for Southeast Asian Refugees. *Journal of Refugee Resettlement* 1(2):18–26.

Whitmore, John K.
1984   Economic Self-sufficiency Among Recent Southeast Asian Refugees in the United States: A Summary. Manuscript, Ann Arbor, Michigan: Institute for Social Research.

Salvadoreans and Guatemalans

They are called the "foot people." They come across the border of the United States from Mexico, pooling all their resources and risking life and limb. Still, the situation they are leaving behind is so intolerable that they find the risk worth taking. Their numbers cannot be documented accurately, but calculations in early 1984 by relief agencies and the Immigration and Naturalization Service (INS) suggested that 500,000 was a conservative estimate. These are Central American refugees coming from Guatemala and El Salvador, where civil wars are raging.

Empirical data on these refugees are just beginning to be collected. The information given here has been obtained from press notices, interviews, and informal articles. Some researchers are beginning to formalize their study in order to make more definite statements regarding this population. Nevertheless, given their numbers and the parameters of their situation, it seems appropriate that a chapter be dedicated to introducing this newest group of refugees.

The struggles waging in Guatemala and El Salvador have their own particular characteristics, and thus the type of person who chooses or is forced into exile is different. At first, the majority of Salvadoreans were young men and women, because they are the most vulnerable. Families would pool their resources in order to get their youngsters out of danger. But in 1982 and 1983, more and more families joined the flight north. Guatemalans are young people also, but they come as families and are predominantly peasants. Some affluent Central Americans have also left their countries and have joined the large Cuban community in Florida and in some of the larger southwestern cities (Lernoux 1984).

The proximity of Central America to the United States has always permitted easy access. Air routes are numerous and wealthy Central Americans in years past have come frequently for tourism, shopping, education, and medical care. Economical travel through Mexico is possible by car, bus, or train, and some enterprising lower-income people have used these means for some time to come looking for better economic options. The latter have blended into the ranks of undocumented Mexicans. However, in order to have a better grasp of the factors that have generated such an unprecedented exodus from this part of the world, it is important to understand the historical roots of the conflict in Central America, even though only briefly outlined here.

The countries of Central America are largely agricultural trading partners of the United States. At the turn of the century, coffee was the chief export. In the early 1900s, bananas were introduced as a commercial crop by the United Fruit Company in Guatemala. By the mid 1900s, cattle were being exported from Guatemala and sugar and cotton became additional important exports both from El Salvador and Guatemala. But in the United States, the image of bananas predominates, hence the pejorative term "banana republics."

As in all agricultural countries, the man–land relationship has been the chief determinant of power. This relationship has been characterized by a land distribution in which a few own large plantations and the majority are land-hungry. Coffee, sugar, and cotton production require a large contingent of harvesters for short periods. Banana production, for the most part, has been in the hands of foreign-owners, who employ large numbers of peasant workers. The relationship between landowners and peasants has often been an exploitative one that on more than one occasion has exploded into conflict.

Background: El Salvador

The current political crisis in El Salvador can be traced to the 1880s, when the government of that country ruled that all collective land should become private property. This was the period of the great international coffee boom, and the laws that were enacted suppressed communal land holdings and paved the way for the concentration of the best agricultural land in the hands of the so-called fourteen families. Peasants were evicted from their property to work on the large estates, and a rural police force was created to make sure they did.

Continuing conflicts over land ownership and the eviction of peasants led to a rural rebellion in 1932. General Maximiliano Hernández Martínez had used military power to annul the electoral process and then turned that same power against agricultural workers and their supporters. The revolt was harshly put down with a toll of more than 30,000 dead. This event was etched into memory as "La Matanza." Many people of Indian descent abandoned their native language and dress in order to hide their identity and save their lives. This era of military rule, despite several attempts to use the ballot box to restore civilian control, has perdured until the present.

Since 1961, when it signed a "General Agreement for Economic and Technical Assistance," the U.S. government has been involved in attempting to modify the feudal land structure of El Salvador. The landowners resisted the efforts to produce a land reform, but the accord also provided for military missions and equipment, which were readily accepted.

As Murat W. Williams, former U.S. ambassador to El Salvador, said in a *New York Times* interview on April 17, 1980:

I told Secretary of State Dean Rusk that I thought our military missions were excessive. Mr. Rusk listened sympathetically and he urged me to write a recommendation so we could reduce them. Alas, strong Department of Defense objections blocked our effort. Within five years of his retirement in 1964, we saw the ridiculous, appalling spectacle of a Salvadorean Army, trained and equipped by the U.S., at war with a Honduran Army, also trained and equipped by us. (Forché and Wheaton 1980)

The land reform and the training of peasant leaders have only exacerbated the enmity between landowners and peasants. They have not changed effectively the land structure of the country. Since 1970, the opposition to military rule and manipulation has slowly gained force, but it has also produced increased repression. In 1976, a new land reform attempt, labeled Transformación Agraria, was proposed by the president, Colonel Molina. The landowners opposed it, but the United States continued to support it as a partial answer to the gigantic gap between the wealthy and the majority of the population, who are incredibly poor. Open hostility to the project and intense persecution of peasant organizations nullified any positive aspects the project might have had. Instead, the government and the landowners sought and gained increased U.S. economic and military aid to put down any efforts by the people to make effective demands.

After 1979, demonstrations and protests became impossible because of the violence with which they were repressed. The death toll from 1979 through 1983 surpasses 34,000. Right-wing military and paramilitary "death squads" search out those who are suspected of opposing the government, while the rebel military forces gain support and strength. Those who are threatened by the conflict flee their homes.

Background: Guatemala

In Guatemala, a government elected in 1944 initiated substantial reforms, including social security, an improved educational system, and a land reform designed to distribute property to thousands of peasants. The largest landowner at that time and the one principally affected by the reform was the United States-owned United Fruit Company. This triggered U.S. intervention. The Central Intelligence Agency helped to organize the coup that brought Colonel Castillo Armas to power. He restored some of the lands to United Fruit and became the first of a series of military governments that have ruled Guatemala to this day.

An opposition movement began in 1960 with an attempted coup by young military officers. They failed but inadvertently attracted the support of peasant groups anxious to restore the process of land reform. This was the beginning of a guerrilla movement that has ebbed and flowed. Since 1979, it has attracted considerable support from the Indian peasants of the highlands. But this support, in turn, produced a massive retaliation that consisted of many of the tactics employed by the South Vietnamese government in the Vietnam War. The violent repression in the countryside includes massacres of entire villages, a scorched earth policy, and the formation of strategic villages. It has caused the displacement of more than a million persons. Some 250,000 of these have fled the country, principally into refugee camps along the border with Mexico. But some have managed to continue their flight across Mexico and into the United States.

Why They Flee Guatemala

The testimonies of those who leave El Salvador and Guatemala attest to the horrors they have endured and from which they are attempting to escape. The generalized violations of human rights in these countries have been documented by such agencies as Amnesty International, Americas Watch, Human Rights Commissions of the United Nations and the Organization of American States, and the Committees for Peace and Justice of the Catholic Church in these countries. The Catholic Bishops of Guatemala, in a 1982 pronouncement, estimated that one million persons in Guatemala had been displaced from their homes and had either gone to cities, were wandering homeless in the countryside, or had left the country.

The displacement is generated through generalized terror, consisting of torturing and massacring publicly in order to intimidate. In the period from March 23 to September 30, 1982, the deaths of 4,004 peasants in Guatemala were documented (Polémica 1983). The peasants were killed in groups that sometimes numbered as many as 500 persons.

The description of the massacre at San Francisco (ARC 1983), a village in the province of Huehuetenango, in northwestern Guatemala, illustrates the tactics of the Guatemalan army. It was recorded by an anthropologist familiar with the region who interviewed survivors. On July 17, 1982, the army came into this Indian village and, under pretext of calling a meeting, led the men into a hall. The women and children were simultaneously taken to the church. The soldiers then shot most of the women. Those who remained alive were separated from their children and taken to some of the homes, where they were killed by blows from machetes. The soldiers then returned to kill the children, by holding them by their feet and swinging them against the walls, to destroy their skulls, or by opening their bellies with a knife. The men were taken outside in groups, their hands tied behind their backs, made to lie face down, and then shot. Two men managed to simulate being dead and escaped during the night. This massacre was conducted by some 600 soldiers and 6 officers.

In an interview, some refugees from the Guatemalan province of Huehuetenango explained how they had fled when they found out what had happened in the neighboring village of Coyá: Army helicopters bombed and strafed the people, and soldiers went in to kill the survivors. Their journey to the United States began by first taking refuge in the forests and hills of Guatemala and then continuing to walk until they reached Mexico. When work and sustenance became impossible there, they continued on to the north, walking or hitching rides until they reached the United States. Once in the United States they made contact with other refugees. Some were actually able to locate relatives and neighbors.

People from urban centers also go into exile because of the terror that prevails. Control is exerted through violent arrests with no judicial process, to be followed by total disappearance. Family members spend days, months, and even years visiting morgues, police stations, and military barracks in search of lost ones. The arrests are carried out by groups of men dressed as civilians who travel in unmarked cars. They occur at any time of the day or night, at home, work, or in the street. There is seldom any official trace of these people, but at the same time, mutilated bodies are found in different parts of the country every day. The Association of University Students from the National University of San Carlos, Guatemala City, in August 1983, published a list of thirty-seven students and professors who had disappeared from January 1982 to August 1983, detailing the circumstances of each apprehension. They range in age from eighteen to fifty-two and represent a cross-section of professions.

Sometimes a family will hear through a network of relatives and friends that a loved one's name has appeared on a death list. Other times the attempt to kill or kidnap an individual fails. When this occurs the family has to choose whether to remain with that risk, to leave as a family, or to attempt to send the person who is threatened into exile. Some choose to go to Costa Rica, Mexico, or another country; others prefer to come to the United States. Two sets of reasons influence the decision, One is the location of family or friends who have preceded them in exile, or perhaps their own previous personal experience in one or another of these countries. The other is the desire to either reconstruct their own lives in exile or continue working in some way for the social, economic, and political changes that will allow them to return safely someday to their native land.

On September 5, 1983, a U.N. subcommission meeting in Geneva approved a resolution recognizing a state of war within Guatemala. The vote was seventeen in favor and three abstentions: the United States, Argentina, and Morocco (United Nations Economic and Social Council 1983). The commission accused the Guatemalan government of having a lack of respect for international law but did not equally accuse the Union Revolucionaria Nacional de Guatemala (URNG), the coalition of armed opposition groups. This resolution allows the URNG to petition international bodies to invoke the international rules of war, to send delegations to aid the victims of the conflict, and to urge other governments to refrain from supplying military aid and advisers to Guatemala while such violations as massacres, forced disappearances, forced resettlement of indigenous communities in strategic villages, and scorched earth tactics continue unabated.

Why They Flee El Salvador

According to the International Committee of the Red Cross (UNHCR 1982), the number of internally displaced people in El Salvador by mid-1981 was 150,000. The U.N. High Commissioner for Refugees (UNHCR) estimated that there were 300,000 Salvadoreans scattered in various countries, mainly in Belize, Costa Rica, Guatemala, Honduras, Mexico, Nicaragua, and Panama. Most of these refugees, a high percentage of whom are women and children, come from poor rural areas, where the civil war has taken its highest toll. In addition, a large number of men and some young women, many of whom bring their families, have come to the United States.

An interim report on the situation of human rights and fundamental freedoms in El Salvador was presented to the U.N. Economic and Social Council. The report was prepared by the Special Representative of the Commission on Human Rights, U.N. Doc. A/36/608 dated 28 October 1981, and concluded that "there has been in El Salvador a consistent pattern of gross violations of these civil and political rights which in many cases has culminated tragically in attempts on human life." The U.N. special representative found on his visit to El Salvador that there was "widespread persecution of opposition political leaders and human rights advocates which frequently ended in murder." In addition to murder, abductions and disappearances were frequent. These, he said, "are designed, on a massive and violent scale, to prevent the exercises of such human rights as freedom of opinion, expression and peaceful assembly, and trade union rights."

The letter from UNHCR (1982) states that it is evident that much of the violence in El Salvador is designed, successfully, to instill fear and submission in the population. "Persons fleeing this kind of violence are bona fide political refugees and not simply war-displaced persons and should under no circumstances be compelled to return. It is immaterial that they have not previously articulated any political opinion or belonged to any political organization."

In September 1983, the Christian Legal Aid Office of the Catholic Archdiocese of San Salvador (SIAG 1983) said that they estimated that 3,000 Salvadoreans had been assassinated during the first half of that year. There had been at least thirty-six major military operations, with an average toll of fifty noncombatant peasants killed during each operation. They calculated that 400,000 persons (8% of the nation's population) had been obliged to relocate in different areas of the country, and that not less than 600,000 had been forced to leave the country as refugees.

Where They Go

Because the economic situation of Mexico and the Central American countries has created massive unemployment and underemployment of their own citizens, refugees have found poor receptivity in those countries. A few camps in Honduras and more in Mexico are being supervised by the UNHCR. However, these camps can barely manage to provide elementary food and medicine. Whenever possible, those who can try to move inland through Mexico in search of work. They soon fall into the stream of Mexican migrants who themselves are moving north to the United States in search of work for subsistence.

The flow of refugees from El Salvador through Guatemala and from Guatemala into Mexico was not clear at the beginning of 1981. Salvadoreans began moving into Guatemala's Pacific Coast plantations and filled in the gap left by the interrupted flow of Guatemalan internal migrants who normally harvest the coastal crops. Meanwhile, displaced Guatemalans began to drift into Mexico's Chiapas coffee plantations, where normally some Guatemalan seasonal laborers are employed.

By mid-1981, however, the presence of Guatemalan refugees became unmistakable, when some 2,000 highland Indians crossed the Usumacinta River into Mexico. The Mexican government wanted to curtail the flow of refugees even as it began, so they deported some of these initial refugees in groups. An international protest arose when it was found that some of those people were murdered on their return to Guatemala. Reluctantly, the Mexican government admitted that refugees were on Mexican soil and allowed international agencies to help deal with the problem. By mid-1982, an estimated 35,000 Guatemalans inhabited makeshift camps in Mexico, along the Guatemalan border. By the end of 1983, some observers calculated that there were approximately 120,000 refugees distributed among thirty-eight acknowledged camps and innumerable small groupings living in isolation.

The UNHCR, in January 1984, declared that 330,500 persons were considered refugees in Mexico and Central America. Of that total, 39,071 Guatemalans and 35,256 Salvadoreans were receiving U.N. aid. The refugee situation in Mexico, along the Chiapas border with Guatemala, is particularly precarious. The incursions of the Guatemalan army into the region are frequent and undeterred. People are abducted or murdered in the camps. The Mexican government and especially the local authorities in the region are ambivalent, when not outright hostile, to the refugees. Those refugees who have some contacts elsewhere venture forth and try to find refuge and sustenance outside the border area.

It is difficult to ascertain how many of these people come to the United States. Because the United States does not readily recognize them as fitting into the official category of "refugees" and seldom grants them asylum, the figures have to be calculated from the deportation statistics and from the reports of private social service agencies who are working with these people. In 1982, it was calculated that about 250,000 Salvadoreans and 60,000 Guatemalans had arrived in the United States. These figures were based on the number of those apprehended since 1979. The INS estimates that for each person they arrest, four or five get through undetected. By 1983, these figures had risen to 500,000— 200,000 in Los Angeles, 100,000 in Houston, 80,000 in Washington, and large concentrations in San Francisco, Chicago, and New York. Ambassador H. Eugene Douglas, U.S. Coordinator for Refugee Affairs, in a public presentation in Houston, in December 1983, stated that his office estimated that there were between 300,000 and 500,000 Salvadoreans in the United States without legal status.

How They Get to the United States

In order to reach the United States, Salvadoreans often have to sell everything they have. They attempt to head for those cities where there are large Salvadorean communities, like Los Angeles, San Francisco, Washington, D.C., and Houston. Some make the long and dangerous trip by land, through Guatemala and Mexico, where they face deportation if caught. Others manage to fly to Mexico. Some obtain false identification papers or get visitors' passes in Mexico and then head for the States. Most pass "without inspection" and thus enter the United States as "undocumented" persons. They solicit the services of "coyotes," people who, for a fee, will smuggle them across the U.S. border.

The danger of such an option has been dramatized by at least two cases that made headlines. One was the fatal crossing of fifteeen persons in July 1980, thirteen of whom died in the Arizona desert after being abandoned by the "coyote." They were unprepared to walk across the desert; the women wore high heels, and they carried their belongings in hand-held suitcases and had a grossly inadequate supply of water. Another group was transported in a freezer truck in Texas, in 1982, and when they could not open the door from the inside, several died of asphyxiation.

Those who have made it and found work attempt to bring relatives left behind. They send money and arrange contacts. Thus they form a kind of human chain. In Houston, there are apartment complexes that house people who all come from the same neighborhood or village in El Salvador. When "coyotes" bring in a group of people, they hold them in a house or an apartment until their friends and relatives pay up the fee. In Houston, in 1983, several Salvadoreans were found murdered, and investigation revealed that they had been killed by the "coyote" because he had not been paid for his services.

Many of the Guatemalans who come to the United States try to make their way to California, where there is a sizable community. Others go to states throughout the country. Like the Salvadoreans, they obtain work much as do undocumented Mexicans. They are hired to do low-skilled construction work, gardening, cleaning of private homes and large buildings, dishwashing, and other service jobs. Because they do not have legal residence, they have to be careful to avoid detection by the authorities. They restrict their use of public services to emergency medical treatment, but some do send their children to school. In Houston, some public school teachers have commented that some of the Spanish-speaking children in their classes draw pictures depicting the horrors they have experienced.

In the southern valley of Texas, where the economic situation for the population at large is precarious, these refugees are seen by many as threats and as interlopers. There is some hostility, but there are also groups concerned with helping them. The goal of these refugees is to move on to larger cities, where there are usually low-skilled service jobs available.

Some of the Guatemalans in the United States are Indian peasants who do not speak Spanish. Some of them have joined the migrant farmworker stream in California and in Florida. In Indiantown, Florida, a group of 250 Kanjobal-speaking Indians from Huehuetenango province in Guatemala came to public notice when seven men and one woman were apprehended in an INS raid on the rundown apartment building in which they lived. They were taken to the Krome Detention Center, where they refused to answer questions or sign voluntary departure forms. This action saved them from being deported to Guatemala. The judge finally released them on their own recognizance, and a group called CORN-Maya has begun the process of helping them submit applications to the INS for political asylum.

U.S. Policy Rationale

Not all those who are apprehended by the INS are as fortunate in getting released on their own recognizance. The U.S. policy toward Salvadoreans and Guatemalans, as directed by the State Department and the Department of Justice, is to consider them deportable illegal aliens who have come to the United States as economic refugees, much as do people who come from Mexico and other Latin American countries.

Golden and McConnell (1983) quote Peter Larabee, director of the INS detention facility in El Centro, California, as saying that Salvadorean refugees "are just peasants who are coming to the U.S. for a welfare card and a Cadillac." Dan McDonald, director of the El Paso detention camps, is quoted as stating, "They are looking for jobs, and the only reason they fear going back is because jobs are hard to find down there. Sure there's violence and they want to escape it, but that doesn't mean they are political."

The INS follows the same general procedures it uses with undocumented Mexicans. The easiest format is to have them sign a voluntary departure form, which obviates the need for a hearing. It requires only that the individual be transported to the border and then released. The process is more costly and complex for Salvadoreans and Guatemalans because they have to be flown by commercial airliner to their own countries. Nevertheless, this has become the routine practice (Richardson 1983). The worst abuse was cited by Carlos Holguin, a lawyer with the National Center for Immigration Rights in Los Angeles. He claims that five- and six-year-old Salvadorean refugees, having been convinced to sign voluntary departure forms in incommunicado interrogation sessions without being able to consult a lawer or family member, have been sent back unaccompanied to El Salvador.

On a commercial flight from the United States to San Salvador in December 1983, two U.S. social scientists observed two INS officers controlling the outside entrance to an airliner's entry tunnel. In the last few rows of the airliner were sitting six frightened Salvadorean peasants. On landing at San Salvador's Ilopango airport, the six men were escorted from the plane by Salvadorean military personnel.

It would seem that the following definition of "refugee" given in the Refugee Act of 1980 is applicable to the numerous Salvadoreans and Guatemalans who have applied for asylum status:

The term "refugee" means (A) any person who is outside any country of such person's nationality or, in case of a person having no nationality, is outside any country in which such person has habitually resided, and who is unable and unwilling to return to, and is unable and unwilling to avail himself or herself of the protection of that country because of persecution or a well-founded fear of persecution on account of race, religion, nationality, membership in a particular social group, or political opinion; or (B) in such special circumstances as the President after appropriate consultation...may specify, any person who is within the country of such person's nationality, or in which that person is habitually residing, and who is persecuted or who has a well-founded fear of persecution on account of race, religion, nationality, membership in a particular social group, or political opinion.

This definition of "refugee" incorporates those found in documents of the United Nations. Among the stipulations cited in such documents is the prohibition of a host country sending people back to the country from which they fled because of persecution or a fear of it. In compliance with the above, U.S. law does allow extended residence to those who seek asylum because they fear for their lives. However, the State Department steadfastly has rejected such treatment for Salvadoreans and Guatemalans on grounds that they come for economic reasons. They base their judgment on conditions that prevailed before 1979, when in fact many people came to the United States because the economic situation of their countries was so poor.

Despite the appearance of fit between the definition of refugee and the situation of most Salvadoreans and Guatemalans who have arrived in the United States during the past four years, the INS operates under a policy of not informing detainees of their right to ask for the services of a lawyer and to apply for political asylum. Detainees are held in detention centers from two to six weeks while they await deportation.

Those refugees who do manage to apply for asylum to the INS are overwhelmingly denied their request, but they can thereby win a respite of two years or so while the hearings are held and appeals are pursued. The most difficult aspect of the hearings involving asylum is the near impossibility of showing satisfactory written proof of persecution in order to qualify. A California immigration judge reviewed the petition of Ricardo Ernandes (*sic*) and found it unsatisfactory. Ernandes, a Salvadorean trade unionist, stated that he had been shot at three times because he was active in the union at the factory in which he worked. Assassins then shot and killed his cousin, leaving a note on his chest saying that they were looking for Ernandes. He was able to identify the men who shot at him as national guardsmen. He was nonetheless denied asylum because "he failed to provide concrete written proof." He told a *Los Angeles*

Times reporter that the only way to satisfy the judge would be to document his death after he was deported home (Golden and McConnell 1983).

The reason for the discrepancy between the legal definition of "refugee" and INS policy seems to be based on the fact that the U.S. government is providing arms and ammunition to El Salvador and military training and military support equipment to Guatemala. A change in Central American refugee policy would be in contradiction with current U.S. political, economic, and military policy toward Central America.

Citizen Response to U.S. Policy

In view of this situation, citizens' groups have evolved two types of aid: legal services and sanctuary. Legal services consist mainly of making asylum applications, assisting during deportation hearings, and educating the refugees as to their rights under the law. The National Center of Immigrants' Rights Inc. in Los Angeles, the Centro Para Inmigrantes of Houston, and Proyecto Libertad in South Texas are three such nonprofit agencies. They were originally founded to help Mexican immigrants rectify their status with the INS. These agencies have found themselves becoming more and more involved with Central American refugees, and more and more frustrated over the INS's intransigence in granting legal asylum status.

In a more dramatic effort to aid Central American refugees, churches in many cities of the United States revived the ancient practice of sanctuary. They have modeled themselves on the underground railroad movement that flourished more than a hundred years ago, created to protect suspected runaway slaves from the Fugitive Slave Law of 1850. This law allowed that suspects could be arrested by request or on sight, without a warrant, and could be turned over to a claimant. The only proof required was the word of a claimant. The current movement calls itself the "above ground railroad" and attempts to transport refugees from the border to safe locations. Rather than trying to keep the movement clandestine, they are appealing to moral principles and counting on public support for what could be seen as civil disobedience.

The practice of sanctuary was more recently reclaimed and reinterpreted in the context of the movement opposing U.S. involvement in Vietnam. Draft resisters and AWOL servicemen entered church sanctuaries with communities of support to express their conscientious objection to the war. The sanctuaries dramatized the fact that the religious congregations opposed the war as immoral.

On March 24, 1982, the Southside Presbyterian Church of Tucson, Arizona, declared itself a public sanctuary for Salvadorean and Guatemalan refugees. Its lead was followed by churches in New York, California, Massachusetts, Ohio, and the District of Columbia. The Wellington Avenue Church of Christ in Chicago, Illinois, declared itself a sanctuary on July 24, 1982, with the public endorsement of more than seventy Chicago-area churches and synagogues.

The decision to become a public sanctuary is a serious one for a congregation, because everyone involved with the project faces possible prosecution on the following charges, for each refugee aided: (1) harboring of undocumented aliens: Section 274 (a), 8 U.S.C. (a): felony, $2,000 and five years; (2) conspiracy to harbor: $10,000 and/or five years; (3) smuggling: $2,000 and/or five years. In March 1984, two religious women and a reporter were arrested, together with two young Salvadoreans (in their twenties) and a baby, as they were traveling by car north from the border. It remains to be seen if they will be prosecuted and how this first move against the sanctuary movement will affect people. To date, there have been no prosecutions and those who are involved believe that their best security, regardless of the political climate, is the most widespread publicity and support.

The basic motivation for sanctuary is a moral and religious commitment. The testimony of the refugees has been a powerful instrument in generating that commitment. In Racine, Wisconsin, the Catholic parish of Cristo Rey chose to offer sanctuary to Salvadorean and Guatemalan refugees. They wrote a letter to the Attorney General stating:

We take this action after much prayer and deliberation. It is our belief that the current policy and practice of the U.S. government with regard to Central American refugees is illegal and immoral. If this is a country based on the inalienable rights of every human person to life, liberty and the pursuit of happiness, we, as American citizens, have the right to call our government to respect these rights where violated. We consider our action to be small and insignificant when compared to the courageous action taken by the refugees who are willing to risk deportation and death that their people might live. (AFSC 1983)

The people at Cristo Rey made this decision after becoming familiar with the life stories of those they had offered to protect. One is a young man, age twenty-three, whom they call Miguel. Miguel's father had been taken by the military two days after a spontaneous protest demonstration in Santa Lucia, Guatemala, held by peasants on strike against large plantation owners. The soldiers pulled the father from his house after midnight, dragged him into a truck, and sped away. Miguel jumped on a motorcycle in a desperate attempt to follow. When he lost sight of the truck he drove to an army barracks, searching for his father. He himself was arrested and taken to a marine base. He offered his family's small farm to ransom his father. Miguel was released and his father and another companion were the only two of fifteen to return alive.

Subsequently, the entire village population fled on a warning that the army was coming. But when they thought it was safe, fifty people returned home only to find the army waiting to kill "subversives." All were massacred, the women after being raped, the children thrown into the flames that engulfed the whole village. Miguel fled Guatemala when he found out that it was he the army had sought, not his father, since they thought he was the leader of the peasant strike. Since his arrival in the United States, Miguel has learned that his brother has disappeared and is feared dead. He is terrified that his mother might be killed next.

The plight of the Sanchez family from El Salvador also had such an impact on the Cristo Rey community that they offered them sanctuary. It was February 5, 1981, at 1 A.M. in El Salvador, when soldiers burst into the Sanchez home. They ordered the mother, father, and six children to the floor. They raped the thirteen-, sixteen-, and eighteen-year-old daughters while forcing the family to watch. Their crime was that one of the daughters belonged to a high school organization. In a subsequent raid, the soldiers took the sixteen- and eighteen-year-old daughters. The father said, "I went crazy, for seven days and nights I searched for my children's bodies in cemeteries and fields." He finally found the body of one of the girls, mutilated and swollen, her severed hand being chewed by a dog. He learned that the other daughter's body had been burned. The newspapers published photos of his daughter's bodies. The family used these to persuade the Mexican Embassy to provide them safe conduct into Mexico. They were offered work on a ranch but soon found that they were starving on the pittance they were paid. They finally found their way to Tijuana, where a smuggler brought them into the United States on $1,500 "credit." Mr. Sanchez still carries his daughters' photos. The pain remains, but it is now shared by the community that has offered the family sanctuary.

Public protest is another means being used to win support for Central American refugees. In January 1984, seven Salvadoreans, accompanied by two North Americans, began a hunger strike at Riverside Church in New York City. They were denouncing human rights violations in their country and demanding that they not be deported back there. An INS spokesman was reported as saying, "The majority of Salvadoreans have been unable to make a strong case for asylum." This hunger strike was just one of many that Salvadoreans and their supporters in the United States have attempted to gain a hearing.

While the "foot people" continued to straggle furtively across the U.S. southern border, Federal government budgets requested additional funds for INS border patrol officers, who will attempt to secure U.S. territory, and for more military equipment and training to help El Salvador and Guatemala to seal their borders, as well as their people's fate.

REFERENCES

AFSC (American Friends Service Committee)
1983   Seeking Safe Haven. Philadelphia, Pennsylvania: Human Rights Program.
ARC (Anthropology Resource Center)
1983   Voices of the Survivors. ARC Newsletter. September.
Forche, Carolyn, and Philip Wheaton
1980   History and Motivations of U.S. Involvement in the Agrarian Reform Process in El Salvador, 1970-1980. Washington, D.C.: EPICA.
Golden, Renny, and Michael McConnell
1983   Sanctuary: Choosing Sides. Christianity and Crisis, 21 February:31–36.

Lernoux, Penny
1984   The Miami Connection. *The Nation* 238(6):186-198. (February 18.)
Polemica
1983   Tribunal Permanente de los Tueblos, Sesion Sobre Guatemala. Special issue, January.
Richardson, Chad
1983   Central American Refugees in the U.S.: A Case of Institutionalized Political Discrimination. Paper presented at the Latin American Association Meetings, Mexico City, Mexico.
SIAG (Servicio de Informacion y Analisis de Guatemala)
1983   *Boletin* 1(2), September.
UNHCR (U.N. High Commissioner for Refugees)
1982   Letter Regarding: UNHCR Mandate Definition of Refugees and the Situation of Salvadoran Asylum Seekers. Washington, D.C.: Washington Liaison Office of the United Nations High Commissioner for Refugees, February.
United Nations Economic and Social Council
1983   Report of the Sub-Commission on Prevention of Discrimination and Protection of Minorities. Thirty-sixth session, agenda item 6.

Soviet Jews

Between 1966 and 1982, about 250,000 Jews were granted exit visas and permitted to leave the Soviet Union. During the first half of that period, most of the migrants opted to go to Israel, where they were warmly welcomed under the Law of Return, which provides citizenship to Jews who come to settle in Israel from anywhere in the world. By 1975, a shift began to occur away from Israel and toward the United States; by 1978, the majority of Soviet migrants were coming to the United States rather than to Israel. Between 1975 and 1980, some 90,000 Soviet Jews arrived in the United States. Others went to Canada, Australia, and New Zealand, along with a minority who continued to prefer Israel.

How many of the remaining two million or so Jews in the Soviet Union have tried to obtain, or are likely to seek, exit permits is not known; nor can one make an informed judgment about how the Soviet government is likely to respond to those requests. Using Soviet behavior in the past as a guide, it appears as if the most significant factor is the quality of Soviet–United States relations. When the atmosphere between the two countries is more relaxed, the Soviets are more lenient in granting exit visas; when tension increases, the number of visas drops sharply. After their invasion of Afghanistan in 1980, the Soviets permitted less than half the previous year's numbers to leave the country. In 1981, only 9,500 Jews were permitted to leave, and in 1983, less than 1,400 were granted exit visas. Using the migrants as a resource for estimating how many more are waiting to come, one would expect, on the basis of their behavior, that many more than the quarter of a million who have already left would like to leave. But it is not clear how reliable a source the émigrés themselves are on this sensitive, complex issue.

THE JEWISH CONDITION IN THE SOVIET UNION

Although the major thrust of this chapter concerns the resettlement and adjustment of the Soviet Jews in the United States, some account of their status and personal circurmstances in the Soviet Union should make their adjustment and reactions to their new life more understandable.

The Bolshevik revolution of 1917 carried with it the promise of a new life for all the ethnic and religious communities that occupied the vast area of the Russian Empire. But for the Jews, especially, the revolution was expected to change their lives. And in the first two decades of Bolshevik rule, before the signing of the Hitler–Stalin pact, the Jews, especially those who had technical and administrative skills, made considerable inroads into Soviet public life.

According to Mordechai Altshuler (1981), assimilation of Jews in Soviet society was eased by the government's perception of the Jews as an oppressed minority who had suffered under the old regime and continued to be subjected to persecution by enemies of the Bolsheviks and were, thus, loyal to the new regime.

This situation created conditions favorable to the integration of Jews, particularly the young, into the Soviet system. Many of these young Jews, who set about their work with extreme fervor in order to change the physiognomy of Russian society, were mainly active within the non-Jewish sectors of society. (Altshuler 1981:154)

Altshuler also noted these factors as contributing to their assimilation: First, a governmental and party apparatus, designed especially for activity within the Jewish populace, aided the new regime in systematically and deliberately attacking forces that helped to maintain Jewish group existence. Among the disbanded "forces" were Jewish political parties, all of which sought to ensure the continuation of Jewish national existence; public institutions of mutual aid, because their existence implied separate group existence; and Jewish educational institutions. Second, a harsh campaign was waged against Jewish and other religions. Finally, Soviet assimilation was accomplished with a feeling of free choice. In contrast to the old regime, under which complete assimilation required religious conversion, the new leadership did not demand individuals to become part of the cultural tradition of another ethnic group.

...rather, he was to participate, alongside members of other national and ethnic groups, in the creation of a new spiritual and cultural tradition and a new life-style, which were to be radically different from anything known heretofore. This new creation was, seemingly, to be of a universal nature, thereby precluding the existence of any elements that contradicted the cultural tradition or customs of Jewish life, which in any case, contained elements of universalism and social justice. (Altshuler 1981:155)

According to Altshuler, a census carried out among Communist Party members in 1927 showed that almost 50,000 Jews were members or candidates for membership; that number represented 4.4 percent of the total party members. Another indicator of the extent of Jewish integration into Soviet society is that there were thirty-three mixed marriages out of every hundred involving at least one Jew in the Russian Federal Republic. The government, during this period, continued to carry on an official campaign against anti-Semitism that included publication of pamphlets denouncing it, educational programs for youth groups, and court actions. The rise of Stalin, the purges of the 1930s, resulting in the famous show trials, and the signing of the Hitler–Stalin pact brought to an end the period of "enlightenment and openness" of Soviet society toward its Jewish community.

Not only did the Second World War result in the death of six million European Jews, most of whom had lived in eastern Europe, but it also left intensely bitter feelings among many of the survivors toward the Soviets for their indifference toward the Jewish suffering during the war. Indeed, in some instances, the local populace cooperated with the Nazis in the annihilation of Jews in the Ukraine and White Russia. The partisan groups and the Red Army also often treated Jews as the "enemy" rather than as victims or allies.

After the war, those Jews who returned to the Ukraine, especially, but to other parts of the western areas of the Soviet Union as well, often encountered open hostility and physical harm by the local residents. Institutionally, also, changes were occurring in the official Soviet behavior toward Jews. Yaacov Ro'i (1981) wrote that in 1948 the Jewish Anti-Fascist Committee and its paper, *Aynikeit*, as well as the Yiddish publications ceased to appear; Yiddish concerts and theatrical performances were stopped; and Soviet Jewry's public figures, such as members of the Anti-Fascist Committee Presidium, Yiddish writers, and other artists, were arrested and imprisoned.

The repression and the systematic exclusion did not end with Stalin's death. To quote Ro'i:

While the virulence that characterized the end of the Stalin period was never again returned to, the post-Stalin period left little room for illusions among those Jews who genuinely sought to assimilate into their non-Jewish environment. Hopes that the Khrushchevian "liberalization" and de-Stalinization would bring a basic change in the Jewish position were quickly dashed. Jews continued to be barred from diplomatic training institutions and from political careers; the party apparatus was almost closed to them; and an evident numerus clausus (i.e., a quota system) was applied in institutions of higher learning. The economic trials of the early 1960s once again discriminated manifestly against Jews qua Jews. Moreover, large numbers of Jews who filled administrative, educational, and other positions in the USSR's national republics and autonomous regions were not only hated by other national minorities as russifiers but became scapegoats for the pressures these minorities applied against the central authorities and were the first to be dismissed from their posts as the various nationalities produced increasing numbers of their own technical, scientific, and administrative "cadres." (Ro'i 1981:168)

In 1960, Jewish students in universities and other institutions of higher learning composed 3.2 percent of all such students in the Soviet Union. In 1964, the percentage dropped to 2.5, and in 1972, it had dropped again, to 1.9. In 1937, there were forty-seven Jews among the Supreme Soviet Deputies; in 1974, there were only six Jewish deputies.

The year of the "Six-Day War" between Israel and the neighboring Arab nations, 1967, is often cited as a turning point in the psyches and behavior of Soviet Jews. The David-and-Goliath nature of the Israeli victory seemed to kindle a small flame among Soviet Jewry, even among young people who had not personally experienced a "Jewish heritage." The existence of Israel, coupled with what Soviet Jews came to view as its heroic and courageous stance, plus the increasing discrimination that they experienced within their own country, fostered the desire on the part of many Soviet Jews to leave their homeland. That desire continued throughout the 1970s and resulted in the emigration of some 250,000 Soviet Jews. During the early 1980s, however, the exodus dwindled; the 1983 total of 1,300 was the lowest in thirteen years. But as emphasized earlier, it is impossible to determine whether the total exodus represents the bulk of those who wished to leave, or whether it represents the government's decision to once again close the doors and forbid the movement of Jews out of the Soviet Union; and if the latter is true, for how long?

According to the 1970 Soviet census figures, there were 2,149,707 Jews living in the Soviet Union: 2,104,651 in urban areas and 45,056 in rural areas. The republics with the largest Jewish populations were Russian Soviet Federated Socialist Republic (RSFSF), 807,915 Jews; the Ukraine, 777,126; White Russia (Byelorussia), 148,011; Uzbekistan, 102,855; and Moldavia, 98,972. After these, the figures drop sharply to 55,382 in Georgia and 36,680 in Latvia. The remaining seven republics contained about 80,000 Jews altogether. The cities with the largest Jewish population were Moscow, 285,000; Kiev, 220,000; Leningrad, 165,000; Odessa, 120,000; Kharkov, 80,000; Kishinëv, 50,000; and Minsk, 50,000.

THE JOURNEY TO THE WEST

The official position that the Soviet government has taken on the issue of Jewish and other ethnic emigration, such as German and Armenian, is that it is sanctioned only on the grounds of family reunification; that is, the desire to facilitate the reunification of families who have been separated by war and boundary changes in Europe. Not everyone, however, who seeks to leave on grounds of family reunification is granted an exit visa. Grounds for refusal include possession of state secrets (military or economic), geographic locations (people living in a "closed area"), military expertise, and possession of other highly valued skills or knowledge. In 1972, the Soviet government instituted a "diploma tax." The tax sought reimbursement to the state for the higher education and academic degrees it had conferred on applicants. Sawyer (1979:195) reports that "graduates of universities and institutions above the high school level were obliged to pay anywhere from 4,500 rubles to slightly over 12,000 rubles, depending on the type of training received and the place of study." The Soviet government suspended the tax in 1973, partly because of world criticism but probably more importantly because it was in danger of losing desired trade concessions from the United States as a result of the tax.

The following paragraph describes what happened to Soviet Jews when they applied for exit visas, even during the period when tens of thousands were permitted to leave each year:

They must ask permission to leave from parents and employers, which generally results in being fired and sometimes in denunciations at public meetings. Frequently pressure is placed upon other family members who have not applied for exit. The potential refugee also must prove that he or she has no outstanding debts, and in many cities this proof entails getting written statements from all retail establishments in the city. The individual must take these risks without any assurance that he or she will, in fact, be permitted to leave. After permission is given to leave for family reunion in Israel, the refugee must renounce Soviet citizenship, a process which is expensive and cuts off any possibility of return. (Leimsidor 1980:35–36)

The exit path out of the Soviet Union—either by plane or, more often, by train, because the emigrants can take more luggage—leads first to Vienna, where separation occurs between those who wish to go to Israel and those who seek resettlement in western countries. If the emigrants opt not to go to Israel, they are moved by HIAS (the Hebrew Immigrant Aid Society) out of Vienna to Rome, where they are likely to remain for several months until they receive the necessary papers for their migration to the United States, Canada, or Australia. Those emigrants who seek resettlement in Israel are placed under the care of the Jewish Agency and are usually moved out of Vienna in a matter of days. The following is an account of the separation process in Vienna and the time spent in Rome.

Those who insist on going to a destination other than Israel, for family or other reasons, and who cannot be persuaded to do otherwise, are transferred to the Vienna HIAS office. There they are met by a Russian-speaking representative of the Jewish Agency who makes a further attempt to persuade them to go to Israel.

Soviet Jews who continue to insist on going elsewhere are sent by HIAS to its Rome office, where still another attempt is made to have them reconsider. It is only then that the Rome office proceeds to process them for immigration to other countries. Most opt for the United States.

The time spent in Rome is filled with tension. The refugees leave Russia with exit visas stamped for Israel. They must now first apply for permission to settle elsewhere. Most of the world (including Italy) is closed to them. At present, their choices are limited to the United States, Canada and Australia...and Israel. Most opt for North America and most will be accepted. But there are applications and interviews—and the specter of those who have been denied emigration. The United States routinely rejects individuals who have been ''voluntary'' members of the Communist Party, a formulation that exempts those who joined because their lives or careers depended on it. Other reasons for rejection are invoked inconsistently. Canada and Australia have different standards, so that individuals barred by one country may be welcomed by another. (Edelman 1977:163)

From the mid- to late 1970s, as the proportion of Soviet emigrants who chose western resettlement over Israel increased, so did the tension between the Jewish

Agency and HIAS, as indeed did anger on the part of the Israeli government
toward the American Jewish community and the U. S. government for providing
the Soviet Jews with a choice between Israel and the United States. That problem
is now moot because the number of Jews who are permitted to leave the Soviet
Union has dribbled down to only a few hundred a year.

THE REFUGEES' SOCIAL AND ECONOMIC ADJUSTMENT

In 1981, a national survey was conducted in fourteen U.S. cities of 900 Soviet
Jewish refugees who had emigrated to the United States. The survey, which was
sponsored by the Soviet Resettlement Program of the Council of Jewish Federations, had two major purposes: to find out about the immigrants' socioeconomic adjustment and to characterize the quality and strength of their Jewish
identities.[1]

To learn about their socioeconomic adjustment, the survey asked about schooling, jobs, and earnings in the Soviet Union, and about the number and types of
jobs they and their spouses have held since they arrived in the United States,
their rates of pay, and their savings. It collected information about the types,
amounts, and sources of financial and other forms of aid they received after their
arrival. It asked them to compare their social status or position, their friendships,
and their cultural life in the United States as opposed to the Soviet Union. The
study explored the problems they confronted in deciding about their children's
education and about their socialization into American society. To learn about
their Jewish identity, it asked about temple and synagogue attendance and affiliation, strength of religious feelings, observance of traditional rituals and practices, and whether they are likely to encourage their children to observe traditional
practices and to affiliate with the American Jewish community.

Fifty-seven percent of the respondents in the survey came from the Ukraine,
22 percent from the RSFSF, 7 percent from White Russia, and 4 percent each
from Latvia and Moldavia. After that, the percentages dropped to less than two
for each of the remaining republics. The cities in the Soviet Union most represented in the survey are among those with the highest numbers of Jews in the
Soviet Union: Kiev, Odessa, Moscow, Leningrad, and Minsk.

When respondents were asked, For what reasons did you decide to come to
the United States?, they answered as follows:

Reason	Percentage
Anti-Semitism in the Soviet Union	49
Children's education future	34
Educational opportunities/university training	8
Family reunion/relatives in the United States	33
Financial/level of income	15
Jewish identity/religious freedom	15
Jobs/career opportunities	18
Spouse's wishes	4

Note: The question was open ended. Respondents were not given a list or set of alternatives from which to choose. They could offer as many reasons as they wanted. The list summarizes the reasons most frequently given. The reponses added up to more than 100 percent because many respondents gave more than one reason.

Anti-Semitism was mentioned more often than any other factor. The next two most frequently cited reasons were the respondents' desire for greater educational opportunities for their children and the opportunity for family reunions with relatives already in the United States. Note that anti-Semitism is cited by more than three times as many people as is the concern about Jewish identity and religious freedom.

Dividing the respondents by the cities in which they were living at the time they decided to emigrate, the percentage who cited "anti-Semitism" as a reason for coming to the United States is indicated for various cities in the following listing:

City	Percentage
Riga	41
Leningrad	42
Moscow	47
Kiev	56
Lvov	64
Odessa	50
Minsk	60
Others	43

Respondents from cities in White Russia and the Ukraine (Minsk, Kiev, Lvov, and Odessa) cited anti-Semitism more often than did respondents from cities in the RSFSF and Latvia (Leningrad, Moscow, and Riga).

Eighty-five percent of the families in the survey consisted of a married couple, with an average of 1.4 children. The mean level of education among the men was fourteen years, and among the women, thirteen years. The educational and technical skills that the immigrants brought with them plus the experience of having lived in large urban centers allowed most of them to enter the U.S. labor force in skilled and technical occupations.

At the time of the survey, 80 percent of the men, who were between twenty-five and fifty-five years of age, were in the labor force full time. Although this proportion is somewhat lower than for the U.S. resident population as a whole, it is impressive when we remember that 75 percent came to the United States in 1979 and later, and the survey was taken in the spring and summer of 1981. The proportion of females in the labor force full time was 57 percent, which is somewhat higher than the U.S. resident female population. Seventy-six percent of the men and 68 percent of the women were working in professional or white-collar jobs or as skilled crafts workers.

Table 11.1. Percentage Reporting Major–Minor Problems in Adjustment

Problem	Major Problem	Minor Problem	No Problem	No Answer
Finding a good job	74	11	15	0
Making new friends	28	27	44	1
Learning English	75	15	10	0
Feeling outside Jewish community	7	20	72	1
Earning enough money for family	47	27	25	1
Providing a good education for your children	33	12	50	5
Indifference of Americans	10	21	68	1
Finding a good place to live	20	19	61	0
Being separated from family	62	19	19	0
Feeling like an outsider	16	21	63	0

Among those employed, 35 percent described themselves as very satisfied with their jobs and 49 percent as somewhat satisfied. Respondents who had been in the United States longer reported higher satisfaction than did newer arrivals. A higher percentage of those with more skills and training were also more likely to be very satisfied with their jobs. The mean male income before taxes was $14,607 in 1980; after taxes it was $11,480. Among women, the mean gross income was $7,627; after taxes it was $6,501.

The biggest problem, reported by 70 percent of the respondents, in their adjustment and resettlement was learning English. Younger respondents (those under thirty) and those with professional or white-collar skills were less likely to report language acquisition as a problem than were the respondents over thirty (53 percent compared with 67 percent) or those with blue-collar backgrounds (60 percent compared with 75 percent).

Finding adequate work was the second most frequently cited problem. There were no significant variations by demographic characteristics or location among the 21 percent who cited that as their biggest problem. No other problem was mentioned by more than 1 percent of the respondents.

When shown "a short list of things with which some immigrants have had problems" and asked to indicate whether each has been a major problem, minor problem, or no problem, the results shown in Table 11.1 emerged. The problems most respondents labeled "major" are individual and personal: finding a good job, learning English, and being separated from family members who are still in the Soviet Union. These are followed by other personal issues, such as earning enough money and providing their children with a good education. Collective or social matters involving ties to the community, Americans' reactions to them, and participation in the the Jewish community are considered major problems by a much smaller percentage.

Learning English is clearly a matter of great concern to a majority of the respondents. The Soviet immigrants rightly perceive it as an important or necessary skill in their socioeconomic adjustment and mobility. At the time of the survey, 50 percent were attending special English classes. When asked to rate their abilities in reading, writing, and speaking English right after they arrived in the United States and again at the time of the survey, their responses were as follows:

English Ability	At Time of Arrival	At Time of Survey
Reading	1.8	3.1
Writing	1.7	2.7
Speaking	1.6	3.1

Note: The rating was done on a five-point scale: 1 means no fluency or knowledge at all in the language; 5 means totally fluent, like a person born and fully educated in that language. Asked to evaluate their ability to read, write, and speak Russian, their ratings were 4.97, 4.95, and 4.96.

By their own evaluations, the Soviet immigrants have made considerable strides since arrival. Comparing scores by age, we see that at both points in time respondents over fifty did not rate themselves as highly as the younger people did:

English Ability	At Time of Arrival				At Time of Survey			
	30	30–39	40–49	50 and over	30	30–39	40–49	50 and over
Reading	2.3	1.9	1.9	1.4	3.5	2.3	3.1	2.4
Writing	2.0	1.7	1.7	1.3	2.9	2.8	2.8	2.1
Speaking	1.9	1.7	1.7	1.3	3.4	3.1	3.2	2.6

How much public assistance immigrant families receive is a matter of interest for policy purposes. Groups who are opposed to immigration for many reasons (i.e., cultural, economic, racial, and social) often make their strongest public argument on economic grounds, specifically that immigrants are a drain on the limited resources of the United States. The amounts of aid we report are based on what the respondents told the interviewers. They have not been separately verified in any way, which means that there may be a variety of errors, both unsystematic and biased. With this in mind, we were able to estimate that the average Soviet immigrant family received $1,722 in public aid during the first twelve months in the United States, about $1,185 during the second, about $1,036 in the third, about $1,018 in the fourth, about $607 in the fifth twelve-month period, and downward from there on. How should one evaluate these amounts? For example, with whom should they be compared—with all U.S. resident families? with other immigrant groups? One relevant comparison is with

Table 11.2. Comparisons Between Life in the Soviet Union and the United States

	Life in the United States			
Comparisons	Better	Same	Worse	Don't Know or Not Applicable
Housing	64	19	17	0
Cultural life	15	14	68	3
Friendships	11	38	49	2
Overall standard of living	75	10	13	2
Social status or position	26	21	47	6
Life as a Jew	89	9	1	1
Work situation (atmosphere)	36	14	45	5
Income	75	7	13	5
Spouse's work situation	30	11	37	22
Spouse's income	55	5	16	24

the amounts of aid that native families receive. In 1975, the average native family received the equivalent of $2,161 in 1980 dollars ($1,420 in 1975 current dollars), according to results from the 1976 Bureau of the Census Survey of Income and Education. Included in that 1975 total is the 1980 equivalent of $1,105 for social security ($735 in 1975 dollars). We see, thus, that even in their first year, Soviet immigrant families receive less public aid than do native families.

Another comparison is with the taxes that these immigrant families pay. On the basis of the income reported by the respondents, we estimated that a Soviet immigrant household paid an average of 22 percent of their income in taxes, which placed their mean tax paid at $4,319. We also estimated that nineteen months after they arrived in the United States, the Soviet immigrants were contributing more to the public coffers in the form of taxes ($1,117 more) than they were taking out in public aid.

From many points of view—the educational and technical skills they brought with them, their labor force participation, and the taxes they pay—the Soviet immigrants seem to be making a good economic adjustment to their new environment and are proving to be an excellent investment for native Americans.

So much for economic matters. What about the Soviet immigrants' social, cultural, and religious adjustment? One of the items included in the survey asked the respondents to compare their life in the Soviet Union against their life in the United States along various dimensions: such as friendships, work situation, social status, life as a Jew, income, culture, housing. Were these aspects better, worse, or the same? Table 11.2 describes the results.

A large majority felt that on objective matters, such as housing and income, their lives were better in the United States. Eighty-nine percent thought that the Jewish aspect of their life was better in the United States. But with respect to the cultural opportunities available to them, to the friends they had made, and to their social status or position, many more respondents favored their life in the Soviet Union over the United States. In comments to the interviewers they complained that the ballet and opera companies in most American cities do not compare favorably, artistically or pricewise, with their equivalents in Kiev, Moscow, or Leningrad, cities from which most of the respondents emigrated. Many of them also felt that they had to accept less prestigious and important positions in the United States compared with those they held in the Soviet Union during the normal (pre-visa application) period of their lives.

Researchers in Israel asked the same questions of Soviet immigrants to that country, and the responses came out looking much the same. Israeli culture did not measure up to what had been available to them in the Soviet Union, and they did not feel that they enjoy as high a social position in Israel as they had achieved in the Soviet Union.

Zvi Gitelman also commented on the Soviet immigrants' feelings about American culture and about their social position. He noted:

The immigrants display a marked ambivalence towards American culture—its freedom and creativity are attractive but its vulgarity and pandering to low tastes are repulsive. They are painfully aware of a decline in their social status. Asked to define the social class to which they belong in the United States, 45 percent say "new immigrant." Almost half the respondents say that in the USSR they would define themselves as "intelligentsia," but only 11 percent do so when asked to define their American social class. On the other hand, 12 percent of the respondents gave "working class" as their class identification in the USSR and exactly the same percentage do so in the United States. Only two people called themselves "lower class" in the USSR, but 24 describe themselves as such in the United States. Nearly 58 percent think their standard of living has risen since their arrival in the United States, and only 13 percent see it as having declined (29 percent say it is the same as in the USSR). (Gitelman 1982:11)

The ethnic composition of the neighborhoods in which the Soviet immigrants live varies by city. For example, 50 percent and 64 percent in Los Angeles and Philadelphia live in mostly Jewish neighborhoods compared with 1 percent in Houston. For the sample as a whole, 26 percent reported living in mostly Jewish neighborhoods. Seventy-two percent said that all their close friends are Jews, and two-thirds of them said that they are all recent Soviet Jewish immigrants. Only a small number have joined Jewish organizations: 16 percent belong to a Jewish community center or a YMHA, 8 percent to a Russian Jewish group, and 2 percent have joined Zionist or Jewish fraternal organizations.

Age turned out to be an important factor in analyzing their responses to all the "Jewish" issues. Respondents who were fifty and older had the strongest Jewish identities and desire for Jewish ties. For example, 73 percent of those fifty and over compared with 46 percent of the thirty-and-younger age-group said that being Jewish was important to them. Sixteen percent of the entire sample described themselves as fairly or very religious in contrast to 36 percent who said that they were not at all religious.

Although fewer than 10 percent of the immigrants claimed that they had obtained any type of Jewish education in the Soviet Union, 79 percent said that they want their children to receive a good Jewish education. Twenty-nine percent enrolled their children in Jewish day schools and 14 percent attend special Hebrew schools in the afternoons. Although the former figure is higher than among American Jews, comparisons are complicated by the fact that Jewish agencies in many communities provide free tuition for the first year of the immigrant child's attendance.

"Jewish" is the label that most respondents think describes them best of all, and "Soviet Jew" is the label most believe is least appropriate or least accurate. They prefer "Russian-American" or "American Jews" to the latter.

CONCLUDING REMARKS

The responses to the Jewish items are tantalizing, particularly in what they promise for the future and in what they leave in doubt. At this stage, there are more questions than answers about how committed and how strong the Soviet immigrant ties are likely to be to the American Jewish community and to the religious, political, and ethnic aspects of Jewish life. Will their experiences living in the United States, with its more open and varied opportunities for Jewish affiliation, strengthen their Jewish identity, or will the absence of fear and the relative lack of anti-Semitism extinguish their interest and their desire for a Jewish identity and for ties with the American Jewish community? Will their energy and drive be consumed by their quest for economic and professional success and social prestige, or will they come to recognize that there are few costs and some benefits to being affiliated with American Jewry? More time, and perhaps later surveys, should provide clearer answers to these issues.

I conclude with a few more facts about the Soviet immigrants' adjustment. If they had to do it over again, 86 percent would immigrate to the United States, 6 percent would go to Israel, 3 percent would go somewhere else but they were not sure where, and 5 percent would remain in the Soviet Union. Five years hence, 34 percent of those who expect to be in the work force expect to be very satisfied with their work life and financial situation; 57 percent expect to be somewhat satisfied.

Taken as a whole, the Soviet immigrants are making a good adjustment in their new lives. After being here only a short time, they are already contributing rather than taking from the public coffers. What they are likely to contribute culturally, spiritually, and otherwise to the Jewish community remains to be seen.

NOTE

1. In each city, the sample frame was obtained from a Jewish resettlement agency, and every Soviet immigrant family that arrived in the United States between 1972 and 1980 and whose "head" was between eighteen and fifty-five years of age at the time of arrival had a chance to be included in the survey. The settlement agency sent letters to people whose names had been randomly selected, describing the survey and asking their cooperation. Each person was then contacted by phone and asked if he/she would agree to be interviewed. The sample was designed so that, within each city, 25 percent of the respondents arrived before 1978 and 75 percent arrived in 1978 or thereafter. Eighty-seven percent of all the potential respondents agreed to participate. The interviews lasted about eighty minutes. Sixty-two percent were conducted in Russian and 38 percent in English. The survey was supported by funds awarded to the Council of Jewish Federation of the Office of Refugee Resettlement, Department of Health and Human Services, Washington, D.C. Rita J. Simon and Julian L. Simon, "The Soviet Jews Adjustment to the United States," unpublished report.

REFERENCES

Altshuler, Mordechai
1981   Factors in the Process of Assimilation Within Soviet Jewry, 1917-1947. In
         Jewish Assimilation in Modern Times. Edited by Bela Vago. Boulder, Colorado:
         Westview Press. Pages 151–163.
Edelman, Joseph
1977   Soviet Jews in the United States. In *American Jewish Yearbook*. Edited by
         Morris Fine and Milton Himmelfarb. New York: American Jewish Committee.
Gitelman, Zvi
1982   Soviet Immigrant Resettlement in the United States. *Soviet Jewish Affairs* 12(2).
Leimsidor, Bruce
1980   Refugees Leave Soviet Union. *World Refugee Survey* 1980:35–36.
Ro'i, Yaacov
1981   The Dilemma of Soviet Jewry's Assimilation After 1948. In *Jewish Assimilation
         in Modern Times*. Edited by Bela Vago. Boulder, Colorado: Westview Press.
         Pages 165–170.
Sawyer, Thomas E.
1979   *The Jewish Minority in the Soviet Union*. Boulder, Colorado: Westview Press.

Vietnamese

Vietnamese refugees account for about two-thirds of the Indochinese refugee population in the United States. Indochinese refugees are by-products of the defeat of non-Communist governments in Vietnam, Laos, and Cambodia; the radical transformation of Indochinese societies in the wake of Communist victory; and continuing warfare and change in that part of the world.

Indochinese people left their homeland to seek haven abroad in two major waves. The first wave occurred as a result of the precipitous fall of Phnom Penh and Saigon in April 1975, in the context of a more or less organized evacuation effort by the United States. The second wave took place in 1978-79, in the wake of the Sino-Vietnamese conflict, the Vietnamese invasion of Cambodia, and the border war between China and Vietnam. This wave was undoubtedly encouraged and, to a large extent, organized by the Vietnamese authorities. In between the two waves and continuing until the present have been trickles of refugees who clandestinely plotted their own departures.

Indochinese refugees are a diverse group. They come from three different countries: Cambodia, Laos, and Vietnam (both North and South). They belong to a variety of ethnic groups: Vietnamese lowlanders, montagnards, Chams, Lao lowlanders, Hmong, Mien, Cambodians, and Chinese. They speak different languages. They have different social backgrounds. Many come from urban areas, others come from rural settings or mountainous areas. Although some have traveled and studied abroad and are highly sophisticated and cosmopolitan, others are less exposed to the Western way of life. There are former government officials, military officers, soldiers, businessmen; but there are also farmers, fishers, and hill people. Refugees left their countries under different circumstances and therefore have different experiences, motivations, needs, and expectations. There are first-wave and second-wave refugees. There are boat people and land people. Although many of them have been resettled in countries of final destination, others are still living in makeshift shelters in Southeast Asia, and a smaller number are in refugee processing centers preparing for final resettlement. This chapter focuses on the Vietnamese refugees, their origin, their reasons for leaving their homeland, their journey to the United States, their resettlement patterns, and their problems.

THE VIETNAMESE REFUGEES: WHO ARE THEY?

Vietnamese refugees were the fallout of the Vietnam War. They came halfway around the world to the United States from an old civilization. Vietnamese think of themselves as descendants of the mythical King Hung, who founded the country more than 4,000 years ago. Recorded history traces the establishment of the kingdom of Nam Viet, a small country in the south of China, to the year 208 B.C. The history of Vietnam is a history of continuous resistance to foreign domination and southward expansion. In 111 B.C., China annexed Vietnam and ruled it for more than a thousand years. Although China succeeded in leaving a lasting cultural influence on Vietnamese society, the Vietnamese still retained their separate and distinct cultural and political identities. Chinese rule was interrupted by revolts, and in 939, Vietnam succeeded in regaining its independence. In the thirteenth century, after defeating the invading armies of Kublai Khan, the Vietnamese began to move southward. They annexed the kingdom of Champa in 1471 and completed their control over the Mekong Delta by the mid-eighteenth century. From a small country based in the Red River Delta, Vietnam now covered an area 1,300 miles long and 100 miles wide along the eastern seacoast of Southeast Asia.

France began its conquest of Vietnam in 1859. By 1844, it was able to force the Vietnamese emperor to sign an agreement formally accepting French control of the country. Although the court succumbed to French pressure, resistance against French rule, led by scholar-patriots and members of the imperial family, continued. The first modern nationalist party, the Viet Nam Quoc Dan Dang (VNQDD), emerged in the 1920s. The aborted uprising at Yen Bay in 1930 led to the execution of all its leaders and the demise of the VNQDD as the dominant anti-French force. It was in this vacuum that the Indochinese Communist Party (ICP) moved in. When the French hold on Vietnam was weakened by the Second World War, the ICP formed the Viet Nam Doc Lap Dong Minh Hoi (Vietnam Independence League), known as the Viet Minh, in 1941. In March 1945, Japanese forces overthrew the French colonial government in Vietnam and encouraged Emperor Bao Dai to declare Vietnam independent from France, which he did. Six months later, when Japan surrendered to the allies, Viet Minh partisans took control of Hanoi and set up a provisional government, with Ho Chi Minh as president. Emperor Bao Dai abdicated in favor of the new government and was immediately appointed its supreme adviser. In the South, government authority was exercised through the Provisional Executive Committee of the South, a coalition of various competing nationalist groups, but Viet Minh control over the committee was much more precarious.

On September 12, 1945, British forces arrived in Saigon to disarm the Japanese. They permitted the French to stage a coup against the Committee of the

South and eventually reestablish their control of South Vietnam before the British departed in January 1946. At about the same time, Chinese troops moved into North Vietnam to disarm the Japanese. With them came the leaders of the Viet Nam Cach Menh Dong Minh Hoi (Vietnam Revolutionary League) and the VNQDD, who had organized the fight against French colonialism from their bases in China. Joining forces with their comrades at home, they demanded a share of government leadership. The ICP was officially dissolved, and a new coalition government was formed to cope with the return of the French.

In March 1946, the new government headed by Ho Chi Minh signed an agreement with France, giving it unhampered access to North Vietnam in return for French recognition of Vietnam as ''a free state...belonging to the Indochinese Federation and to the French Union.'' The nationalists immediately accused the Communists of being too compromising on Vietnam's independence. The Communists used the breathing spell given by this agreement to move against their opposition. Caught between the Communists and the French, prominent nationalist leaders, one by one, left the government and went into self-imposed exile. In December 1946, the French provoked an incident in Hanoi to move against the Viet Minh. The colonial war began.

After the Chinese Communists took control of mainland China, the Viet Minh openly acknowledged its Communist ties. The ICP was reinstituted as the Vietnam Workers' Party, and the Democratic Republic of Vietnam established diplomatic relations with China and Russia. At the same time, the French, unable to defeat the Viet Minh on the battlefield, attempted a political solution. They agreed to the return of ex-Emperor Bao Dai who, as ''head of state,'' would have authority over the internal affairs of a unified Vietnam, while France still retained control over foreign relations and defense. France now could claim that it was at the front line of the cold war, helping a nationalist government in its struggle against communism. The United States moved to accord diplomatic recognition of the Bao Dai government and increased its financial support to the French military effort in Vietnam. The colonial war in Vietnam took on new dimensions: communism vs. nationalism and totalitarianism vs. democracy.

In 1954, after the French were defeated at Dien Bien Phu, an international agreement ending the Vietnam war was signed at Geneva. Vietnam was demarcated at the seventeenth parallel; the North came under the control of the Communists and the South belonged to the nationalists. The Final Declaration, which the United States and the Bao Dai government refused to sign, provided for national elections to be held in 1956 to reunify the country. In June, a new set of agreements was signed between France and Vietnam, providing the basis for genuine independence. Ngo Dinh Diem was appointed prime minister with full power. South Vietnam was in a state of near chaos when Diem came back from self-exile. He began to take control of the armed forces, arranged for the withdrawal of French troops, and pulled the country together. By 1956, a new constitution was proclaimed and Diem was elected president of the Republic of Vietnam. His government was also able to resettle almost a million refugees who went south to flee the Communist regime, many of whom were among those who left Vietnam in the 1975 exodus.

The year 1956 went by without the elections to reunify the country as envisioned in the Geneva Final Declaration. In 1959, the first government post was attacked by guerrillas. In 1960, the National Front for the Liberation of South Vietnam (NFLSVN) was formed to lead the war against the government. The Front was tightly controlled by the Vietnam Worker's Party through its Central Office for South Viet Nam (COSVN). The United States was committed to help Diem to mount a counterinsurgency campaign against the rebels. In 1962, the U.S. Military Assistance Command was established and antiguerrilla special forces were sent to Vietnam. As the war went on, Diem became increasingly authoritarian and eventually was overthrown in 1963 by the military in a coup d'etat, acquiesced to by the United States. The 1963 coup was followed by a period of political instability and military setbacks in South Vietnam. To stop this deterioration, the United States decided to send troops to South Vietnam and began to bomb North Vietnam. On the other hand, China and Russia also poured massive aid into North Vietnam, and the Socialist Republic of Vietnam increased its infiltration into South Vietnam. The war began to escalate. On Tet 1968, the Front launched a general offensive in several major cities throughout South Vietnam. It was a costly military campaign in terms of human lives, but it turned out to be a political victory for Hanoi. The United States, knowing it could not win a quick military victory, decided to quit. Troop withdrawal, "Vietnamization," and diplomatic negotiation began. In 1973, a cease-fire agreement was concluded in Paris. It provided for the total withdrawal of all U.S. combat forces but not North Vietnamese forces. U.S. aid to South Vietnam was cut and "Vietnamization" could not proceed as planned. By 1975, the correlation of forces was utterly in favor of the Communists. Under the probing attack of Communist forces, President Thieu decided to redeploy South Vietnamese forces to defensible areas. The withdrawal from Pleiku and later from Hue turned into a rout. As Communist forces advanced toward Saigon, the American-organized evacuation went into high gear. This hasty operation was able to evacuate 130,000 Vietnamese but did not succeed in bringing out many Vietnamese who would be endangered by a Communist victory. Hundreds of thousands of Vietnamese who grew up with the idea that they were fighting for a good cause alongside a committed ally were left to languish in the various concentration camps throughout Vietnam.

WHY DID THEY LEAVE?

Vietnamese refugees left their homeland for a variety of reasons. Many left because of the fear of communism, fear of imprisonment, execution, expected loss of social status and political freedom. These are the predominant reasons among first-wave refugees. The ethnic Chinese left because of racial and economic discrimination and because they were forced to leave (even Chinese who lived in North Vietnam for generations and who belonged to the working class were asked by the government to leave for fear that they might become China's fifth column in Vietnam). Religious leaders and their followers (the Catholics and the Buddhists) left to avoid religious discrimination and persecution. Some left in panic, especially among first-wave refugees; others left because life had become hard and unbearable to them and held no future for their children. It has been a common practice for Vietnamese parents to sacrifice everything to provide opportunities for their children to leave the country. (This accounts for the fact that children and young people compose the majority of second-wave refugees. It is estimated that young people under twenty-five account for 60 percent of the current refugee population.) Economic hardship is no doubt one of the reasons but not really the root cause of the risky departure of many refugees. Many people, especially those who were released from reeducation camps and those who were associated with the former government or with the American war efforts, were discriminated against in their homeland. They did not get rations to buy the necessities of life from government stores; they could not get jobs; they were forced to go to the new economic zones, where their life became hopeless (many have come back to the cities to lead an illegal and barely subsistent life); and their children were deprived of the chance to enter colleges and universities. Under these circumstances, they naturally suffered from economic hardship, they could not make ends meet. Their economic hardship did not result primarily from the overall economic situation in their countries, but because they were discriminated against politically and socially.[1] Continued conflict and warfare in Indochina (the Sino-Vietnamese conflict and the border war of 1979, the Cambodian-Vietnamese conflict, and the Vietnamese-sponsored military campaign against the present regimes in Indochina), political repression, as well as worsening economic and social conditions and tales of a good life abroad have been other causes of the flow of refugees. So long as these reasons remain, the world will continue to see more refugees coming out of Vietnam.

THE FLOW OF REFUGEES FROM VIETNAM

By January 1984, the total number of Indochinese refugees had amounted to more than 1.5 million, of which approximately 220,000 left during April 1975 and about 1.3 million left between May 1975 and the end of 1983. The biggest wave of refugees took place between March 1978, when the Vietnamese government began to enforce its socialist economic policy, especially against ethnic Chinese who resided in Cholon (Ho Chi Minh City), and July 1979, when, under international pressure at the U.N. Geneva Conference on Indochinese Refugees, the Vietnamese government pledged to take "firm and effective measures" to stop the flow of refugees for a "reasonable period."[2] It is estimated that this mass exodus added about 400,000 to the refugee population.

Basically, four types of refugees have come out of Vietnam: the first-wave refugees, the second-wave refugees, the escapees, and the orderly departures.

The first-wave refugees left Vietnam during the spring of 1975 as Communist forces advanced toward Saigon and the United States began to airlift its non-essential employees out of Vietnam. Leaving before April 29 were Vietnamese dependents of U.S. servicemen and government workers,[3] people who worked for foreign companies and were not within draft age, people who knew the Americans who organized the airlift, those sponsored by Vietnamese-Americans living in the United States, and those who could talk or bribe their way into the U.S. processing center at Tan Son Nhat airport. Leaving in panic on April 29, the day when U.S. military and civilian personnel were requested to leave within twenty-four hours, was anyone who could come to one of several designated locations in the city or get into the embassy or onto waiting barges at the Saigon River. This evacuation was organized by the U.S. government.[4] Those who left before April 29 (and a few who left on that date) boarded the planes at Tan Son Nhat airport and were flown to Clark Air Base in the Philippines. Those who left on April 29 were flown by helicopters or taken by barges to waiting naval ships that carried them to Subic Bay in the Philippines. From the Philippines, refugees were flown to Guam and then to one of four refugee camps in the United States, waiting for security clearance and sponsors to get them out of camps.[5]

The second-wave refugees left Vietnam during the 1978-79 period, at the height of the Sino-Vietnamese conflict. Resenting ethnic Chinese control of private business in South Vietnam, and fearing the possibility of a Chinese fifth column in Vietnam, the Vietnamese government clamped down on Chinese in business and forced them to leave the country. This evacuation was unofficially organized by the Vietnamese authorities, therefore labeled by refugees as ''unofficial departure.'' People who wanted to go had to register and pay in gold for a place in the boat. This was done through an intermediary called the organizer. When all the arrangements were made, they were told to assemble at a designated location, where they were brought to the waiting boat. Security agents would escort their boat out of Vietnam's territorial water. Second-wave refugees were predominantly ethnic Chinese, about 250,000 of whom went to China. But there were many Vietnamese who were able to buy false papers and register themselves as Chinese for the purpose of these ''unofficial departures.''

The escapees plotted their own departures. Although a few took the land road through Kampuchea into Thailand, the majority took to the sea. They pooled resources to buy boats and gasoline for their trip; they recruited a navigator (usually a former navy man); they forged their papers; they bribed local security agents; and they left clandestinely, usually in the darkness of night, for the sea in a small and unsafe boat. Theirs was the riskiest type of departure. If caught by the authorities, they would be imprisoned. Once on the high seas, they fell prey to the turbulent sea and the pirates who roamed the Gulf of Thailand. Except for a few Chinese and Vietnamese who got a place in the two or three well-publicized big boats and arrived promptly and safely at ports of destination, most second-wave refugees shared the same risks as the escapees once they were on the high sea. Even if they survived the angry waves, mechanical failure, the lack of food and water, multiple robberies, assaults, and rapes, they still had to suffer humiliation, mistreatment, and possibly internment by the countries of first asylum. It is estimated that half the boat people were drowned at sea or killed during their journey in search of freedom and compassion.[6] Like the second-wave refugees, escapees landed first in countries neighboring Vietnam in Southeast Asia, where they lived in makeshift camps and began their long wait to be screened and accepted by countries of final resettlement.

The orderly departure program is the result of the 1979 Memorandum of Understanding between Vietnam and the U.N. High Commissioner for Refugees, with the endorsement of all resettlement countries, including the United States. Orderly departures were those who were permitted to depart directly from Vietnam to countries of resettlement. The majority of them had family ties with people already living abroad, but the United States also accepted former employees of its mission in Vietnam and other Vietnamese who were closely associated with the U.S. effort in Vietnam before 1975. The orderly departures left Ho Chi Minh City by Air France plane for Bangkok for visa processing and then on to the United States. Theirs was and is the safest trip out of the country but not the easiest. They had to obtain entry permits from the country of destination and exit visas from the Vietnamese government. The waiting period was usually long, from two to five or more years, depending on one's connections, circumstances, luck, bribery, policies of the respective government, and the status of their relations.

As the number of boat people leaving Vietnam decreased, the number of orderly departures increased noticeably in 1980, doubled in 1981, and has steadily increased ever since, totalling 39,475 by the end of September 1983. There are two reasons for this. First, the plight of the boat people and international pressure during the 1978-79 period forced Hanoi to put a tight control on clandestine escapes by boat and relax its control on legal exits. Second, Hanoi hoped a liberal emigration policy might help to improve its relations with the Western nations, especially with the United States, at a time when Hanoi was diplomatically isolated because of its stance in Kampuchea.

VIETNAMESE REFUGEES IN THE UNITED STATES

By September 30, 1983, the United States had received a total of 678,057 refugees from Indochina, close to two-thirds of whom entered the United States between 1979 and 1982, during the period of the refugee crisis. Vietnamese refugees accounted for about two-thirds of all Indochinese refugees in the United States. Until 1980, more than 80 percent of Indochinese refugees coming into the United States were Vietnamese. This ratio has since declined as refugees from Cambodia and Laos began to arrive in large numbers. In both 1982 and 1983, arrivals from Vietnam were just under 59 percent of the total (see Table 12.1).

Table 12.1 Number of Indochinese Refugees and Percentage of Vietnamese Admitted into the United States, 1978-82

	1978	1979	1980	1981	1982	1983
Total	20,397	80,616	166,727	132,447	72,155	39,167
Pecentage of Vietnamese	89	85	78	53	59	59

Source: Office of Refugee Resettlement and Immigration and Naturalization Service.

Vietnamese refugees in the United States are a mixed group. They include people at different stages of resettlement. A large number of Vietnamese refugees are professionals, many of them graduated from major universities and military academies in Europe and North America, and are familiar with the Western way of life and work ethic. But others come from rural areas and have a much more traditional outlook. With some exceptions, the group that entered the United States in the 1975-78 period tended to include more people with urban and professional backgrounds; the group that came into the United States between 1979 and 1982 tended to include more ethnic Chinese and people with rural backgrounds. The first group had a higher level of education and was more fluent in English. The second group included many people whose skills were not readily transferable to work in an industrialized economy. Educational background, English proficiency, and the length of time they resided in the United States can explain why the labor force participation of the first group has been higher than that of the second group.

Vietnamese refugees resettled in every state and many territories of the United States. Despite the initial government attempt to disperse the refugees throughout the country, secondary migration has led to heavy concentration of refugees in a few states. Seventy-five percent of all Indochinese refugees live in only twelve states (California, Florida, Illinois, Louisiana, Massachusetts, Minnesota, New York, Oregon, Pennsylvania, Texas, Virginia, and Washington). California has the largest refugee population (248,900), followed by Texas (54,900) and Washington (31,000). California and, until 1982, Texas have been magnets for the secondary migration of Vietnamese refugees. Secondary migration may be prompted by a variety of reasons: climate, employment opportunities, reunification with relatives, accessibility to social services, and the pull of established ethnic communities. Vietnamese refugees in Louisiana are predominantly Catholic. The nation's capital area (including Washington, D.C., northern Virginia, and suburban Maryland) has a larger number of professionals working for international organizations and for federal and local governments. Texas and California have a large number of entertainers, writers, journalists, English-as-a-second-language teachers, and blue-collar workers. Ethnic Chinese tend to ingather in New York and especially in California, where they are engaged in the restaurant business, groceries, retail sales, and commercial real estate. Southern

California, with its warm climate, its large population of Vietnamese refugees, its thriving Vietnamese business community along Bolsa Avenue, all the important Vietnamese-language newspapers, and the possibility to lead a social life close to the one at home, has been called by Vietnamese "the refugee's capital."

Heavy concentration of refugees, especially new arrivals, in certain locations may strain local resources and tax their coping capability. This concentration also tends to lead to the establishment of ethnic enclaves. On one hand, this may be regarded as a healthy development, because it gives the uprooted refugees a sense of identity, of belonging. It facilitates the exchange of information and mutual help, thereby aiding the resettlement process, reducing anxiety and mental distress. It shelters the weak and disadvantaged who could not function effectively in mainstream Amerian society. It also can play a beneficial economic role as a tourist attraction, and it contributes to a diversity of cultures that has been the pride of the United States. On the other hand, the formation of ethnic enclaves may lead to the development of a subculture, a social ghetto, a shelter for criminals, and a source of instability and ethnic conflict. This has not happened to Vietnamese refugees.

Economically, Vietnamese refugees have made a quick adjustment to American society. Although persistent dependence on income support is still found chiefly among the youngest and the oldest refugees and those with little education and little or no ability to use English, labor force participation of the refugees has steadily improved over time. Labor force participation rates of refugees who have been in the United States for five years or longer tend to be even higher than those of the general population. According to an Office of Refugee Resettlement survey, the labor force participation rate of Indochinese refugees in 1982 (the majority of whom were Vietnamese) was 72.1 percent for those who entered the United States in 1975 and 74.3 percent for those who entered the United States in 1976-77, as compared with 64.1 percent for the general U.S. population. A 1980 survey of the Bureau of Social Science Research showed a positive correlation between the level of education, fluency in English, length of residence of the refugees in the United States, and their labor force participation.[7] Vocational training is also a factor in helping refugees to find jobs and become self-sufficient. In a relatively short span of time, the majority of refugees have found jobs or set up their own businesses. A large number of refugees are working in low-status jobs in the electrical and electronic industries and in the machine trades. Most refugee-owned businesses so far have been family businesses that cater principally to their ethnic clients (restaurants, laundries, grocery stores, hair salons, and tailor shops). Some have engaged in car dealerships, insurance, sales, and real estate. Others have opened medical and dental offices. A few are engaged in wholesale, import–export, and manufacturing.

Behind an appearance of economic success, Vietnamese refugees, especially the older ones, have not done equally well in social and psychological adjustment. Most have not made a conscious effort to integrate themselves into American society. They join professional organizations only when they have to. Few join social clubs and interact extensively with other Americans. Their social friends are predominantly Vietnamese. They lead a dual life—one in the office among their American co-workers and another at home and during off-hours among their Vietnamese compatriots. This phenomenon is prevalent especially among the educated and Westernized elements, for not only have they felt a loss of status, but also a loss of motivation. The study of the Bureau of Social Science Research mentioned earlier indicates that although 13 percent of Vietnamese refugees interviewed saw an improvement in their lives, about two-thirds rated their lives as less satisfying than they felt their lives had been in Vietnam. This discrepancy between economic success and psychological well-being is also supported by a survey of Vietnamese living in the southern Gulf Coast and in northern California (Starr and others 1979). The findings show that economic success and psychological well-being are not consistently related among Vietnamese refugees, and that the refugees who have greater educational attainment, higher social status, greater English proficiency, and less traditional Vietnamese outlook, people generally thought of as better equipped for adjustment, tend to earn higher income, but also have more serious mental problems. A "Vietnam syndrome" similar to the one experienced by a number of American veterans of the Vietnam War is probably a major factor causing this withdrawal, this pessimistic outlook, this negative attitude toward social participation among people culturally and professionally equipped for it. Most of them felt betrayed when South Vietnam was lost to the Communists. Most felt that the United States-organized evacuation in 1975 was not meant to include them. Most feel that the version of Vietnamese history currently prevalent in the American media and intellectual circles is distorted and unfair to them and to the cause they believed in and fought for. Most feel that they are losers and that there is no use explaining the complexity of the Vietnam War to people who do not understand it or arguing with those who refuse to accept their viewpoint.

This "Vietnam syndrome" is felt most acutely by former Vietnamese soldiers, especially by those who bore the brunt of the fighting and did not know why they had to withdraw during the last month of the war without having a chance to fight, and by some generals who felt guilty about their performance during the critical hours, and by Vietnamese who left the country after having spent years in Communist "reeducation camps." Their manifestation of the "Vietnam syndrome" is generally less passive than the educated and the professionals who are doing well economically in the United States. Although many of them withdraw from social participation, others have joined the various resistance movements, hoping one day to liberate their country from the present regime. For these people, their presence in the United States is only temporary; their future is not in the United States, but in a liberated Vietnam. Many of them are active participants in protest demonstrations against either the Public Broadcasting System's slanted history of the Vietnam War, or the human rights violations by the Hanoi government, or the "National Shame Day" commemoration.[8] Leaders of the movements know full well the difficulty of their task, but they believe that their movements do have an immediate beneficial effect, which is to restore a sense of self-confidence and self-respect to the refugees about their role and their historical heritage.

A different type of active political participation can be found among younger Vietnamese and people who are concerned about their long-term role in the United States. Citizenship has been acquired, and ad hoc and permanent groups have been formed to work in support of certain legislation or political candidates, especially in areas in which there are heavy concentrations of Vietnamese.

The elderly refugees have their special problems. They are too old to compete effectively in the labor market. They usually do not have independent means of transportation or cannot drive. Their traditional outlook and their lack of English proficiency do not equip them well to function effectively in the mainstream society. Although they are becoming more dependent on their children, the latter are having less and less time for them. They can hardly find comfort in the company of their grandchildren, who tend to speak English more fluently than Vietnamese and have a much more American outlook. For the older refugees who feel isolated in a changing family environment and in a strange world beyond the family, the need for peer support is obvious. Places of worship (such as Buddhist temples) and mutual assistance associations (such as the Vietnamese Senior Citizens Association) can provide them with friendship and assistance. Participation in social and cultural activities of these organizations can give them a sense of self-worth and permit them to play a constructive role as bearers of Vietnamese culture and tradition.

Vietnamese women are no less victims of changing circumstances. Many have to abandon their traditional role in the family and become breadwinners. They are often not equipped, professionally or mentally, to cope with an unfamiliar western world of work, with all its difficulties and temptations. There are cases when they also have to cope with sullen husbands who find it hard to adjust simultaneously to their loss of status and the changing role and behavior of their wives. This situation can cause serious tension in the family and can affect the welfare of the children. In a few cases, it has led to breakups. On the whole, the Vietnamese family, which emphasizes the group over the individuals, has weathered the storm of change rather well. In many cases, the concept of extended family, where relatives live and pool their resources together, has helped them to achieve economic self-sufficiency in a relatively short time.

If the adult refugees are faced with difficulties in their social and psychological adjustment, they can find much solace in their children. Vietnamese children are doing well in schools. Many Vietnamese have been valedictorians in their graduating classes. Others have graduated from colleges and universities and are pursuing careers in government and in the private sectors. A noticeable pattern among first-generation Vietnamese students has been their overwhelming concentration in science and engineering over the humanities. Vietnamese children have represented the United States in international sports competition. Vietnamese refugees have produced for the United States the first female West Point cadet, a champion of Rubik's Cube, a concert violinist, a world-class classical guitarist, and even an astronaut-in-training. The future seems to hold great promise for young Vietnamese in the United States.

BEYOND INITIAL RESETTLEMENT

The United States government and the voluntary agencies have done a remarkable job in resettling a massive influx of Vietnamese refugees into the United States in the aftermath of an unpopular war. This success has been aided partly by the traditional American compassion for refugees, partly by Vietnamese culture, which emphasizes the need to live in "harmony with the environment," and partly by the refugees' capability (gained throughout their turbulent history) to accommodate to changing circumstances.

Becoming economically self-sufficient is the immediate goal of newly arrived refugees. Given the characteristics of Vietnamese refugees, this goal can be easily attained by an effective program of English language instruction and vocational training, coupled with an income support policy based on the right combination of incentives and disincentives that do not discourage people working at their first low-level jobs. A great majority of Vietnamese refugees have become self-sufficient. They have fulfilled the traditional role of new immigrants in providing America with a wealth of labor for low-status jobs. Some of them have even achieved a high degree of economic success. As the refugees become self-sufficient and move beyond the initial stage of resettlement, they will interact more frequently with other ethnic groups. Increased interaction leads to both cooperation and conflict, especially conflict between the refugees and people at the lower rungs of the social ladder who feel their position threatened by the newcomers. It is in the interest of both the host country and the refugees to minimize conflict and promote cooperation between ethnic groups. Government cannot legislate away conflict, but civic leaders, both American and Vietnamese, and the opinion makers can at least minimize its impact by avoiding the temptation to exaggerate, distort, and stereotype.

Two things distinguish the Vietnamese refugees from other refugees and immigrants who have set foot in America: the exposure of the boat people to the horror of pirates' attacks and their perception of injustice done to their collective image.

The plight of the boat refugees is well known. About 70 percent of the refugee boats are attacked by pirates in the Gulf of Siam, not once, but several times. Atrocites committed against the refugees include robberies, assaults, murders, multiple rapes, and abductions. It is estimated that 50 percent of people who left Vietnam by boat never reached the shore. Survivors have to live the rest of their lives with the indelible mark left by pirate atrocities. This mental suffering is incredible, especially to the victims of multiple rapes and to their children and husbands. For these people, social and psychological adjustment may become impossible. Pirate atrocities against helpless refugees must be stopped. They must not be ignored or allowed to continue.

Finally, because they are losers in an unpopular war, the Vietnamese refugees feel their collective role in the Vietnam War has been misinterpreted and distorted by the winner and by the mass media in the United States. The swiftness and unanimity with which they reacted to ABC's "20/20" program on the "Vietnamese Mafia" and PBS's thirteen-part series on "Vietnam: A Television History" revealed a significant difference between the image of Vietnamese refugees, their legacy, and history as projected on the American TV networks, and the refugees' own perception of themselves, their legacy, and history. For them, the PBS series' claim to be definitive history, and its use as educational material, are particularly disturbing when they think of the possibility that their children may have to grow up with that kind of historical distortion. This perceptual conflict over the history and the roots of a new group of immigrants in this country will be a topic of public debate for some time. For those who advocate a reconciliation between the United States and the Socialist Republic of Vietnam after a bitter war, it may be wise to think first about reconciliation right here, at home, with a sizable group of new Americans.

NOTES

1. Interviews with recently arrived refugees who escaped from Vietnam after being released from "reeducation camps" about the reasons for their dangerous escape invariably provide an answer like, "We knew the chance of making it to safety was only ten percent, but we'd rather die than live with 'them.'"

2. Until spring 1978, the flow of refugees from Vietnam was about 2,000 to 5,000 per month. Mass exodus began in March (22,000) and April (62,000) 1978 and leveled off in May (60,000) and June (60,000) 1979. By August, the flow was down to 6,000. UNHCR data on refugee arrivals in Thailand, however, presented a slightly different picture. Refugee arrivals in Thailand numbered 34,316 in 1977, doubled to 69,140 in 1978, peaked at 200,000 in 1979, went down to 113,867 in 1980, and tapered off to 43,260 in 1981. This is due to the fact that the UNHCR figures also include the "land" people coming out from Cambodia and Laos during the same period.

3. The term "dependents" was interpreted loosely to include not only spouse and children, but also the spouse's parents, brothers, sisters, and sometimes other relatives. This made it possible for many Vietnamese who, through friendship or bribery, could pass themselves as spouses or dependents of U.S. citizens to get a place on the planes.

4. This admirably executed airlift operation succeeded in evacuating many Vietnamese but failed to fulfill its initial objective, which was to evacuate all Vietnamese whose lives would be endangered by the Communist takeover.

5. Camp Pendleton in California, Fort Chaffee in Arkansas, Eglin Air Base in Florida, and Fort Indiantown Gap in Pennsylvania.

6. For a detailed description of the Vietnamese boat people, their journey, and the dangers they faced, see Grant and others (1979) and USCR (1984).

7. For further details, see Dunning (1982).

8. April 30, the day when Saigon fell to the Communist forces, is remembered by Vietnamese refugees as "National Shame Day."

REFERENCES

Dunning, Bruce
1982   *Survey of the Social, Psychological, and Economic Adaptation of Vietnamese Refugees in the United States*. Washington, D.C.: Bureau of Social Science Research.
Grant, Bruce, and others
1979   *The Boat People*. New York: Penguin Books.
ORR (Office of Refugee Resettlement)
1983   *Report to the Congress: Refugee Resettlement Program*. Washington, D.C.: U.S. Department of Health and Human Services.
Starr, Paul D., Alden Roberts, Rebecca LeNoir, and Nguyen Ngoc Thai
1979   Adaptation and Stress Among Vietnamese Refugees: Preliminary Results from Two Regions. In *Proceedings of the First Annual Conference on Indochinese Refugees*. Fairfax, Virginia: George Mason University.
USCR (U.S. Committee for Refugees)
1984   *Vietnamese Boat People: Pirates' Vulnerable Prey*. New York: American Council for Nationalities Service.

A Selective Annotated Guide
to the Literature

The following is a limited inventory of useful items regarding refugees in the United States. In making the selection, I have been guided by three principles. The first is relevance: I have tried not to stray from the specifics of refugees in the United States into the distractions of refugees in other countries, other immigrants to the United States, or the situations of refugees in their countries of origin. The second is availability: Items that are not readily available are excluded, such as out-of-print reports, articles in defunct or rare journals, and papers presented at meetings. A reasonable university library should suffice; where it may not, an address is included. The third is parsimony: I have refrained from any multiple references to a single source; there are thus no separate references to items found in a single listed book or journal volume. Multiple citations of individuals are also avoided, as are multiple citations to similar kinds of items. The result is a bibliography that, in the pursuit of utility, excludes many good items. I bear the responsibility for these trade-offs in selection, as well as for the annotations, all of which are my work and reflect my reading of the items in question.

Aguirre, Benigno E.
1976   Differential Migration of Cuban Social Races: A Review and Interpretation of the Problem. *Latin American Research Review* 11(1):103–124.
    Analysis of the factors leading to the predominantly white racial composition of those Cubans coming to the United States. The author reviews the existing data on the various waves of Cuban refugees and notes that although occupational levels have gradually fallen, racial homogeneity has increased. The explanation offered is that Afro-Americans are seen as "both a major bulwark of the revolution and one of its main beneficiaries." The tendency for black Cubans in the United States to have a distinctive geographical distribution is also mentioned. 22 pages.

American Council for Nationalities Service
Biweekly *Refugee Reports* (20 West 40th St., New York, NY 10018)
    Biweekly newsletter on current developments regarding refugees and the refugee program. The newsletter focuses on the U.S. refugee program and is probably the best single source for an updated knowledge of legislation, policy, and program directions. Lead articles are followed by program update, resource, and statistics sections.

Arden, Harvey
1981   The Wanderers from Vung Tau: Troubled Odyssey of Vietnamese Fishermen. *National Geographic* 160(3):378–395.
Review of the experiences of a small community of Vietnamese in Biloxi, Mississippi. Arden notes the hard work that has gone into their efforts at fishing in the United States, and the community tensions resulting from cultural differences and economic competition over somewhat limited resources. The cohesiveness of these families over time—many moved south from North Vietnam together in 1954—and their ability to generate capital for boat building are particularly noteworthy.

Ashmun, Lawrence F.
1983   *Resettlement of Indochinese Refugees in the United States: A Selective and Annotated Bibliography*. DeKalb: Northern Illinois University, Center for Southeast Asian Studies. (Exclusive distribution by the Cellar Book Shop, 18090 Wyoming, Detroit, MI 48221)
Bibliography through 1981 on Southeast Asian refugees, including books, dissertations, articles (journals, magazines), program documents, and miscellaneous papers. Ashmun incorporates and adds to a variety of existing bibliographies to produce a useful compendium. Indices and relevant (ERIC, DAI, etc.) order numbers are included. 207 pages—1,037 entries.

Bach, Robert L., and Jennifer B. Bach
1980   Employment Patterns of Southeast Asian Refugees. *Monthly Labor Review* 103(10):31–38.
Analysis of Southeast Asian refugee employment in the United States based on the Immigration and Naturalization Service Alien Address Report and Opportunity Systems Incorporated surveys. Bach and Bach note that refugee labor force participation rates are lower than those for the U.S. population as a whole but rise consistently with length of residence in the United States. Data also indicate that refugees consistently work more hours per week than the general U.S. population but still, in many cases, have marginal earnings.

Balaran, Paul, Diana L. Morris, and Patricia K. Biggers
1983   *Refugees and Migrants: Problems and Program Responses*. New York: The Ford Foundation. (Office of Reports, Ford Foundation, 320 E. 43rd St., New York, NY 10017)
Working paper representing a consensus view of several divisions within the Ford Foundation involved with the causes and effects of international migration both to the United States and to other countries. The first half of the report coherently summarizes the various aspects (domestic, international, economic, institutional, legal, etc.) of refugee and other migrant movements; the second half describes the Foundation's current and future grant activity in the area. The report is of particular interest because of the Ford Foundation's involvement and influence regarding refugee issues. 64 pages.

Barger, W. K., and Tham V. Truong
1978   Community Action Work Among the Vietnamese. *Human Organization* 37(1):95–100.
Overview of the constraints and options of community action work based on experience

with a Vietnamese association in Lexington, Kentucky. The authors were involved in facilitating the incorporation of the association and the establishment of a small model business. They recommend the following as basic elements in such work: (1) establishing communication and mutual respect, (2) identifying areas of mutual involvement, (3) negotiating roles, (4) identifying goals with emphasis on the community's explicit interests, and (5) assessing the nature of the community.

Baron, Roy C., Stephen B. Thacker, Leo Gorelkin, Andrew A. Vernon, William R. Taylor, and Keewhan Choi
1983   Sudden Death Among Southeast Asian Refugees: An Unexplained Nocturnal Phenomenon. *Journal of the American Medical Association* 250(21):2947–2951.
    Review of the sudden unexplained deaths of fifty-one Southeast Asian refugees from 1977 to 1982. A variety of case-study material, results from questionnaires, and autopsy findings are adduced to determine the causes of these sudden nocturnal deaths, almost universally of males and disproportionately common among Laotians. No clear explanation emerges, although stress is suggested as a significant factor.

Bender, Lynn Darrell
1973   The Cuban Exiles: An Analytical Sketch. *Journal of Latin American Studies* 5:271–278
    Brief analysis of the Cuban refugee flow largely in terms of the factors affecting the departure decision. "Without question, Cuba's most successful 'export' from the very beginning of the Castro period has not been revolution, but the physical removal of its domestic enemies." Bender notes the generally upper-class origins of most refugees and their decreasing involvement in formal political opposition to Castro. A brief description of the different periods of Cuban emigration is also presented.

Boone, Margaret S.
1980   The Uses of Traditional Concepts in the Development of New Urban Roles: Cuban Women in the United States. In *A World of Women: Anthropological Studies of Women in the Societies of the World.* Edited by Erika Bourguignon. New York: Praeger. Pages 235–269.
    Analysis of the changing roles of Cuban immigrant women in the United States, based largely on the author's fieldwork in the Washington, D.C., area. The author notes the traditional schism between male and female roles in Cuba, but also the significant equality and importance of women in some public domains. In the United States, Cuban women have maintained a semblance of ideal traditional roles. They have also participated actively and effectively in the world of work. The major portion of the article involves a description of various women's roles, both formal and informal.

Boone, Margaret S., Editor
1981   *Metropolitan Ethnography in the Nation's Capital.* Special issue of *Anthropological Quarterly* 54(2).
    Set of seven articles (plus editor's introduction) on different ethnic groups in the Washington, D.C., area. Separate articles deal with Vietnamese (Haines, Rutherford, and Thomas), Cubans (Boone), and Hungarians (Schuchat), as well as Sephardic Jews, Palestinians, Armenians, and Serbs. Together, the articles are particularly useful in dealing

with the maintenance of dispersed ethnic communities and with the unique effects of the nation's capital on immigrant and refugee adjustment. 55 pages.

Brodsky, Betty
1982   Social Work and the Soviet Immigrant. *Migration Today* 10(1):15–20.
   Review of the role of the social worker as it applies to relationships with recent Soviet refugees. In reviewing key aspects of the refugees' cultural and social background, Brodsky argues for (1) greater informality in the social worker's relationship with the client, (2) fuller attention to the importance of the extended family to the Soviet client, and (3) expanded emphasis on providing the client with practical help in adjusting to American society. The description of the divide between public and private life in Russia is particularly cogent.

Burton, Eve
1983   Surviving the Flight of Horror: The Story of Refugee Women. *Indochina Issues*
         No. 34. (Center for International Policy, 120 Maryland Ave. NE, Washington,
         DC 20002)
   Account of the hazards faced by Vietnamese refugees whose boats are prey to the attacks of Thai pirates. Based on her work with refugee women, Burton relates not only the rape and abuse experienced by these women, but also the long-lasting effects on them, effects that mar their subsequent adjustment to the United States, undermine their possibilities for happiness, and may keep them isolated from their ethnic communities. 7 pages.

Casal, Lourdes, and Andres R. Hernandez
1975   Cubans in the U.S.: A Survey of the Literature. *Cuban Studies* 5:25–51.
   Review of the existing literature on Cubans in the United States through 1974. The discussion is organized in terms of the following twelve topics: (1) causes of the migration, (2) demographic composition, (3) exiles as sources of information about Cuban society, (4) assimilation and acculturation, (5) political behavior and attitudes, (6) family and sex roles, (7) mental health, (8) occupational adjustment, (9) youth problems, (10) special "at risk" groups (such as the black and the elderly), (11) relationships with other ethnic groups, and (12) impact of the Cubans on U.S. society. A short annotated bibliography is included.

Catanzaro, Antonino, and Robert J. Moser
1982   Health Status of Refugees from Vietnam, Laos, and Cambodia. *Journal of the
         American Medical Association* 247(9):1303–1308.
   Report of results from medical evaluations of 709 Southeast Asian refugees in San Diego. Screenings, all conducted within two months of arrival, indicated a variety of medical problems, including anemia, hepatitis, and intestinal parasites. The authors present findings separately for Vietnamese, Cambodians, Hmong, and Laotians and stress the considerable variation in the health problems faced by all of these groups.

Cooney, Rosemary Santana, and Maria Alina Contreras
1978   Residence Patterns of Social Register Cubans: A Study of Miami, San Juan,
         and New York SMSAs. *Cuban Studies* 8(2):33–49.
   Examination of the residential patterns of middle- and upper-middle-class Cubans in

three urban areas, based on data from the Cuban Social Register (1974) and the U.S. census. Cubans are most segregated by class in San Juan and least segregated in New York, with Miami falling in between. In all three cities, social register Cubans "live in high quality neighborhoods differing from other upper-middle-class areas only in terms of ethnic exclusivity." The high degree of residential clustering of upper-class Cubans in San Juan is attributed by the authors to the homogeneity of the original migrant stream to Puerto Rico.

Downing, Bruce T., and Douglas P. Olney, Editors
1982   *The Hmong in the West: Observations and Reports.* University of Minnesota, Southeast Asian Refugee Studies Project. (Center for Urban and Regional Affairs, 313 Walter Library, 117 Pleasant St. SE, University of Minnesota, Minneapolis MN 55455)

Collection of twenty papers originally presented at a research conference on the Hmong held in 1981. The conference was the first of its kind in the United States, and the papers, although varying in topic and method, represent an important advance in research on this refugee population. A keynote historical review by Yang Dao is followed by separate sections on cultural continuities and changes, Hmong language and communication, issues in Hmong learning of Western languages, and resettlement problems and prospects in the United States. 401 pages.

Dunning, Bruce B., and Joshua Greenbaum
1982   *Survey of the Social, Psychological, and Economic Adaptation of Vietnamese Refugees in the U.S., 1975-79.* Washington, D.C.: U.S. Department of Health and Human Services. (Social Security Administration, Office of Policy, Office of Research and Statistics. Report identification: SSA Publication No. 13-11755, December 1982)

Executive summary of a far longer report on a survey of 555 Vietnamese refugees living in the Los Angeles, Houston, and New Orleans areas. An overview of the study itself is followed by summaries of the refugees' backgrounds, their economic adjustment to the United States, their social/cultural adjustment, and their perception and use of services. This is an important data set, particularly strong in its inclusion of attitudinal and social information and in its equal representation of the five yearly entry cohorts from 1975 to 1979. 43 pages.

Eckels, Timothy J., Lawrence S. Lewin, David S. North, and Danguole J. Spakevicius
1982   *A Portrait in Diversity: Voluntary Agencies and the Office of Refugee Resettlement Matching Grant Program.* Washington, D.C.: Lewin and Associates. (Lewin and Associates, 1090 Vermont Ave. NW, Washington, D.C. 20005)

Final report of a study of the Matching Grant Program conducted under contract to the federal government. The program involves a match of up to $1,000 for each refugee served by participating voluntary agencies; the match is calculated on a dollar-for-dollar basis. The report describes the operation of the program and, in particular, the variations in the way different agencies use the program. Those served through the program include Soviet Jews, Armenians, Poles, Rumanians, Afghans, and Ethiopians. 125 pages.

Edelman, Joseph
1977   Soviet Jews in the United States: A Profile. In *American Jewish Yearbook, 1977*. Edited by Morris Fine and Milton Himmelfarb. New York: The American Jewish Committee.
Useful overview of the Soviet refugees who had come to the United States through the end of 1975. The author covers the following areas: general migration patterns; the problem of dropouts (*noshrim*); places of origin in the Soviet Union; age and sex distribution; geographical distribution in the United States; problems in adjustment and integration; job placement (with emphasis on the problems of professionals); and the current stress on the issue of Jewish identification.

Erickson, Roy V., and Giao Hoang
1980   Health Problems Among Indochinese Refugees. *American Journal of Public Health* 70(9):1003–1006.
Report on the findings from 194 medical evaluations of Indochinese refugees seen at the University of Connecticut between June 1979 and January 1980. The prevalences of intestinal parasites, tuberculosis, tuberculin skin test positivity, hepatitis B carrier state, and other infectious diseases were similar to those noted in a variety of previous studies. However, significant levels of hematologic, dermatologic, psychiatric, and endocrine abnormalities were also detected.

Fagan, Richard R., Richard A. Brody, and Thomas J. O'Leary
1968   *Cubans in Exile: Disaffection and the Revolution*. Stanford, California: Stanford University Press.
Analysis of the factors leading to exodus from Cuba, with emphasis on the period from 1959 to 1962. The findings are based on 209 self-administered questionnaires and some cross-correlations with the files of the Cuban Refugee Center in Florida. Different chapters deal with the following areas: (1) demographic characteristics, including comparison with the general Cuban population; (2) attitudes toward the revolution; (3) levels of political participation before, during, and after the revolution; and (4) analysis of the individual reasons for exile. The book emphasizes the exodus for what it implies about the Cuban revolution. 120 pages of text, plus appendices.

Feingold, Henry
1978   Soviet Jewish Survival, American Jewish Power. *Midstream* 24(2):11–22.
Analysis of the historical similarities and connections between Soviet and American Jewry. Feingold notes that both American and Soviet Jews have been caught up in a process of secularization and assimilation into a wider society, although in the Soviet Union, these processes have had a more forced nature. In regard to recent Soviet Jewish emigration, the major conclusion is that the prime reason for emigration is the perceived decline in future upward mobility, rather than any actual restriction in current activities.

Feldman, William
1977   Social Absorption of Soviet Immigrants: Integration or Isolation. *Journal of Jewish Communal Service* 54(1):62–68.
Review of the social integration of Soviet Jews in Cleveland, Ohio, based on a survey of 148 families drawn from the caseload of the Jewish Family Service Association. In general, the émigrés have adjusted well, with rapid rises in English language competence

and income levels. A continuing residential concentration in the heavily Jewish neighborhood of Cleveland Heights is notable, as in general increase in Jewish religious activities. Feldman concludes that the Soviet Jews are relatively satisfied with their new life and actively desire to be part of the American Jewish community.

Ferree, Myra Marx
1979   Employment Without Liberation: Cuban Women in the United States. *Social Science Quarterly* 60:35–50.

Analysis of labor force participation and domestic roles of Cuban women in the Miami area. The research included interviews with 122 Cuban-born women selected through random sampling of telephone listings of Spanish surnames. The importance of female labor participation for the level of household income is noted, but the major conclusion is that this extensive participation by Cuban women in the labor force is not in conflict with the maintenance of their traditional domestic roles in the home.

Finnan, Christine R., and Rhonda Ann Cooperstein
1983   *Southeast Asian Refugee Resettlement at the Local Level: The Role of the Ethnic Community and the Nature of Refugee Impact.* Menlo Park, California: SRI International. (333 Ravenswood Ave., CA 94025)

Final report of a two-part study conducted under contract to the federal government. Part I examines the structure and function of refugee communities, including the importance of kinship groups, informal social networks, and formal organizations, and the variety of tangible and intangible supports provided through such social relations. Part II examines the nature and dimensions of the effects that refugees have on the localities in which they settle, including such topics as housing, employment, public assistance, and education. The report is based both on secondary analysis and on field research in five counties across the United States. 259 pages.

Gitelman, Zvi
1978   Soviet Immigrants and American Absorption Efforts: A Case Study in Detroit. *Journal of Jewish Communal Service* 55(1):72–82.

Review of the adjustment of Soviet Jews, based in part on interviews with a random sample of 132 refugees in Detroit. Gitelman stresses the need to understand the differing backgrounds of Soviet Jews, particularly the distinction between "Westerners" and "heartlanders." Major findings from the survey are (1) high levels of general satisfaction with life in the United States, (2) positive economic expectations for the future, (3) disappointment with the isolation and lack of sociability among Americans, (4) concern about crime, and (5) ambivalence about the level of social freedom in the United States.

Goldstein, Edgar
1979   Psychological Adaptations of Soviet Immigrants. *American Journal of Psychoanalysis* 39(3):257–263.

Informal overview of psychological problems faced by Soviet refugees, written by a former Soviet psychiatrist. Particular problems noted are (1) the "totalitarian state" that the refugee carries within himself; (2) an unclear sense of ethnic and religious identity; (3) the great loss of status as an immigrant in the United States; (4) a letdown as refugees realize that they are less important to the United States than they had expected; and (5) a strong tendency to deny psychological problems.

Grant, Bruce, Michael Richardson, et al.
1979   *The Boat People: An "Age" Investigation.* New York: Penguin Books.
    Review of the dramatic exodus by sea of refugees from Vietnam in the late 1970s.
The book is an admirably written and compelling narrative based on the reports of
correspondents for the Australian newspaper, the *Age.* It is particularly useful in sorting
out the different flows by time (1976-79), by cause (e.g., the increasingly anti-Chinese
stance of the Vietnamese government), and by route (e.g., the flows east and north from
northern Vietnam versus those south and west from southern Vietnam). 225 pages.

Harding, Richard K., and John G. Looney
1977   Problems of Southeast Asian Children in a Refugee Camp. *American Journal
         of Psychiatry* 134(4):407–411.
    Description of the efforts made to meet the mental health needs of Vietnamese children
at Camp Pendleton in 1975. The authors found that children generally received strong
emotional support from their multigenerational Vietnamese families and adapted well to
their new surroundings. However, children separated from their families demonstrated
emotional vulnerability, and their foster placement as unaccompanied minors presented
serious problems. Some of these problems stemmed from the sponsoring process that
removed these children from families to which they were attached in an informal way.

Howell, David R., Editor
1982   *Southeast Asian Refugees in the U.S.A.: Case Studies of Adjustment and Policy
         Implications.* Special issue of *Anthropological Quarterly* 55(3).
    Series of five articles by anthropologists, with an introduction by the editor about the
role of anthropology in refugee resettlement and public policy. Articles deal with segmentary kinship among the Hmong in Minnesota (Dunnigan), refugees in the fishing
industry in California (Orbach and Beckwith), ethnic solidarity among the Hmong in
California (Scott), community influences on the occupational adaptation of Vietnamese
refugees (Finnan), and the overall interactions of refugee kinship and American public
policy (Haines). 62 pages.

Huyck, Earl E., and Leon F. Bouvier
1983   The Demography of Refugees. *Annals of the American Academy of Political
         and Social Sciences* 467(May):39–61.
    Overview of the size, source, destination, and causes of current refugee movements.
Acknowledging distinctions among political, environmental, and economic refugees, the
authors review the world situation by region: Africa, the Middle East, Europe, Latin
America, and Indochina. The article concludes with a consideration of future trends in
refugee movements. Most data derive from the USCR's World Refugee Surveys (see
separate citation) of 1981 and 1982.

Jacobson, Gaynor I., et al.
1979   A Symposium on the Soviet Immigrant. *Journal of Jewish Communal Service*
         56(1):50–76.
    Set of papers on Soviet refugees delivered at the annual meeting of the Conference of
Jewish Communal Services in Toronto, 1979. The following papers are included: "Today's Jewish Immigrant" (Jacobson), "Impact of Soviet-Jewish Culture on the Problem-
Solving Process" (Dorf), "New Culture Learning in the Day-Care Center" (Jacobs),

"How the Center Helps Russian Jews" (Schrag), "Soviet Jewish Resettlement in the Small Community: Working with Volunteers" (Bienstock), "Resettlement of Soviet Jews in Toronto" (Gold), "Prenatal Group for Soviet Immigrants" (Cunningham and Dorf).

Justus, Joyce Bennett
1976   Processing Indochinese Refugees. In *Exploratory Fieldwork on Latino Migrants and Indochinese Refugees*. Edited by Roy S. Bryce-Laporte and Stephen R. Couch. Washington, D.C.: Smithsonian, pp. 76–100.

Report on exploratory fieldwork carried out at Camp Pendleton in 1975. The research included both interviews and participant observation. Specific findings include the overreporting of previous occupation (particularly unnerving, considering the importance placed in most research on the occupational background of refugees), misunderstanding of the resettlement process, and strong desires for secrecy. This work is invaluable in delineating the divergence between the perceptions of the refugees and those of camp management.

Kelly, Gail Paradise
1977   *From Vietnam to America: A Chronicle of the Vietnamese Immigration to the United States*. Boulder, Colorado: Westview Press.

Review of the initial Vietnamese refugee exodus of 1975. The book is based on written documents and on the author's interviews conducted at Fort Indiantown Gap. The first part of the book is a compelling account of the exodus, including a description of the types of people who were able to get out of Vietnam. The second part concerns the camp experiences of the refugees, with emphasis on the areas of education and cultural orientation. The third section describes the initial adjustment of the refugees after being sponsored out of the camps. Although Kelly has been criticized for her thesis that the United States tried to force the refugees into being ordinary immigrants, events since 1975 suggest that she may be more correct than it appeared at that time. 254 pages.

Kinzie, J. David, Kiet Anh Tran, Agatha Breckenridge, and Joseph Bloom
1980   An Indochinese Refugee Psychiatric Clinic: Culturally Accepted Treatment Approaches. *American Journal of Psychiatry* 137(11):1429–1432.

Report on the evaluation and treatment of fifty Indochinese patients at a clinic established by the authors in 1978 in Portland, Oregon. Most of the patients seen at the beginning of the program were psychotic and severely impaired. However, later patients suffered from a wider variety of problems. A flexible approach to treatment was adopted that would be compatible with the cultural expectations of the refugees. One of the results was an emphasis on the medical approach of the physician. The process by which the clinic gained acceptance in the community is also discussed.

Knoll, Tricia
1982   *Becoming Americans: Asian Sojourners, Immigrants, and Refugees in the Western United States*. Portland, Oregon: Coast to Coast Books.

Informal textbook approach to the causes, processes, and consequences of Asian immigration into the western United States from 1848 to the present. The book is split about evenly between earlier immigrants and more recent refugees. Separate chapters deal with the Chinese, Japanese, Filipinos, Koreans, Vietnamese, Laotians, Cambodians, and overseas Chinese (from Southeast Asia). Knoll emphasizes the personal stories of the immigrants, rather than more aggregate or abstract research. The book is well written and well balanced. 350 pages, with maps, chronologies, and photographs.

Kogan, Deborah, Patricia Jenny, Mary Vencill, and Lois Greenwood
1982   *Study of the State Administration of the Refugee Resettlement Program: Final Report.* Berkeley, California: Berkeley Planning Associates. (3200 Adeline St., Berkeley, CA 94703)

Final report of a study conducted under contract to the federal government. Based on field visits to nine selected states, the authors describe and analyze the influence of the general state context on the refugee program, the structure of the program within the overall state government, the design of the program, issues of coordination at the state and local levels, and the ways in which accountability is maintained within the program. A concluding chapter presents suggested standards for examining the management of the program and a set of key program issues. The resulting portrayal of the refugee program is balanced, thoughtful, and sometimes provocative. 166 pages.

Kritz, Mary M., Editor
1983   *U.S. Immigration and Refugee Policy: Global and Domestic Issues.* Lexington, Massachusetts: Lexington Books (D. C. Heath and Company).

Series of articles originally presented at two conferences in 1981. Separate parts deal with the international context, global refugee problems, domestic impacts in the United States, Caribbean migration, pluralism in the United States, and general conceptual and policy issues. There is an introduction by the editor and a foreword by Victor Palmieri, former U.S. coordinator for refugee affairs. 415 pages.

Kunz, E. F.
1973   The Refugee in Flight: Kinetic Models and Forms of Displacement. *International Migration Review* 7(2):125–146.

Uniquely influential article on refugee flight and transit. Kunz's basic contention is that the kinds of dynamics (''kinetics'') through which the refugee moves from country-of-origin to eventual resettlement in themselves condition various ultimate refugee outcomes. His distinction between anticipatory and acute refugee movements, his analysis of ''vintages'' and forms of displacement, and his general emphasis on the need for comparative work on different refugee flows are all widely echoed in the literature on refugees.

Lin, Keh-Ming, Laurie Tazuma, and Minoru Masuda
1979   Adaptational Problems of Vietnamese Refugees: Health and Mental Health Status. *Archives of General Psychiatry* 36:955–961.

Report on approximately 300 interviews conducted with Vietnamese refugees in Seattle, Washington. Based on separate administrations of the Cornell Medical Index in 1975 and 1976, the authors note high and continuing levels of physical and mental dysfunction. There were also shifts between 1975 and 1976, specifically an increase in anger and hostility, but a decrease in feelings of inadequacy.

Liu, William T., Maryanne Lamanna, and Alice Murata
1979   *Transition to Nowhere: Vietnamese Refugees in America.* Nashville, Tennessee: Charter House.

General description of the 1975 Vietnamese refugees from the time of departure to initial sponsorship and resettlement in the United States. The research was conducted at Camp Pendleton, with an emphasis on mental health problems, and included the use of various standardized protocols, such as the Cornell Medical Index. The authors also cover the general demographics of the refugee population, American public reactions, and the special problems of unaccompanied children. 214 pages.

Marsh, Robert E.
1980   Socioeconomic Status of Indochinese Refugees in the United States: Progress and Problems. *Social Security Bulletin* 43(10):11–20.

Review of existing data on employment, income, and receipt of public assistance by Indochinese refugees in the United States. The article is largely based on the first six surveys conducted by Opportunity Systems Incorporated but also includes a section on OASDHI-covered earnings written by Harold Grossman. In general, the early refugees showed significant improvement in employment and earnings levels by the end of 1978. Marsh suggests that more recent refugees are likely to face more difficulties because of their lower educational and occupational background.

Masuda, Minoru, Keh-Ming Lin, and Laurie Tazuma
1980   Adaptation Problems of Vietnamese Refugees: Life Changes and Perceptions of Life Events. *Archives of General Psychiatry* 37:447–450.

Analysis of the coping and adaptation problems of Vietnamese refugees in Seattle, Washington. Data derive from about 300 interviews conducted during 1975 and 1976, with an emphasis on the Social Readjustment Rating Questionnaire (SRRQ). Results indicate a high level of life changes during the evacuation year of 1975 but also indicate continuing high levels of change during 1976. In particular, problems associated with work, finances, life-style, marriage, and school continued to adversely affect the refugees and, in fact, increased during 1976.

Mattson, Roger A., and Dang Dinh Ky
1978   Vietnamese Refugee Care: Psychiatric Observations. *Minnesota Medicine* 61(1):33–36.

General observations on the situation of Vietnamese refugees during their brief stay on Wake Island in 1975. Authors note the age distribution, class structure, large family groups, and general good health of the refugees. Relatively few adjustment problems appeared. Of those that did occur, the following were the major ones: (1) problems with the high protein and fat in the American diet; (2) frequent psychosomatic complaints, such as headaches, stomach pain, and insomnia; and (3) some anxiety during the ultimate move away from Wake.

Mesa-Lago, Carmelo, and June S. Belkin
1982   The Cuban Exodus: A Symposium. Special combined issue of *Cuban Studies* 11(2) and 12(1).

Series of four articles, with separate comment sections, on the Cuban exodus to the United States. The articles address (1) the incorporation into the United States of 1970s arrrivals (Portes, Clark, and Lopez); (2) the Cuban entrants of 1980 (Bach, Bach, and Triplett); (3) the political structure of the Cuban community in the United States (Azicri); and (4) a comparison of Cubans and Mexicans in the United States (Bailey). Comments on the articles are provided by E. Rogg, G. Fernandez, E. Baloyra, and L. Perez. 103 pages.

Montero, Darrel
1979   *Vietnamese Americans: Patterns of Resettlement and Socioeconomic Adaptation in the United States*. Boulder, Colorado: Westview Press.

General description of the demographic characteristics of the early Vietnamese refugees and their adjustment to the United States through 1977, based largely on the first five surveys conducted by Opportunity Systems Incorporated under contract to the federal government and provided to interested researchers. A general model of what the author terms "spontaneous international migration" is also presented. 72 pages of text, plus front matter and appendices.

Muecke, Marjorie A.
1983   Caring for Southeast Asian Refugees in the USA. *American Journal of Public Health* 73(4):431–438.

Overview of key problems medical practitioners are likely to face when treating refugees from Cambodia, Laos, and Vietnam. After providing brief cultural backgrounds, Muecke (lucidly) explains and "demystifies" typical practitioner problems, including (1) essentials of etiquette in initial patient contacts, (2) use of interpreters, (3) gaining patient consent, (4) reasons for client unresponsiveness, (5) cultural restraints, (6) social supports, and (7) traditional attitudes toward healing.

Nicassio, Perry M.
1983   Psychosocial Correlates of Alienation: Study of a Sample of Indochinese Refugees. *Journal of Cross-Cultural Psychology* 14:337–351.

Assessment of Southeast Asian refugee alienation based on interviews with 460 heads of household in Illinois in 1979. The sample included, and separate analyses were conducted for, Vietnamese, Cambodians, Hmong, and Lao. Overall, Lao and Vietnamese tended to be less alienated than Hmong and Cambodians. However, the key correlates of alienation appeared to be lack of economic progress, low English proficiency, and a great self-perceived difference from nonrefugee Americans.

North, David S., Lawrence S. Lewin, and Jennifer R. Wagner
1982   *Kaleidoscope: The Resettlement of Refugees in the U.S. by the Voluntary Agencies*. Washington, D.C.: New TransCentury Foundation. (New TransCentury Foundation, 1724 Kalorama Rd. NW, Washington, D.C. 20009)

Final report of a study conducted under contract to the federal government. An overview of the fifteen voluntary agencies involved in the resettlement of refugees is followed by separate chapters on the allocation process, structural and organizational issues, services provided to refugees, and refugee use of public assistance programs. Although sympathetic to the great variability among the voluntary agencies and their at least historical seniority in resettlement, the report generally favors more uniform and rationalized program operations and stronger government oversight. 139 pages.

Office of Refugee Resettlement
Annual *Report to the Congress: Refugee Resettlement Program*. Washington, D.C.: U.S. Department of Health and Human Services. (Office of Refugee Resettlement, 330 C St. SW, Washington, D.C. 20201)

Annual report to the Congress on the operations, accomplishments, and goals of the refugee program during the preceding fiscal year. The reports typically include reviews of the overall program, with emphasis on domestic assistance. Particularly useful are sections on refugee population characteristics and economic adjustment. Extensive appendices include tables on arrival rates, nationality, state of destination, etc.; reports from other public and private agencies; and a list of state refugee coordinators.

Office of the U.S. Coordinator for Refugee Affairs
Annual   *Report to the Congress: Proposed Refugee Admissions and Allocations.* Washington, D.C.: U.S. Department of State. (Office of the U.S. Coordinator for Refugee Affairs, Department of State, Washington, D.C. 20520)
Annual report to the Congress on proposed admissions of refugees for the coming fiscal year. The report is submitted to Congress late in the summer and is the basis for the legislatively required consultations between the administration and Congress regarding the number of refugees to be allowed entry. The report reviews the program for the preceding year (both domestic and overseas aspects) and outlines admissions by region. About 70 pages.

Portes, Alejandro
1969   Dilemmas of a Golden Exile: Integration of Cuban Refugee Families in Milwaukee. *American Sociological Review* 34:505–518.
Classic article about the integration of Cuban families in Milwaukee, based on forty-eight in-depth interviews conducted jointly with husbands and wives. Portes's general hypothesis is that the level of integration is a function of the rewards available from current socioeconomic status. The correlation between economic rewards and level of integration is described as a result of the rational-individualistic ethic of those Cubans who came to the United States.

Portes, Alejandro, and Robert L. Bach
1980   Immigrant Earnings: Cuban and Mexican Immigrants in the United States. *International Migration Review* 14(3):315–341.
Analysis of the determinants of earnings among recent Cuban and Mexican immigrants. The study is based on interviews with 427 Cubans and 439 Mexicans at the moment of arrival and three years later. The authors examine the applicability of dual labor market theory to the results of their multivariate analysis and find the results confirm the importance of structural features of the labor market in predicting income levels. For the Cubans, however, ethnic businesses appear to blur the differences beetween the primary and secondary labor markets.

Portes, Alejandro, Samual A. McLeod, and Robert N. Parker
1978   Immigrant Aspirations. *Sociology of Education* 51(4):241–260.
Analysis of the nature and determinants of occupational, income, and educational aspirations among Cuban and Mexican immigrants to the United States. The article is based on interviews with 822 Mexican and 590 Cuban immigrants at their places of arrival in 1973-74. Aspirations of these immigrants are compared with the actual attainments of Americans of similar ethnic origin and are found to be modest and realistic. The results of multivariate analysis suggest that aspirations are set through a rational assessment of past attainments and skills.

Rahe, Richard H., John G. Looney, Harold W. Ward, Tran Minh Tung, and William
T. Liu
1978   Psychiatric Consultation in a Vietnamese Refugee Camp. *American Journal of
          Psychiatry* 135(2):185–190.
Review of the authors' experience providing psychiatric consultation at Camp Pendleton
during 1975. Their major recommendations as a consulting team were related to the stage
of camp development: Early recommendations concerned easing adaptation to the camp
setting; later efforts included creating a psychiatric crisis clinic and carrying out a mental
health survey (CMI, RLCQ) with a random sample of refugees. Many of their recommendations were successfully implemented, but the authors do note problems in ade-
quately identifying the camp's structure and particularly in resolving the problems facing
unaccompanied minors.

Rogg, Eleanor Meyer
1974   *The Assimilation of Cuban Exiles: The Role of Community and Class.* New
          York: Aberdeen Press.
Influential description and analysis of research conducted on Cuban refugees during
1967-68 in the New York City area. The research was conducted under funding from
the Department of Labor and included interviews with 250 randomly selected Cubans in
the high-density Cuban area of West New York, New Jersey. Rogg focuses on the
relationships between adjustment and the presence of a strong ethnic community, and
between adjustment and occupational and class backgrounds in Cuba. Other areas covered
include the restructuring of family relations, ethnic relations, and intergenerational conflicts. 241 pages.

Rubin, Burton S.
1975   The Soviet Refugee: Challenge to the American Jewish Community Resettle-
          ment System. *Journal of Jewish Communal Service* 52(2):195–201.
Reflective article on Jewish communal services and their appropriateness to Soviet
refugees. Rubin reviews the misfits between the values and behavior of the service agencies
and the attitudes and experiences of Soviet Jews. He concludes that it ''seems abundantly
clear that our ability to adapt and redefine our social services, as well as our attitudes,
are as vital and important for the successful immigration of the Soviet Jew as is his own
ability to adapt and modify his value system to our own cultural milieu.''

Rumbaut, Ruben D., and Ruben G. Rumbaut
1976   The Family in Exile: Cuban Expatriates in the United States. *American Journal
          of Psychiatry* 133(4):395–399.
Frequently cited overview of the adjustment of Cubans in the United States, with
emphasis on the interplay between uprootedness and the opportunity for new accomplishments. The authors note the following factors in explaining the relative success of Cuban
adjustment: (1) high occupational and educational levels, (2) formation of vigorous ethnic
communities and the support they furnish in maintaining a positive ethnic identification,
and (3) an effectively organized reception by the United States.

Salter, Paul S., and Robert C. Mings
1972   The Projected Impact of Cuban Settlement on Voting Patterns in Metropolitan
          Miami, Florida. *Professional Geographer* 24(2):123–131.

Analysis of the current and projected impact of Cubans on the political system in Miami. The article is based on voting patterns, estimated ethnic concentrations, and a street corner survey of 502 Cubans. The results indicate that Cubans "will have a strong tendency to support candidates who take a strong anti-communist position, particularly in international affairs, and who in general express conservative ideals." Salter and Mings's contention that Cuban voters would turn Miami from a traditional Democratic stronghold to a source of conservative strength has been at least partially borne out by subsequent events.

Shaw, Robert, Jr.
1977   Preventive Medicine in the Vietnamese Refugee Camps on Guam. *Military Medicine* 142(1):19–28.
Review of the health situation in, and general management of, the refugee camps on Guam in 1975. Major medical-related problems included water supply, food, waste disposal, insect and rodent control, and disease surveillance and control; major refugee complaints were conjunctivitis, upper respiratory tract infections, diarrhea, skin problems, gastroenteritis, and other relatively mild problems. Shaw also reviews camp management and suggests areas in which improvements could be made, such as communication, understanding of cultural differences, and recreation.

Simon, Rita J.
1983   Refugee Families' Adjustment and Aspirations: A Comparison of Soviet Jewish and Vietnamese Immigrants. *Ethnic and Racial Studies* 6(4):492-504.
Comparison of Soviet and Vietnamese refugees, based on interviews of parent/adolescent-child pairs in Chicago. Because Southeast Asian and Soviet refugees are rarely the subjects of a single research effort, Simon's findings of differences (particularly in economic adjustment) and similarities (e.g., parental expectations for the children) are particularly intriguing.

Skinner, Kenneth A., and Glenn L. Hendricks
1979   The Shaping of Ethnic Self-identity Among Indochinese Refugees. *Journal of Ethnic Studies* 7(3):25–41.
Analysis of the development of ethnic identity among Indochinese refugees, with emphasis on college students at the University of Minnesota. The refugee's major options for self-identification are as a refugee, as a member of a particular group (such as Vietnamese or Lao), or as an Asian-American. The authors note the different rewards for self-placement in each of these categories. Minnesota college students, for example, have access to considerable financial support as members of the Asian-American minority. Potential problems with other minorities are also discussed.

Special Service for Groups
1983   *Bridging Cultures: Southeast Asian Refugees in America: Social Work with Southeast Asian Refugees.* Los Angeles, California: Asian American Community Mental Health Training Center. (SSG, 1313 W. 8th St., #201, Los Angeles, CA 90017)
Reader on Southest Asian refugees designed to be part of an overall curriculum module that also includes a slideshow and videotape. Seventeen selections of varying quality deal with cultural background, general refugee program policy, community organization, and

social work experience with refugees. The volume is generally current to 1980, although some selections are limited to earlier years of the Southeast Asian refugee influx. 298 pages.

Starr, Paul D., and Alden E. Roberts
1982   Community Structure and Vietnamese Refugee Adaptation: The Significance of Context. *International Migration Review* 16(3):595–615.

Examination of the significance of the social context of the receiving community on the adjustment of Vietnamese refugees in the United States. The analysis is based on interviews with 350 refugees in 1978 in northern California and along the central Gulf Coast. Starr and Roberts argue, on the basis of statistical analysis, that although refugee background characteristics have important effects on adjustment, such features of the local community as employment opportunities, ethnic heterogeneity, and general educational level also have demonstrable effects.

Stein, Barry N.
1979   Occupational Adjustment of Refugees: The Vietnamese in the United States. *International Migration Review* 13(1):25–45.

Influential article on the occupational adjustment of Vietnamese refugees to the United States. Data on the refugees come largely from the first five Opportunity Systems Incorporated surveys funded by the federal government and cover the period from 1975 to mid-1977. Stein's emphasis is on downward occupational mobility, and he suggests that after four years in the United States refugees are likely to be close to their permanent economic status. The article benefits greatly from its attention to comparative information on other recent refugee groups.

Stein, Barry N., and Sylvano M. Tomasi
1981   Refugees Today. Special issue of *International Migration Review* 15(1–2).

Collection of thirty articles and documentary notes on various aspects of refugee exodus and resettlement, of which about a fourth bear on the recent resettlement of Southeast Asian refugees in the United States. The volume, the first effort of its kind in the United States, brings together the disparate perspectives of research, policy, and program operation, as well as a good range of comparative material from different countries. The contributions are organized into separate sections on policy, resettlement, and adjustment, with initial sections on more theoretical issues and a concluding and useful article by Stein on some likely parameters of the refugee experience as a field of study. 398 pages.

Szapocznik, Jose, Mercedes Arca Scopetta, Maria de los Angeles Aranalde, and William Kurtines
1978   Cuban Value Structure: Treatment Implications. *Journal of Consulting and Clinical Psychology* 46(5):961–970.

Examination of the relationship between cultural variables and psychological treatment models for Cubans in the Miami area. The article is based on clinical experience and on research with more than 500 Cuban and native-born American adolescents. By developing four factorially derived subscales, the authors demonstrate that Cuban immigrant adolescents tend to prefer hierarchical social relations, subjugation to nature, and actions phrased in the present tense. Anglo-Americans, on the other hand, prefer individuality, mastery over nature, and a future orientation. In discussing treatment models, the authors stress that the therapist must accept the importance of his or her authority and emphasize concrete objectives.

Taft, Ethel
1977   The Absorption of Soviet Jewish Immigrants—Their Impact on Jewish Communal Institutions. *Journal of Jewish Communal Service* 54(2):166–171.

Assessment of the effects of recent Soviet émigrés on the Jewish community in general and on Jewish social services in particular. Taft suggests that long-range effects will be limited because of the current institutional rigidity of American society and the lack among the émigrés of any strong Jewish involvement. However, there have been some discernible effects including increased cooperation between family and vocational services, expansion in the range of activities provided by Jewish centers, and redefinition of the role of clients in the formulation of social service policy.

Teitelbaum, Michael S.
1980   Right Versus Right: Immigration and Refugee Policy in the United States. *Foreign Affairs* 59:21–59.

Review of the policy implications and alternatives regarding immigration to the United States. Teitelbaum notes the rising level of immigration, the predominance of Spanish speakers, and the laxness of Immigration and Naturalization Service enforcement practices. He emphasizes the need for the development of a coherent policy that fulfills three conditions: (1) adequate expression of traditional American humanitarian values; (2) protection of the civil liberties and human rights of U.S. citizens and legal immigrants; and (3) actual enforceability. The effects of immigration on labor markets, fertility, and political consensus are stressed.

Tepper, Eliot L., Editor
1980   *Southeast Asian Exodus: From Tradition to Resettlement: Understanding Refugees from Laos, Kampuchea, and Vietnam in Canada.* Ottawa, Canada: The Canadian Asian Studies Association. (Distributed in the United States by the University of Chicago Press)

Collection of thirteen articles, plus an introduction by the editor. Part I includes separate background chapters on Vietnam, Cambodia, Laos, and the overseas Chinese; Part II provides additional contextual information on such topics as agricultural background and first-country asylum; Part III addresses issues of resettlement in Canada (policy, cultural factors, community relations, economic adjustment, and psychological problems). 230 pages.

Thernstrom, Stephan, Ann Orlov, and Oscar Handlin, Editors
1980   *Harvard Encyclopedia of Ethnic Groups.* Cambridge, Massachusetts: Harvard University Press (Belknap Press).

Extensive compilation of group descriptions and thematic essays on key issues in immigration. The selections vary in quality and approach, but the volume remains an important reference tool. Refugees, except for Cubans, are not well covered; Southeast Asian refugees, for example, are treated under the single entry of "Indochinese." The thematic essays—some useful overviews—are now being published separately. 1,076 pages.

Tillema, Richard G.
1981   Starting Over in a New Land: Resettling a Refugee Family. *Public Welfare*
            39(1):34–41.
Informal review of one congregation's experience in sponsoring a five-member Hmong
family who had already spent five years in a refugee camp in Southeast Asia. Tillema
describes initial health problems, cultural conflicts over medical practices, problems in
dealing with social service agencies, congregational resources, and educational issues.
Major recommendations involve the utility of explicit service plans and the need to
coordinate a wide variety of public and private resources.

United Nations High Commissioner for Refugees
Monthly *Refugees: News from the United Nations High Commissioner for Refugees.*
            (Public Information Section, UNHCR, Palais des Nations, CH-1211, Geneva
            10, Switzerland)
Newspaper-type periodical providing current information on refugees throughout the
world. This is a particularly valuable source not only because of its global coverage and
perspective, but also because of the UNHCR's broad definition of refugees and deep
involvement in asylum provision. *Refugees Magazine* is provided as a supplement to this
newspaper.

U.S. Committee for Refugees
Annual   *World Refugee Survey*. New York: American Council for Nationalities Service.
            (20 W. 40th St., New York, NY 10018)
Annual magazine-style publication on refugees throughout the world. Although the
format varies from year to year, the major portion is a series of articles on different
issues, ranging from general policy and program concerns to the specific situations of
particular refugee groups in countries of temporary and permanent asylum. Also included
are summaries of refugee statistics, useful publications, and relevant organizations. About
70 pages.

U.S. Department of State
Annual   *Report to the Congress: Country Reports on the World Refugee Situation.*
            Washington, D.C. (Bureau for Refugee Programs, Department of State, Wash-
            ington, D.C. 20520)
Companion volume to the annual report on *Proposed Refugee Admissions and Allocations* submitted to Congress by the Office of the U.S. Coordinator for Refugee Affairs.
Region by region and country by country, the report reviews current developments in
both sending and receiving countries. Based largely on information supplied by U.S.
diplomatic missions, the report sometimes gives a varying depth of information for
different countries but is nonetheless a useful source. About 125 pages.

U.S. General Accounting Office
1983   *Greater Emphasis on Early Employment and Better Monitoring Needed in
            Indochinese Refugee Resettlement Program*. Washington, D.C. (U.S. GAO,
            Document Handling and Information, P.O. Box 6015, Gaithersburg, MD 20760)
            Report identification: GAO/HRD-83-15, March 1, 1983.
Review of the refugee resettlement program conducted at the request of the House
Committee on the Judiciary. The report focuses on four major problem areas: (1) a family

reunification policy that has caused significant concentrations in few localities; (2) the great extent to which refugees are receiving public cash assistance; (3) an insufficient emphasis on rapid employment for refugees; and (4) the fragmented management of the program. 122 pages, of which more than half are devoted to public and private organizations' comments on the report itself.

U.S. General Accounting Office
1982   *Improved Overseas Medical Examinations and Treatment Can Reduce Serious Diseases in Indochinese Refugees Entering the United States.* Washington, D.C. (See 1983 entry for address.) Report identification: GAO/HRD-82-65, August 5, 1982.

Report on the incidences of serious diseases among Indochinese refugees and the existing or necessary procedures to identify and treat such diseases. The report suggests that serious diseases too frequently go undetected and untreated. GAO recommends the improvement of treatment overseas as the safest and most cost-effective solution to the problem. Most recommendations have now been implemented. 66 pages.

U.S. General Accounting Office
1979   *The Indochinese Exodus: A Humanitarian Dilemma.* Washington, D.C. (See 1983 entry for address.) Report identification: ID-79-20, April 24, 1979.

Particularly useful review of the Southeast Asian refugee situation, published during the tremendous boat exodus from Vietnam but before the considerable expansion in U.S. resettlement. Separate chapters discuss the growth of the refugee problem in Southeast Asia, the role of the international agencies, camp conditions in Southeast Asia, U.S. selection and processing of refugees, and the resettlement program in the United States. (A list of the four previous GAO reports on Southeast Asian refugees is given on p. 99.) 106 pages.

Vignes, A. Joe, and Richard C. W. Hall
1979   Adjustment of a Group of Vietnamese People to the United States. *American Journal of Psychiatry* 136(4):442–444.

Brief review of research conducted mainly with fifty newly resettled Vietnamese families in Baton Rouge, Louisiana. The major focus of the research was the construction of a social adjustment index, which was then tested for statistically significant correlations with age, religion, income, education, and marital status. The only significant relationship was with income. More generally, Vignes and Hall suggest that the Vietnamese are adjusting well, although they do echo other research that has found that previously high-status individuals face particular problems because of the extent of their downward mobility in the United States.

Wain, Barry
1979   The Indochina Refugee Crisis. *Foreign Affairs* 58(Fall):160–180.

Review of the Southeast Asian refugee problem from 1975 to 1979. Wain discusses the different waves of refugees (ethnic Vietnamese, ethnic Chinese, highland Lao minorities) and analyzes them in terms of Hanoi's foreign policy vis-à-vis the Soviet Union, China, and Southeast Asia. The major recommendation is for direct U.S. negotiations with the Vietnamese government, since it remains the most important instigator of the refugee flows.

Westermeyer, Joseph, Tou-Fu Vang, and John Neider
1984   Acculturation and Mental Health: A Study of Hmong Refugees at 1.5 and 3.5
        Years Postmigration. *Social Science and Medicine* 18(1):87–93.

Assessment of changes in Hmong refugee self-ratings, based on eighty-nine respondents interviewed initially in 1977 and reinterviewed in 1979. Although there were few social changes in their lives, there were distinct changes (improvements) in self-rating. There was a particularly significant reduction in depression (SLC-90 and Zung scales). Nevertheless, distress remained higher than that reported for other populations.

Wilson, Kenneth L., and Alejandro Portes
1980   Immigrant Enclaves: An Analysis of the Labor Market Experiences of Cubans
        in Miami. *American Journal of Sociology* 86(2):295–319.

Analysis of the mode of incorporation of Cuban émigrés into the U.S. labor market, based on 427 follow-up interviews conducted during 1976-77. The authors review classic theories of a unified economy, more recent theories of dual labor markets, and the growth of the Cuban enclave in Miami. Multivariate analysis confirms the distinction between primary and secondary labor markets but adds a third possibility—an enclave economy associated with immigrant-owned businesses. Enclave workers exhibit distinct characteristics, such as a higher utilization of previous occupational skills, than is typical in the secondary labor market.

Winsberg, Morton D.
1979   Housing Segregation of a Predominantly Middle Class Population: Residential
        Patterns Developed by the Cuban Immigration into Miami, 1950-74. *American
        Journal of Economics and Sociology* 38(4):403–418.

Statistical analysis of shifts in ethnic residential concentration in Miami from 1950 to 1974. Winsberg notes that although Cubans have assimilated economically, they have not assimilated residentially. Initial analysis of the data indicates the rapid expansion of Cubans throughout the city. The net effect, however, has been a significant rise in residential segregation involving not only Latins, but also blacks, Jews, and the elderly.

Index

Contributors

Robert L. Bach received the Ph.D. in Sociology from Duke University in 1978 and is currently Assistant Professor of Sociology at the State University of New York at Binghamton. He has written numerous articles on immigrant and ethnic groups in the U.S. labor market. He is coauthor of *Latin Journey: Mexican and Cuban Immigrants in the United States*, published by the University of California Press in 1984.

Susan Huelsebusch Buchanan received the Ph.D. in Anthropology from New York University. Her major area of research is migration, with particular emphasis on Haitian immigration to the United States. She has conducted a study for the federal government on recent Haitian entrants, and has authored a forthcoming book on Haitian immigrants in New York City. She works for the Cuban Haitian Resettlement Program of the Community Relations Service, U.S. Department of Justice.

Frederick J. Conway received the Ph.D. in Anthropology from the American University, where his major research focused on religious conversion and health practices in Haiti. In 1980 he served as an advisor to the Cuban-Haitian Task Force in Miami and as acting director of the Krome South camp for unaccompanied Haitian minors. Since that time he has been involved with the analysis of forestry projects in West Africa and served most recently as the coordinator of a large agroforestry project in Haiti.

Timothy Dunnigan received the Ph.D. from the University of Arizona in 1969, and is currently an Associate Professor of Anthropology at the University of Minnesota in Minneapolis. His major research interests include socioeconomic change, linguistic acculturation, and ethnicity. Focusing on both Native American and Southeast Asian cultures, he has published articles on the Pima, Ojibwe, Dakota Sioux, and Hmong.

May Ebihara received the Ph.D. from Columbia University in 1968 and is currently an Associate Professor at Lehman College and Doctoral Faculty at the Graduate Center, both of the City University of New York. She is one of only three people, and the only American, to have done ethnographic research among Khmer peasants. She served on the Southeast Asia Council of the Association for Asian Studies from 1980 to 1982 and is currently on the Indochinese Studies Committee of the Social Science Research Council. She continues to write on Cambodian history and society, while turning more toward research on the history of ethnology in the United States.

David W. Haines received the M.A. in Southeast Asian Studies and the Ph.D. in Social Anthropology. He has written various articles on the economic and social adjustment of Southeast Asian refugees, as well as on Vietnamese history and mainstream American society. He worked for four years for the U.S. refugee resettlement program where his responsibilities included the design and oversight of evaluation research and the conduct of policy research regarding the overall administration of the refugee program.

Margarita B. Melville received the M.A. in Latin American Studies and the Ph.D. in Anthropology from the American University. She lived and taught in Guatemala from 1954 to 1967, has traveled extensively through Central America, and also conducted field research among the Mapuche Indians in Chile in 1973-75. Currently an Associate Professor of Anthropology and Mexican American Studies at the University of Houston, she has authored various articles on Mexican Americans, ethnicity, and Central America, coauthored *Guatemala: The Politics of Landownership*, and edited *Twice a Minority: Mexican-American Women*.

Nguyen Manh Hung received the Ph.D. in International Relations from the University of Virginia in 1965, following study at the School of Law of the University of Saigon. He was a professor at the National School of Administration in the Republic of Vietnam, and then Deputy-Minister of National Planning and Development. He has written numerous papers, articles, and books in both Vietnamese and English, and is currently Associate Professor of Government and Director of the Indochina Institute, at George Mason University.

Douglas P. Olney is a Ph.D. candidate in Anthropology at the University of Minnesota where he is conducting research on ethnicity, kinship, and politics in the Twin Cities Hmong community. He was responsible for the compilation of *A Bibliography of the Hmong*, now in its second edition, and is coeditor of *The Hmong in the West*. He has also written several articles on the Hmong in Minnesota.

Rita J. Simon received the Ph.D. from the University of Chicago in 1957, and was at the University of Illinois until coming to the American University in 1983 as Dean of the School of Justice. She has published widely on criminal justice topics, turning more recently to issues of migration, women in migration, and the interaction of public opinion and immigration policy. She has been active in various professional societies and journals, including current editorship of *Justice Quarterly* and prior editorship of the *American Sociological Review*.

John L. Van Esterik received the Ph.D. in Anthropology from the University of Illinois and a degree in public management from Indiana University. He recently completed a study of Lao refugees for the Office of Refugee Resettlement of the U.S. Department of Health and Human Services, and continues to write on the adjustment of the Lao in the United States. He is currently the manager of a refugee services program in Ithaca, New York, at the Tompkins-Seneca-Tioga Board of Cooperative Educational Services.

John K. Whitmore received the M.A. in Cultural Anthropology and the Ph.D. in Southeast Asian History from Cornell University. He has taught Southeast Asian and Vietnamese history at both Yale University and the University of Michigan, as well as conducting research and writing on various aspects of early modern Vietnamese history. He is currently working on Southeast Asian refugee survey projects at the Institute for Social Research, University of Michigan.

DATE DUE
